"Wherever there was sh... ...or war zone—Raful was there. Battle-scarred, he is a living testimony to Israel's struggle for survival."
— Yitzhak Rabin, former Defense Minister and Prime Minister of Israel

"...a genuine work of literature. It is hard to understand the secret of Israel without this account of Eitan's early days in the Jezreel Valley, without this wonderful portrayal of Israel's inception."
— Shimon Peres, former Prime Minister of Israel

"The life of farmer, soldier and political leader—Raful is the quintessential Israeli story. It is an adventurous saga of toil and ideals, perseverance and hope, tragedy and triumph. Reading his book is like shaking hands with the soil of Israel and its spirited sons."
— Benjamin Netanyahu, Israel's Deputy Minister of Foreign Affairs and former Ambassador to the UN

"General Eitan is one of the outstanding military leaders that Israel has brought forth. His unconventional character and approach have played a major part in his military career. He can be termed a unique commander who left an indelible mark in Israel's military history."
— Chaim Herzog, President of the State of Israel, author *The Arab–Israeli Wars*

"General Raful Eitan is a great representative of Israel's fighting spirit."
— Ezer Weizman, former Defense Minister of Israel

MORE ADVENTURE-FILLED
Biographies & Historical
Fiction from S.P.I.

A division of
Shapolsky Publishers, Inc.

___

☐ **A DRY LEAF IN THE WIND:** *A Saga of Pre-War Russia* **by Wolf Goodman.** Written with sweep and skill, this gripping epic captures the turbulent era of post-revolutionary Russia. "In Russia's grim winter of 1919–1920, a crippled, eight-year-old Jewish boy becomes a diminutive Everyman riding out powerful currents that throw his life into confusion...Drawn in convincing detail" — *Publishers Weekly*
(ISBN: 1-56171-070-9 — $4.95)

___

☐ **ESCAPE INTO DARKNESS:** *The True Story of a Young Woman's Extraordinary Survival During World War II* **by Sonia Games.** A vivid and gripping wartime saga from the pen and heart of a beautiful, resourceful young woman who transcends the destruction of her family, her community and even her very identity. Games tells a spellbinding story of tenacious survival that includes aiding the Underground Resistance throughout war-ravaged Europe.

   "Reminiscent of *Anne Frank's Diary of a Young Girl*...a true heroine, defying death." — *Library Journal*
(ISBN: 1-56171-096-2) — $4.95)

___

☐ **A FORGOTTEN MAN:** *A Combat Doctor's Tour of Duty in Hell!* **by Carl Bancoff.** A brilliantly haunting true-to-life story about a good man and the people he touched during war. Carl Bancoff (himself a Vietnam veteran) has captured a time, a place, and an experience that America is at last ready to remember.

   "Riveting...superbly crafted. A tough, gritty depiction of modern warfare. Bancoff deserves excellent marks."—*Philadelphia Daily News*
(ISBN: 1-56171-095-6 — $4.95)

- -

Buy them at your local bookstore or use this convenient coupon for ordering.
National Book Network • 8705-C Bollman Place • Savage, MD 20763
Order Toll Free: 800-462-6420 or 301-459-8696 • FAX 301-452-2118

Please send me the books I have checked above. I am enclosing $ _____
(please add $1.95 to this order to cover postage and handling—50¢ for each additional book). Send check or money order—no cash or C.O.D.s. Make checks payable to National Book Network. Maryland residents please add appropriate sales tax.

Name _____

Address _____

City _____ State _____ Zip Code _____
Allow 2 to 3 weeks for delivery.

A
SOLDIER'S
STORY

The Life and Times
of an Israeli War Hero

by General Raful Eitan, M.K.

A division of Shapolsky Publishers, Inc.

S.P.I. BOOKS

A division of Shapolsky Publishers, Inc.

Copyright © 1992 by Raful Eitan

Reprinted from *A Soldier's Story*, written by Raful Eitan with
Dov Goldstein, translated by Eliot A. Green, a 1991
Shapolsky Publishers hardcover edition

For any additional information, contact:
S.P.I. BOOKS/Shapolsky Publishers, Inc.
136 West 22nd Street
New York, NY 10011
(212) 633-2022
FAX (212) 633-2123

ISBN: 1-56171-094-6

10 9 8 7 6 5 4 3 2 1

Printed and bound in the U.S.A.
by Ringier America, Dresden, TN

This book is dedicated to my childhood friends, with whom I shared my early years of joy and hard work. This book is also intended as a token of appreciation to my comrades-in-arms in the Palmach during the War of Independence — the paratroopers, tank crews, and airmen.

I honor those fighting men who fell in combat and gave to the Jewish State the ultimate sacrifice. They were valiant men of combat who understood we had no choice but to be victorious — at any cost.

To them, and all the others I met along the way, I give my deepest appreciation and love. I could not have achieved all I did without their support. The State of Israel could not have survived without their talents.

ACKNOWLEDGMENTS
AND INTRODUCTION

My deepest gratitude to my wife, Miriam, and my daughters, Rutti, Galia and Nurit. Their advice and criticisms greatly helped in developing this book from an idea to a reality. My deepest thanks to journalist Dov Goldstein who edited the Hebrew manuscript and assisted in the English translation. Without his aid and collaboration it is doubtful that this book could have been written at all.

In addition, my sincere appreciation to Mr. Craig Frank, who prepared and edited the English edition of this book. I could not have found a more qualified individual.

My sincerest thanks to my publisher, Ian Shapolsky, who took this complicated mission on his shoulders.

This book has been written in an effort to present the story of my life, from the time of my childhood until my entry into the Israeli political arena as a member of the eleventh Knesset.

In writing this book I have relied mostly on my memory, although I have also referred to written records of events, particularly in my discussion of the 1982 Peace for Galilee War. The Jewish people and the State of Israel have witnessed many historical events during my lifetime. I have had the honor to participate in many of these. In recounting them in this book, I have found it difficult to include the name of every individual who participated along with me. I ask those brave individuals whose names I have failed to include to forgive my oversight. Their contributions were noble and deserving of mention.

I have spent my life serving my country and my people. In today's world one might be ashamed to make such a bold statement. Yet, I am proud. The opportunity to serve was the only compensation I desired, the only reward I sought.

To the families of Israel's beloved fallen soldiers I would like to express my prayer that your hearts not remain forever empty and in pain with the void left by your sons, brothers, fathers and husbands. We will forever keep a place for them in the glorious history of the resurgence of the Jewish people in their homeland, for they made the supreme sacrifice to allow the dream to become reality. They, like every Israeli, fought for our only country, so that it may remain free and enlightened. Only through our will to sacrifice will we successfully maintain our sovereignty, and thus, control over our own destiny.

I would like to thank the many friends who have stood by me through the good times and the bad. I couldn't have achieved all I have without you.

Raful Eitan
Tel Adashim, Israel
1991

Contents

A SOLDIER'S STORY

Part One:
THE WAR OF
INDEPENDENCE

1

"Jump!"

There are some words that become engraved in your memory. They take on a meaning far beyond their true importance and stay with you all your life. For me "jump" has been one such word. It has been with me since my days in the Palmach, the elite fighting unit of the pre-State Haganah.

I was assigned to Company "G" of the Palmach. We spent most of our time on patrol. We also handled special intelligence functions such as preparing beaches for the landing of unauthorized Jewish immigrants. Our company was organized in 1946 on Givat Ha-Shlosha, and later at Mishmarot and also contained the Palmach's Arab platoon.

We spent about four months at Givat HaShlosha. A routine day consisted mainly of work and military training. The unit was not very cohesive in the beginning, and functioned more like a group of individuals gathered together for a common purpose. We had not all arrived at the base at the same time, which gave those who arrived first the feeling that they were in some ways the veterans of our unit. The fact that they had arrived no earlier than a week before the rest did little to stifle their feelings of responsibility and privilege. I arrived in the middle of the organizing period and was neither a veteran nor a rookie.

When I first arrived I quickly learned that being the new kid on the block had its disadvantages. It wasn't long before one of the "veterans" in the platoon confidentially informed me that he was assigned to carry out a special mission that evening, and as a result, I was being called upon to replace him on kitchen duty. It was only later that I learned that while I was reporting to the kitchen, he was reporting to his special mission — the local movie theater in Petah Tikva.

Kitchen duty was considered the worst of all the work details. The conditions were difficult and the work was depressingly boring, yet this particular night I was not bored. I was kept alert receiving my first informal lesson on the power of deterrence. I was assigned the task of slicing onion rings. Standing before me was a new immigrant, a young woman a little older than I. Her task was to peel potatoes and she did so with a broad, mechanical motion. After peeling each potato, she'd toss it into a pot of water beside me. After a few minutes, I was soaking wet from the spray of her tossed potatoes. Glancing at her, I realized she had failed to notice that her actions were getting me wet. Not knowing what to do, I moved closer to her. Soon the situation had deteriorated to the point where she was sprinkling me with water and I was slicing my onions right under her eyes. Within a few moments I was dripping water and she was dripping tears. As often happens, a compromise was reached without the use of the spoken word, as she ceased tossing her potatoes into the water and I moved my onion slicing away from her eyes.

The idea behind the Palmach was noble. We were going to support ourselves by working the land and simultaneously train to be soldiers. The notion was that our work would draw us closer to the land we would be defending, which in turn would serve as a motivational force during battle, turning us into aggressive, daring soldiers. The greatness of this concept is not diminished if I mention that we didn't particularly enjoy the farm work. I had come to the kibbutz with a distinguished background. I was raised on a moshav, an alternative type of collective farm, called Tel Adashim, and was very good with horses.

This skill awarded me a very prestigious task. I was responsible for the removal of all kibbutz trash.

To assist me in my chores I was given a rickety old wagon, pulled by an equally old mare named Lilka. The odds were about even as to whether the mare would die before the old wagon fell apart. Each morning I would steer my wagon and Lilka to the back of the kitchen. Leading from the kitchen and dining room was a concrete channel. All the garbage was thrown into this channel and collected at the bottom, where a gate behind the kitchen prevented spillage. My task was to open the gate, collect the garbage with a hoe, pile it onto my wagon and transport it to the dump, where I then unloaded the trash. Riding to the dump just outside the farm, I would sit on the pile of garbage, separated only by a piece of torn sack or a narrow board. That was my work and as odd as it may sound, as unpleasant as the work was, it allowed me to feel I was doing my small part to help in advancing the larger goal of national liberation.

The training we underwent was often extremely difficult and the conditions were always harsh. Although history has afforded the Palmach a kind reputation, I have little doubt that were we to force today's army recruits to endure the conditions and training exercises we were exposed to, there would be a great outcry in all of Israel. I remember one particularly frightening episode which serves as an example of the seriousness with which military maneuvers were taken. The exercise required that the unit divide itself in half. Group A was assigned the task of delivering a note to a pre-determined location. Group B was told to prevent the delivery. During the exercise, a member of Group A was captured. When he refused to disclose the location of the secret delivery, his mouth was forced open and filled with sand. Unable to speak or even breathe, the boy made a desperate motion, indicating the secret location. Only then would the others remove the sand from his mouth.

The treatment was rough and demanding. Any form of self-indulgence was perceived as a sign of weakness and was not tolerated. Every failure was declared the result of a lack of manhood. We accepted this treatment in good spirit and with great enthusiasm. We understood that Jews did not have the luxury of making errors. We knew that this period was our hardening period, the period that would turn us into soldiers worthy of the title "Palmachnik." We worked hard, we trained hard, and we slept very little. We made do with very few supplies and little food. We were aware of the history of the times and this served to motivate us.

We left Givat HaShlosha without great sorrow and arrived at Kibbutz Mishmarot without much joy. I was one of five soldiers sent in advance to prepare our site for the rest of the platoon. When we arrived we saw that tents were already set up and we had little to do but wait for the platoon to arrive on the next day.

When the unit arrived, we were all addressed by a middle aged man from the kibbutz named Yoske, who spoke eloquently about the virtues of labor. He informed us that our work day was to begin at four o'clock each morning, at which time we were all to meet at the corner near the barn.

The next morning we all gathered as instructed near the barn. Yoske greeted us, looked us over sternly and instructed us to follow him. We walked through the barn, along an orchard path and into a large ditch. At the end of the ditch, built into the edge, was a small building. As we entered this building we were amazed to find various types of machines and equipment.

Yoske immediately explained that we had arrived at an underground Haganah weapons factory. Our task was going to be the production of hand grenades. Yoske explained that we were not going to be producing the Polish type of grenade, which was a friction grenade, but rather a new kind of explosive called the Mill grenade. We were told that we were the first unit engaged in the production of this weapon.

We worked very hard. In the beginning we were allotted two days for setting the grenade castings, with the explosive filling being placed on the third day. Soon, however, we were completing the castings in one day and pouring the explosives on the second day. We worked according to a schedule which often called upon us to work twenty-four hours straight without sleep. We would produce two thousand grenades on a regular casting day. The task of manufacturing weapons also served to motivate us and gave us a deep sense of mission. We understood that the weapons we were involved in producing would one day be used in the defense of Jewish lives and the freedom of a Jewish homeland.

Our duties at the weapons factory were interrupted only by the need for military training and patrols. Our platoon leader, Chaim Poznanski, whom we called "Poza," trained us in land navigation and night fieldcraft. He wanted us to learn to contend with the darkness and its hidden noises. Poza would lead us between Arab villages, teaching us to conceal our tracks and move silently through the night.

During this time our unit was assigned its first operation. The mission was to gather intelligence data and photograph an Arab village in the Galilee. We rode by bus to the north and embarked at Rosh Hanikra, along the Lebanese border. We then walked along the Wadi Karkara until we reached Eilon, where we stopped for the night. We were seven boys and three girls. Poza had fallen in the wadi and was not with us due to a knee injury. We were being led by our squadron leader, Giora. We were armed only with a pistol, which was wrapped in cellophane and carried in a jam box, and one hand grenade, which I carried.

The next morning we left Eilon planning to walk along the Wadi Koren. A friend, Noni, and I were chosen to serve as scouts and walked ahead of the group searching for a way to get around the waters of the wadi. In doing so, we lost eye contact with the rest of our unit.

In the peaceful silence we suddenly heard our compatriots shouting for us to stop walking. While waiting for further instructions we were approached by an Arab armed with an English rifle. He led us down to where the rest of our unit was being held by another Arab, also with an English rifle. We were instructed to place our belongings on a large rock and move to a tree a few feet away. Under the tree we turned to Giora for a plan that might provide for an escape. Using few words and hand signals we decided that Noni, Dov Greitzer, and I would attack the Arab closest to us (who was no longer armed, having given his weapon to the second Arab) as Giora, who still had the pistol in the jam box, shot the Arab farthest away. We decided we would move on Giora's command. The attack word was to be "Jump."

Hiding behind us, Giora removed the gun from the jam box and cellophane. Suddenly, ripping through the stillness came the command, "Jump!." Noni, Dov, and I jumped on the Arab closest to us and rolled with him a few feet to the shallow waters of the wadi. We wrestled with the Arab, drowning him, all the while waiting to hear Giora's shot ring out. There was no shot. Giora's gun jammed and all we heard was the empty clicking sound of the pistol's hammer. Click, Click, Click. Three times the gun failed.

The jamming of the gun, however, gave the other Arab the opportunity to regain his senses. He soon began shooting at us with one of the English rifles. I was sure that our fate was sealed. How could one pistol that wouldn't shoot outgun two English rifles?

To this day the image is still vivid. A large man standing only five feet away aiming his rifle at us, shooting wildly, and missing his targets. When he used up all ten bullets in the first rifle, he retreated behind a large rock about ninety feet from us. From this vantage point he resumed his shooting with the second rifle. Luckily, his aim did not improve.

By now Giora had given up on his pistol and was calling out for me to throw my grenade. I took the old, wet grenade hidden under my shirt, pulled the safety pin, and threw it toward the large rock protecting the Arab. I counted until three, but heard only silence. The grenade did not go off. The only sound I heard was another shot from the English rifle.

The Arab we had jumped on was now dead, having been drowned. Noni and Dov were sitting on his back going through his pockets where they found the solution to our problem, a Parabellum pistol. Dov immediately took the gun and began firing at the Arab behind the rock. After Dov fired a few shots, the Arab fled.

After taking a few moments to pull ourselves together, we decided to continue our mission. Noni and I resumed our roles as scouts, but now only a few feet ahead of the group. We hadn't walked very far when shots were fired at us from a short distance in front of us. We recognized the man firing on us as the Arab who had fled only minutes before. We evaluated the situation and determined that it was foolish to continue to battle this man. We were aware of the dangers of our situation, for only a few feet behind us lay a dead Arab we had drowned. We had to be careful in this part of the country or we could find ourselves severely outnumbered. We were already outgunned. We decided to return to Mishmarot.

Today, the Parabellum pistol is on display in my office, having been given to me by kibbutz Eilon when I was General of the Northern Command. A friend notified me that the pistol was at the kibbutz. I contacted the kibbutz and they invited me to share with them the history behind the pistol. After hearing the story, they decided I should have it. Today it serves as a reminder of the first time I managed to defy death.

The early days in the Palmach were not only times of animosity with our

Arab neighbors. Once, on a long hike through the south, our unit ran out of water. By the time we reached Ein Gedi many men were fainting. Desperate, our leader, Poza, two other soldiers, and I set out to find water.

As we approached a well we spotted three Bedouin Arabs with German rifles sitting in front of it. Because I did not know whether their intentions were hostile, I held on tightly to the knife in my pocket. Poza approached the Bedouins and began to address them in Arabic. In a short time they were smiling and soon we began laughing together. The faces of the Bedouins had become relaxed and friendly and we all drank from the well. Upon hearing the fate of the rest of our unit, our new friends brought out big water skins, filled them with water, loaded them on the backs of their donkeys and came with us the few miles to where our unit was waiting for us. That night they joined us for dinner and a campfire where we shared songs and anecdotes.

In the Palmach we came to know the Land of Israel by walking through her valleys and climbing her hills. We learned to triumph over adversity and to push ourselves beyond what we had thought were our personal limitations. We walked for hours, carrying fifty pounds of supplies on our backs. Our motivation was survival, our love of the land, and our dream that it would one day be ours.

We worked, we trained, we had dangerous encounters with Arabs. We were a Palmach squad in Palestine, 1947. When I went on to lead a training squad in Givat Adah later that year, I tried to train my recruits, despite the lack of proper weapons and insufficient supplies, by passing on my determination and motivation.

The time was immediately after the November 29, 1947, United Nations' decision to partition Palestine and we understood that our War of Independence was on the horizon. We were going to need great courage and the will to sacrifice. We were going to need the hunger for freedom that had caused us to act bravely and fearlessly when given the command "Jump!" only a short year before.

2

A Poor but Happy Childhood

In today's social environment of materialism, it might be thought that my childhood was unhappy. Yet I only have happy memories. Although my family had to do without many things we now consider basic, not to mention appliances and luxury items, we judged our difficult conditions by how those around us lived. We were very poor but understood our situation to be the normal conditions of life. We knew no other way of life, and so we were happy with the little we had.

I was born on Moshav Tel Adashim in the Jezreel Valley in what is today northwest Israel. My exact date of birth was at one time in question, but my father and the Muktar of the village, Mamonov, remember the date as January 11, 1929. I was born into poverty as a result of poverty. Once my mother's pregnancy was determined my parents realized that they were unable to have another child. Already with four children, they realized that the economic hardships the family was forced to endure would only worsen with an addition to the family. They also sought to spare the child-to-be the discomforts and disadvantages of growing up poor. The decision was made to abort the pregnancy. Yet, there was no abortion because my father could raise only 1.20 pounds of the two pounds needed to pay the doctor's fee and the doctor would not extend credit. And so I was brought into this world.

Tel Adashim was first founded before the First World War by members of the defense organization HaShomer. HaShomer was

an organization similar to the Palmach in that they too supported
themselves by farming during the day, while serving as guards at
night. The first group of settlers consisted of seven or eight families.
They lived in semi-private shacks and worked very hard. When the
First World War began, the routine of the settlement was interrupted as many of the men joined the British army. Soon after the
remaining settlers left for other places in the country. My mother
went back to her family in Kfar Saba and my father served as a scout
in the British army. His assignment was to lead the Australian
division northward.

Throughout my childhood my father shared with me his experiences in the British army. He told delightful stories and
frightening stories. Many had lessons and morals that I remembered
many years later and brought with me into various battle situations.
He often applied what he had learned to the problems and trials he
faced daily. He taught by example and expected me to draw the right
conclusions. He taught me self-control, courage, and resourcefulness. Whenever we were frightened and demoralized by the seemingly insurmountable obstacles which stood before us, he would tell
us, "You are alone in the desert and you must learn that you will be
alone in the desert many times in your life. Nobody will come to
your aid and no one will rescue you. What will you do when you're
alone in the desert?" By word and deed he inspired me to face
challenges and struggles without fear. He gave me the firm sense
that a man who struggles and does not give in is the master of his
own fate. I was taught I should never surrender, even when things
are bitterly tough and the obstacles are large and menacing.

When the war ended we were living in Petah Tikva, close to the
country's center. Not long after my father's return to us, he once
again found himself fighting, this time defending the settlement
from Arab attackers during the 1921 Arab riots that swept across
the country. It was during these riots that my family suffered its first
loss, as my cousin was killed defending Petah Tikva.

Tel Adashim was re-established in 1923. A small group of original
members were joined by some of the defenders of Tel Hai and some

of the original members of Mahanayim and Ruhama. I was born six years after the Moshav's rebirth. Tel Adashim was a classic Zionist settlement. We had no electricity. No running water meant we had to bring water from a distant well a few times a week. The same water was used for bathing, cleaning dishes, and other household uses. New clothing or a pair of new shoes were beyond our dreams. My mother sewed our pants and shirts from any cloth that came to hand and mended our torn clothing until there was no more cloth left to mend. Each article of clothing went through several strange metamorphoses, being handed down from child to child until each of us had benefited from its services. When we had all outgrown the garment it was passed on to another family in the village, where it continued its voyage. We were a village of Jews with a vision and a dream and we worked together and struggled together to realize our dream. A use was found for everything, if not in one family, then in another. All the families in the village acted as one.

My earliest personal memories are of the village kindergarten. Our teacher's name was Haya. In the summer, and sometimes in the winter, we walked to school barefoot. I remember that in the winter we got a lot of mud on our feet and Haya used to spend a whole hour cleaning the mud from between our toes, and drying and warming our feet. When my kindergarten class advanced to elementary school most of us already knew how to read and write. The first thing I read independently was the headlines of the newspaper "Davar," which was brought to the village regularly and was the channel linking the villagers with what was happening in the country and around the world.

Our poverty and the difficult conditions did not detract from our desire and will to learn. Our village school assembled in three buildings, shacks that had been used by the original settlement: a school building that my older brothers and others had built during the mid-1920's, as well as a community building that also housed the village library, and the office of the village secretary. The building most conducive for learning was the school building, which had two floors. However, in the interest of fairness, classes were moved from building to building and every class would also at times meet in the shacks and the community center, where conditions were extremely difficult. Our studies were not at the top of the Moshav's list of priorities. The need for us to "lend our shoulders" for the hard work of building a settlement often disrupted our studies. The status of a young boy or girl was therefore determined by his or her ability to master the chores of the farm. Respect was granted to those who worked hard, learned to milk the cows alone, knew how to harness a horse without any assistance from an adult, and were permitted to plow the fields without adult supervision.

With our responsibilities divided between the fields and school, we were often the center of a debate as to which, working or learning, was more important. Many teachers understood the demands of the Moshav and allowed schoolwork to take a lesser role. Others demanded we emphasize our studies, often creating friction. Yet we learned to juggle our dual roles and approached both work and our studies with sincerity and enthusiasm.

There were also many wonderful experiences. Many of my fondest memories are drawn from this economically difficult and physically straining time of my life. Simple things were joyful, such as the baking of bread. Every house had a baking oven and every family in the village baked bread in its own house. For us baking day was a holiday. I particularly looked forward to baking day because I enjoyed my job, which was to feed the oven with two containers of corn stalks to maintain the proper temperature. The night before, my mother would knead the dough in a big tub, where it would stay until the next day. The following afternoon she would place the dough in the oven along with the meat of birds, such as starlings, pigeons, and bulbuls, that we had hunted during the week. The meals on baking day were always a simple pleasure.

The streets in Tel Adashim had no official names. The villagers had named them after events in the Moshav history, or a person who lived there, or a special characteristic of the particular street. Therefore the street that always accumulated a great amount of mud in the winter was called Mud Street. Like all the other streets, Mud

Street was not paved, and travel over it in the winter with a horse drawn wagon was always a difficult and complex operation. Although the street has since been paved, like the others in Tel Adashim, it still bears the name it was given by the original settlers.

Within the village there were various places of importance. Among these were the village secretary's office, the dairy, the blacksmith's shop, the general store, and the mill. The most important object in the Moshav was a bell that hung from a special framework of beams next to the dairy. The bell was a large container made of thick, heavy metal and a heavy iron clapper was used to strike the container, sending the sounds far and wide. It was the instrument that unified the village and notified everyone of important news. It rang three times a day to signal the opening of the dairy. This meant it was time to milk the cows and for farmers to bring their milk in. The bell was also used to call the villagers to general meetings and to sound the alarm in case of fire or any other serious, sudden danger. For each purpose there were specific rings. For the dairy there were six rhythmic rings, and for warnings of an emergency, there was quick, steady ringing. Older children were allowed to wield the clapper and ring the bell, which was a sign you were growing up. The person responsible for ringing the bell was a big, strong man named Nathanson. Nathanson was also the dairyman (the man who received the milk from the farmers), the man who received the eggs, and, later on, the manager of the general store. He was quiet and well liked by everyone. Nathanson and the bell were so identified with each other that they became a single concept, so much so, that the bell was eventually placed on his grave.

The dairy was a regular meeting place. There people brought their milk cans, exchanged greetings, and told stories. There was a bulletin board there too. Each day a bus would arrive at the dairy to transport the full, heavy urns of milk from the village to the Tnuva cooperative, the company that processed and distributed milk to all the Jewish settlements. The back half of the bus was shared by milk cans and chickens, while the front half was for passengers.

The village flour mill was also a kind of symbol of independence from the outside world. The farmers brought wheat, barley, and corn they had grown to the mill and took away flour and various kinds of feed for their animals. Eventually, the mill was shut down, and the village had to depend on a big mill in Afula, a nearby town.

The village flock was a source of pride too. Our herdsman was a man named Galili. We used to look forward to the flock's return from the pasture before dark. Among the animals was a gigantic ram named Og. As the flock approached the waiting children, Galili used to stop the animals, and we would jump up on big, good natured Og and ride him. Fifteen children used to hold on to each other and to Og's long fleece, leading the rest of the flock to the fold.

In the winter we took shelter from the cold in the blacksmith's shop. We used to crowd around the hot bellows and wait to listen to what the blacksmith had to say. We became expert in firing the coals. We would hold the horse's leg while he was being shod. That was an unforgettable experience.

The winter provided us with more entertainment than did the other seasons. The wagons made deep ruts in the heavy mud with their wooden wheels rimmed with iron. Seeing a wagon making slow progress, the horses pulling and the farmers shouting and sometimes the draw shaft breaking was an exciting sight. Once, a truck sank deep into the mud and all the children immediately gathered at the scene to help the tractor extricate the vehicle. These incidents were exciting and challenging and served to raise our spirits.

The only source of entertainment on the Moshav were movies, which were delivered to us every six weeks by a man driving a green van. The movies were such a central part of our lives that people actually counted the passage of time by the number of weeks between films. On movie day there was an air of expectancy that began early in the afternoon. In the winter the films were screened in the community building and there was practically no room for movement. In the summer the movie was shown outside, on a screen made from a stretched white felt sheet which was placed on the wall of the general store. Although the screenings were not until nightfall, the road in front of the general store would become crowded as early as noon. People carried bundles of straw, chairs, even couches, and set them up in front of the movie wall to reserve a place for their families.

The children on our Moshav were very zealous and were not afraid to take the initiative when we thought we were right. When the Moshav decided to build a new community center, the children enthusiastically pitched in, dragging rocks, mixing concrete and plaster and doing as much of the heavy work as possible. When the building was almost completed we presented a request that four gymnastic rings, used to support a horizontal bar, be set into the stage floor. Many of us were active gymnasts and we were interested in performing at the new community center's dedication ceremony. To our dismay and anger one of the higher Moshav committees denied our request. Feeling wronged, a few of us secretly entered the new building and installed the four rings, carefully covering them with flour tiles. On the night of the dedication everyone was surprised when we removed the tiles, set up our horizontal bar and presented our exciting gym performance. The members of the Moshav were not really angry with us. They had always encouraged us to be innovative and bold. Many even praised our act of defiance.

We had a special relationship with the animals on the farm. Horses in particular were granted special status because they were our primary means of transportation. My family had two mares, one named Geulah, a beautiful white horse, and Shunamit, which was grey. These horses are woven into my childhood memories as if they were members of the family. Shunamit was slightly wild, but Geulah had a good disposition. My father treated them gently and they responded by being disciplined and obedient. I must confess to never liking Shunamit very much. Much of my displeasure was due to an accident one afternoon when I was a small boy. I was playing in the hay in the feeding wagon while Geulah and Shunamit were eating. Shunamit lifted the hay and ate until at some point she accidentally put her huge teeth into my belly. My parents immediately rushed me to the doctor in Afula, who prescribed two rabies shots each week. These injections were very painful, and I panicked and screamed each morning I was scheduled to go to Afula. As a child, I was unable to forgive Shunamit and did not feel as close to her as I had before the accident.

Our horses were important for reasons other than that they served a functional purpose. They were a source of adventure and entertainment. We learned to ride at age six or seven and could gallop at an even younger age. The horses were also key players in our childhood games, as the children of Tel Adashim fought mock Wild West battles with the children of the nearby villages of Balfouriya and Merhavya. We rode our horses as we shouted battle cries to scare away Arab herdsmen whose flocks had entered our fields. We even played Ben Hur, removing the backs of our wagons and hitching our horses to the two front wheels.

A dream of every child on the Moshav was to own a bicycle, although each family was too poor to provide one. One day a boy was given a bicycle by a distant relative. This boy immediately became the crowned king of all the kids in the village. We were all nice to him and even willingly paid him in treats and money for a chance to ride his bicycle. He was enterprising enough to allow those without the immediate means of payment to ride his bicycle on credit.

A few years later many of the Moshav's youth discovered the secret of working for a salary outside of the Moshav. In the nearby village of Gideon I got a job thinning out corn that earned me seventeen grush a day. I was determined to realized my dream of owning a bicycle. After a short while, although I hadn't earned enough money on my own, my father contributed a bit of money and I bought a used bicycle for two pounds. I was very excited and eager to embark on my first ride. With the movements of an experienced rider, I swung my leg up and saddled the bicycle. As I turned the pedals, anticipation high, the old thing fell apart. In my whole life, I can't remember feeling as heartbroken as I felt then. I junked the broken bicycle and persisted in my dreams for a better one. When I was fifteen years old I worked and saved my money until I had accumulated sixteen pounds. My older brother and I traveled to Haifa and bought a shiny new bicycle. I loved that bicycle and later gave it to my nephew when I joined the Palmach.

We were kept nearly bald as children. Two of the village's farmers were in charge of haircuts. When a boy's hair grew wild, he was forced to get a haircut. The barbers would sit us down on a log, dip their shears in a container of kerosene to disinfect them, and then plow a furrow right through the center of the wild hair. This was done to create a "fait accompli" and served as a preventive measure against our running away. Once the center was quickly chopped off, the barbers would then finish the haircut strip by strip until we were completely bald. At first, we weren't embarrassed by our haircuts, but once the children from the neighboring villages began to tease us, we became uncomfortable with the way we looked. At some point we discovered Noah, the barber in Afula. His price for a magnificent haircut was a half grush, not an insignificant sum for most of us. Noah would cut our hair painstakingly, and he even placed a white sheet on our shoulders to prevent the cut hair from falling down our backs. Since finding half a grush was a difficult task, Noah also agreed to accept payment in the form of an egg. We used to walk the five kilometers to Afula on foot with the egg in our pocket. We would get our hair cut and then hand Noah the whole egg. He was happy with his egg and we were pleased at having averted baldness yet one more time.

In addition to work outside the Moshav, there was a farmer in the village named Engel who was a regular source of income for us. In the evening he used to sit on a big round rock at the entrance to his yard and we would bring him the various insects we had caught that day. Our treasures included hornets and beetles and other pests which damaged the crops and fruit plantations. We would bring them packed in match boxes so Engel could inspect them and decide on their worth. Every insect had its price and Engel would pay us in cash. His willingness to pay had converted us all to ardent hunters, and we stalked the fields searching for valuable prey. The price often included swollen fingers and hands as we were forced to endure the stings of numerous insects. The most valuable pest, rewarded by the greatest sum from Engel, was the mole. For a mole Engel was willing to pay up to half a pound. At last we had our chance at wealth.

The village clinic was one of our most important institutions. The doctor at the clinic, the wife of one of the farmers, was a Russian woman named Sofa. I felt close to Sofa, not only because she was the village doctor, but also because she had served as my wet nurse. She and my mother gave birth at the same time, and Sofa willingly breast-fed me upon discovering that my mother was unable to nourish her newborn.

My mother was born in a small village in the Ukraine to the Orloff family who were farmers and carpenters. There were nine children in the family and they all came to Israel in 1904. The family concentrated in Petah Tikva, but my mother soon left for Sejera where she had found work. It was in Sejera that she met my father. After they got married my parents lived in numerous settlements as they searched for work and the place they wanted to live. My father was one of the founders of the Jewish defense and pioneer organization HaShomer. When the First World War broke out, my family moved to Kfar Saba and Petah Tikva to stay with my mother's family while my father was at war. It was during this time that my brother Yosef, whom I would never know, was killed as he fell off a wagon in Kfar Saba. My mother was a good, loving woman, quiet and strong, and her personal stamp can be seen on my character.

My most vivid memories are connected with my mother's family, the Orloff-Nishris. I loved traveling to my mother's family. We would travel to Kfar Saba in a bus which was fitted with a series of thick nets over the windows so as to protect us from the stones which were thrown at Jewish buses as we would pass the Arab villages of Jenin, Tul-Karem, and Kalkiliya. We would visit my mother's brother, my uncle Tzvi Nishri, who was the first gymnastics teacher in the Jewish Yishuv and he used to teach me new gymnastic movements. My mother's sister also lived in Kfar Saba. She was a kind woman, but her husband was a hard, tough man who was not very kind to us. Our visits to my aunt's house were highlighted by the mandarins and other oranges that we used to pick from their trees.

My mother had a brother who lived in an area of Tel Aviv called Kerem Ha Teymanim, or Vineyards of the Yemenites. It was during a visit to my uncle's house at the age of ten that I saw the sea for the first time. I immediately fell in love with Tel Aviv. My uncle's house was big, particularly when compared to our house at the Moshav. It had steps leading up to the entrance door and a flat roof that I spent hours sitting on. After my first visit I returned to the Moshav and shared my experiences with my friends. Although they were a little suspicious of my tales of a flat roof and stairs leading to the door, they were openly doubtful when I relayed that my uncle's house had a piano and that his daughters each knew how to play it. In their minds, wealth to this degree could only be the result of a fanciful dream.

My mother's parents are buried in Petah Tikva and I discovered their gravestones not long ago. My mother also has a nephew buried there. His name was Palo "Ze'ev" Orloff and he fell in the defense of Petah Tikva. He was the first person in our family to fall in the Arab war against the Jews. My mother died in 1963.

My father came from the Ukraine to the Jewish Homeland at the age of seventeen. He arrived with his older brother Yosef, who had been involved in the revolution of 1904. The Turks were very suspicious of him and sent him back to Russia. On the ship back to Russia, Yosef hanged himself. My brother Yosef, who was killed in Kfar Saba, was named after him.

My father helped found Ha Shomer while in Sejera. He too came from a family of farmers. He had golden hands that were skilled in all kinds of work in wood and iron, as well as agriculture. He brought from Russia a carpenter's plane that he had received from the grandfather of his grandfather. This tool was probably over one-hundred years old, but it was still usable.

My father was a motivated and brave man who taught me the value of work, how to make do with little, the importance of patience, and to be an independent person. He taught without compulsion and without rebuking, by personal example. He would always remind us that we are "alone in a desert" and that we must rely on ourselves to overcome obstacles. When a problem arises, the only option is to stick to the original goal, accept the pain, and invest all your ability in solving the problem. He would often assign chores to me that were seemingly impossible just so that I would be forced to improvise and devise a solution to my dilemma. For example, if I was asked to load the plow onto the wagon at the end of an exhausting day of plowing, my father would not give much thought to the fact that the plow was much heavier than any weight I could lift alone. He would simply step aside and smoke his pipe, waiting for me to figure my way around my natural limitations and complete the task. The image is still very vivid in my mind: a young boy struggling with a heavy plow while his father stands nearby blowing smoke rings toward the sky.

I live my father's advice to this day. I do not believe in asking for favors or help. I believe in completing a task with my own two hands. In addition, my father taught me to ride a horse, to shoot a rifle, to work hard, to know my way in the great outdoors in both night and day, to identify animal tracks, and to live independently in the open country. As early as seven or eight years old, my father put me on watch duty at night. He used to send me to far off posts and watch me from a distance. Although my mother was fearful, my father understood that these assignments would provide me with the knowledge and experience I would need later to survive. In fact, moving through the dark, silent night rid me of fear and gave me courage.

Much of my love for the Land of Israel was taught to me by my father, as was the belief that we had a duty to defend it. Many of our serious conversations were held in the late afternoons as we prepared to milk the cows. My father would share stories about the Jewish struggles in Israel, the Turks, the First World War, and the British. I used to sit spellbound, listening to every word, hoping that sunset was far off, so that our conversation would not be interrupted by the chore of milking the cows.

My father was very active in defense and security matters. I

learned a great deal from the security and defense strategy meetings
that were often held in our house. He also spoke, read, and wrote
fluent Arabic and had close ties with the Arabs of the neighboring
villages. He was often their guest and in turn regularly hosted them
in our house. He cultivated close and complex security ties with
them. My father also had close ties with British officials and they
too visited our house on various occasions. He had dreamed and
spoken about an independent Jewish state ever since I was a little
boy. There were times as we sat on the milking stools in the dark
barn that he would bring me into his dream of a Jewish State, "a
State of our own."

My father lived in our independent Jewish State for ten years,
until his death in 1958. His last request was that our farm in Tel
Adashim should never be called by a stranger's name. I am proud to
have fulfilled his request. Despite my long army service, I never cut
my links to the farm, and when I left active service in 1983, I made
the farm in Tel Adashim my beloved home.

I was born during the bloody Arab riots of 1929. The men stayed
in Tel Adashim to defend the farms. The women and children took
shelter in Kibbutz Mizra. I was seven during similar riots in 1936.
We felt the echoes of battle. We heard shots and saw the fields of
our Moshav burning, set ablaze by Arabs. Someone from our village
was stabbed by Arabs. The village mules were stolen. There were
fights with Arabs in the fields. Nobody had to tell us that there was
a situation of conflict between us and that the Arabs simply did not
want Jews living in the area. We felt it. As a result of Arab hostility,
I have lived through many wars, several times almost getting killed.

Our need to defend ourselves prompted my father to teach me
how to fire a gun at a very young age. In fact, my first injury related
to security activities came when I was seven years old. My father was
teaching me how to shoot a hunting rifle that was too heavy for me
to hold properly. As I shot at a piece of scythe my father had placed
on the ground, the rifle bucked, hitting me below my eye. My face
was swollen for a whole week.

The Jews had two primary tasks: work and security. They were

always linked together and were seen as the keys to independence.
As a ten year-old boy I served as a liaison runner between guard
posts to assist the newly established settlement of Gal-Ed. During
that year I was also brought into the "Gadna," the youth wing of
the Haganah. There my training included signaling and field craft.

I was ten years old when the Second World War began. There
was one radio receiver in the village. In the evenings, everyone in
the village, adults and children, gathered around it, crowded head
to head and listened to the news of the war.

As a child my process of maturation was quick. I skipped over
many intermediate steps and was handed responsibility at a young
age. At age thirteen I finished elementary school. A ninth grade class
was not organized and we scattered to our parents' farms. We
worked and were kept busy with Haganah matters. Before the
Second World War, a second well had been dug in the village with
a big drill that was rotated by hand with the help of a long bar. Soon
afterwards they installed pipes to the houses, providing us with
running water. Electricity soon followed. Our standard of living was
improving. Our focus, however, remained on the security issues of
property and life.

3

The Palmach —
A Way of Life

The Second World War sharpened our feelings of vulnerability and we began to feel the danger the Arabs posed to our existence. Many of the adults from the Moshav enlisted in the British army, including my older sister. When they would arrive home on weekends for leave, I would stare at them with envious eyes, admiring the splendor of their uniforms and service caps. A great joy to me at the time was to wrap myself in my sister's military tunic and parade around the Moshav, walking tall and proud.

A short time before I turned seventeen years old, my neighbor Shlomo Granov, who was two years older than I was, joined the Palmach. When he would return to the village on leave, he would share his experiences in the Palmach, which made many of the boys eager to join as well. I was very excited about joining the Palmach, and with anxious anticipation I approached my father, asking him to allow me to join. Although I sensed his concern, he answered without hesitation. His reply was simple, "There is much work to be done on the farm and you are an excellent worker. Yet, you should go for a year. You have to go."

The event which sealed my decision was "Black Shabbat," a day of massive British arrests of Jews involved in the Jewish defense underground. The arrest of many members of the Palmach angered me and finalized my decision to begin my active participation in the struggle for Jewish independence. Not knowing exactly how to join the Palmach, I asked my neighbor Shlomo, who sent me to Kibbutz

Sarid and told me to ask for a man named Haim Zinger. I was told
to tell Zinger that Shlomo Granov sent me. After a brief interroga-
tion, Zinger told me that I was to wait one week and then travel to
Kibbutz Givat HaShlosha. Once there, I was to report to a man
named Shlomkeh.

When I returned home and announced I had been accepted into
the Palmach there was neither joy nor sadness in my home. I knew
my parents were sad to see their child leave and concerned about
assuming all the chores of the farm, but I also knew that they were
proud. When the week passed, my mother and father walked me to
the bus. My mother had put my sweater in a small haversack, and it
was all I carried. I was told I would receive socks, and perhaps even
shoes, from the Palmach. As I kissed my parents goodbye and
boarded the bus I had no way of knowing I was taking my first steps
in a career of military service that was going to last thirty-seven
years.

My experiences at Givat HaShlosha, as I have already said, were
both difficult and inspiring. The role of the Palmach, however,
changed with the passage of the United Nations resolution calling
for partition. On the night the United Nations' passed the resolution and called for the creation of a Jewish State, I was granted a one
day pass. Upon my return home I was overtaken by my exhaustion
and went directly to sleep. Throught the night I was awakened by
loud celebrations, but did not participate, despite the efforts of my
father to awaken me. I was simply too tired. The next morning I was
picked up by van and taken to Givat Ada where I was engaged in the
training of a Palmach platoon. The atmosphere at Givat Ada was
festive and although I shared in the joy at the United Nations'
resolution, I reminded everyone that there was in fact little to be
happy about. "Now our war is going to begin," I told them, and in
a short while war indeed broke out.

During the course of training, my platoon had several incidents
with Arabs. Between November 1947 when the United Nations
passed their resolution and May 1948 when the State of Israel was
declared, there was a civil war of sorts between Jews and Arabs in

British mandatory Palestine. We were involved in many minor actions. We were ordered to set up an ambush on the Benyamina - Pardess Hannah road and to attack any Arab transportation of goods that passed. Although we lay there for a full day, no Arab transports passed us. In another incident, we were ordered to destroy a portion of Arab Caesarea that had expanded onto Jewish soil.

The Palmach was preparing for what seemed like certain war once the British departed in May 1948. We were short on supplies, weapons, and ammunitions. The situation was so severe that I even took advantage of an opportunity to purchase bullets from an Indian soldier I met in a cafe in Benyamina. I paid three pounds for thirty rifle bullets.

At the beginning of 1948 the Palmach's loosely structured platoons and divisions were brought together at Sarona, now the Israeli army's major administrative base in central Tel Aviv, where we were organized into a cohesive army. This resulted in many soldiers being reassigned into newly formed platoons, companies, and divisions. Weapons were distributed, mostly Czech rifles, and M.G.34 machine guns, which had also been obtained through Czechoslovakia. We were also given new army clothing, cigarettes, soap, razor blades, and chocolate.

Once the unit assignments and distribution of goods were completed, my group was sent to Hulda. With no formal military base, we set up camp in the streets and our administration center in a barn. It was being rumored that we were going to be assigned the task of breaking through the siege of Jerusalem. That evening officers arrived and took command of the platoons that I and the other sergeants had trained. Our platoon commander was David "Dado" Elazer, who later rose to Chief of Staff and commanded the Israel Defense Forces during the Yom Kippur War. I was named platoon sergeant.

The next day a convoy was organized to bring needed supplies to troops and Jewish civilians in Jerusalem. Our objective was to carve a passage from Hulda to what is today Mishmar David, by securing the road to Sha'ar Hagai, where the road to Jerusalem begins its climb into the mountains. The platoons were spread out along the length of the convoy. About a mile from Hulda the front of the convoy came under fire from an Arab ambush and suffered heavy losses. Our platoon suffered four dead. It was a terrible slaughter. We were not organized for a counterattack and could not even rescue our wounded. During the day and most of the night, the wounded were abandoned to our attackers. Once the attackers had left, we went to retrieve the bodies of our beloved compatriots and discovered their burned and mutilated bodies. One of our drivers, who managed to hide from the Arabs, told us that the Arabs had abused the wounded, and then poured fuel on them and burned them alive. This was the first time that I had been exposed to this type of atrocity and it taught me that the Arab soldier came from a different culture, with a different fighting ethic.

After a day of reorganizing, we once again set out for Jerusalem. We reached Kiryat Anavim without any resistance, but received intelligence reports that the Kastel, a fortified police outpost used by the Turks and British and situated on the road to Jerusalem, had fallen to the Arabs, effectively blocking our passage to Jerusalem. I was ordered to take my platoon in an armored car a few miles up the road to pick up any Jewish soldiers who might have escaped the Kastel alive. We reached the foot of the Kastel and approached cautiously. There we found two of our soldiers wounded and hiding under a storm drain. We managed to bring them back with us to Kiryat Anavim, arriving before dark. That night we re-captured the Kastel without any Arab resistance. We stayed at the Kastel for two days, after which another unit came to secure control over the strategic fort. We returned to our base to once again organize and prepare for our breakthrough to Jerusalem.

I had never been to Jerusalem and was very excited to be involved in what I saw as an historic effort to reach our ancient city. As a result of my enthusiasm I was assigned to ride in the first car of the convoy. All went well until we passed Upper Motza and approached what is today Beit Zayit. Near Beit Zayit, our convoy was shot at from an Arab village called Kfar Kolonia, where the Jewish town of Mevassaret Tzion is today. The shots punctured the tires of our armored vehicle and we had little choice but to return once again to Kiryat Anavim. The rest of our convoy returned with us.

Incidents such as this, not uncommon during the War of Independence, illistrate the poor state of the weapons and equipment we had to fight with. Were it not for the intelligence, courage and dedication of the Jewish fighter, our troops would never have broken through the Arab military line and reached Jerusalem.

The next mission our unit was assigned concerned the broadening of the corridor leading up to Jerusalem. Our objective was to capture five Arab towns from what is today the village of Shoresh to Mevo'ot Yerushalayim. The first village we captured was Kfar Kolonia. The Arab defenses in the village were formidable and the fighting was heavy, yet we were victorious, and even captured a British soldier named Taylor who was working with the Arab gangs.

Most of our strikes took place at night. We were trained to exploit the darkness and found that night attacks maximized the element of surprise. We traveled on foot and had very few weapons. In addition to rifles and light machine guns, we also had some two-inch mortars and a few eighty-one millimeter mortars. We attacked Beit Surin successfully and assaulted Sova twice, until it too was secured. Our strategy was to capture a town at night, destroy all the buildings, and withdraw by morning, leaving the task of maintaining control over the area to another Palmach unit.

After this series of assaults, Dado was promoted to company commander and left our unit. I was assigned the duties of acting platoon commander. In this capacity I helped lead an action that was to be ill-fated and a terrible tragedy. The plan called for a coordinated effort by three Palmach platoons: one was to capture Beit Iksa, another was to reach Nebi Samuil, and the third, my unit, was to block the axis between Nebi Samuil and Biddu.

It was a cloudy night and very dark. As we approached Nebi Samuil my unit separated from Poza's, whose targets were the village and the mosque. I positioned my unit and we prepared to perform our function. Suddenly, and as if by an act of sorcery, the clouds and

fog lifted and daylight fell upon us without warning. I was able to
see Poza's unit charging Nebi Samuil in three columns, and in front
of me I noticed an Arab unit a short distance away. We opened fire
and almost immediately one of our squad leaders was shot in the
lower chest. We successfully evacuated him and continued to push
the Arabs back.

The timing of the attack was wrong, however. I was able to see
that Poza's unit was not doing well and that the attack had been
broken. At ten o'clock in the morning I was ordered to return my
unit to base. On the way back we found dead and wounded soldiers.
We placed the wounded on our backs and brought them back with
us. We had no choice but to leave the bodies of our dead in the fields.

In the fighting for Nebi Samuil we lost ten soldiers. All of the
commanders in Poza's unit were killed in the first round of the
fighting. The Palmach officer was often the first to die, as officers
were always the men who led their troops into battle. Leading troops
meant being in the front. This tradition is still alive today as the
slogan "follow me" is taught to all officers in the Israel Defense
Forces.

We reached Jerusalem on the eve of Passover 5708 (1948) and
were based in a former British military courthouse. On our second
day in Jerusalem we received an order to capture a British armored
car that was equipped with a two-pound cannon, which was a very
powerful weapon by the standards of that time. Our intelligence
information reported that the British drove the armored car on a
fixed route on the way to the maintenance garage. Two of our squads
squeezed into two taxicabs as we waited in ambush along a side
street. As the vehicle passed us, we drove behind it until it reached
the garage. When the three British soldiers got out of the car we
immediately surrounded them and, threatening them with our
weapons, disarmed them. With us was a French volunteer who had
served in the French underground, the Maquis, during World War
Two, whose task it was to drive the vehicle to our hiding place.
Unfortunately, also present at the garage were Jewish workers who

were concerned that they would be seen by the British as accomplices. They asked us to beat them, to dispel any suspicions, and sadly, we complied.

The armored car reached safe refuge in Kiryat Anavim where it was hidden under a pile of hay and straw. It was to play an important role in many battles to come, particularly the battle for Katamon. As a reward for securing the vehicle we were treated to a beer and a plate of cooked peas at the Vienna Café. For us it was the equivalent of a holiday meal.

As the seventh day of Passover approached there was talk that we were going to attack Katamon. Unlike the Israel Defense Forces of today, preparation for an attack did not include such basics as surveillance of the field, models of the objectives, or preparatory maneuvers. We were simply told to capture a specific place and were left to our own intelligence and courage to help us succeed.

It was raining heavily on the day of the operation. We assembled in the late afternoon and began our march toward Katamon. Not far from our objective we were spotted by Arab guards, who fired in the air. Rather than risk attacking without the benefit of surprise, we retreated back to our initial position.

During this time, different areas of Jerusalem were controlled by Arabs, Jews, and the British. The Jews controlled the Jewish Quarter in the Old City and all of the New City except for the Arab neighborhoods. The Arabs controlled the southern neighborhoods and the areas south of the city. Katamon was a vital strategic area because it dominated this whole region.

The following day we once again set out to conquer Katamon. I was leading a platoon in Company A. Company B was the attacking unit. There was a light rain as we marched through the Valley of the Cross, making the rocks slippery and the ground muddy. Company B positioned itself for the attack and opened fire. After a short while they had succeeded in securing the Monastery, a large, solid structure. Our Company was called in to take a defensive posture and we positioned ourselves along the stone wall outside of the Monastery. We knew the Monastery must not fall back into Arab hands, since it was situated on the edge of Katamon and served as a key control point for the Jewish neighborhoods in the north and the Arab areas to the south and east.

By dawn we were under heavy pressure from a large scale Arab counterattack. The terrain was such that the Arabs were able to fire at us from close range, advancing under the cover of bushes, trees, and stone terraces. We were two companies, approximately 120 men, fighting a combined Arab force of more than one thousand troops.

The first soldier from our unit to fall was Avraham "Semyon" Veiser from Petah Tikva. He was killed as he bravely crossed a path that was dominated by Arab fire to bring ammunition from the Monastery to our position outside. I found Semyon's body as I too crossed the path seeking to reach our ammunition supply. I succeeded in returning to our positions with two boxes of Bren gun ammunition. It was hellfire. We were being fired upon from a very close range.

The Arabs were attacking the Monastery's western entrance in great strength. The soldiers defending the small western gate were slowly losing control. Dado ordered my platoon to attack the Arabs from the northwest. We were a small unit of only five men, one machine gun, and Dado, who joined us. We spread out, opened fire and charged ahead. As soon as our machine gunner opened fire, he caught a bullet in the trigger guard, severing a few of his fingers and putting the machine gun out of action. As we approached the gate, I saw an Arab behind a rock aiming his gun at me. The next memory I have is of lying on the ground with a bullet in my head. As strange as it may seem, my thoughts as I lay there were focused on the fact that I was dripping blood on the scarf my friend, Motti Efrati, had lent me the night before, and that I would not be able to return such a blood soaked scarf to him. I was fully conscious and Dado grabbed me and brought me into a room in the Monastery that was crowded with our dead and wounded.

The pressure on the Monastery was mounting and the number of our soldiers being wounded grew in direct proportion. We could not get out of the Monastery and reinforcements were not able to reach us. An armored car we had acquired from the British just three days before was in the Jewish neighborhood of Bayit veGan. Although its cannons fired several shots at the Arabs, their pressure did not weaken and they effectively had us surrounded.

At 10:30 in the morning, the decision was made to attempt to break through the Arab line and abandon our position. There was little reason to continue to hold the Monastery and we knew that our defenses would soon be overrun. The Arabs were using armored cars they had captured in previous battles with our forces and were only a few feet from the Monastery wall, having succeeded in blasting a hole through it. One of our soldiers threw a whole sack of explosives at the vehicles, chasing them away, yet this did little to change the severity of our situation.

Although I was wounded, I was anxious to return to the fighting and requested permission to man a position. I was brought to a room with windows facing east that had Christian sacramental objects on the walls and many of our dead lying on the floor wrapped in sheets. I noticed the body of my friend Aryeh Haikin and began to feel weak and groggy. I overcame my weakness and took my position, which was on a chair that had been placed high on top of a table. In this position I was able to shoot through the window at Arabs climbing the stone wall of the Monastery's eastern edge. Although I was weak, with great concentration I was able to hold my rifle steady enough to aim and succeeded in hitting at least two enemy soldiers. The Arabs returned my fire, but to no avail, as I was deep inside the room.

As the time of our departure arrived, the wounded who could walk were organized and prepared to be taken with us. Those who were unable to leave were handed a hand grenade. The decision would be theirs: allow themselves to be taken prisoner or commit suicide. I too was provided with a grenade. Although it is not an easy decision to make, my mind's eye pictured all the mutilated bodies of the Jewish soldiers I had seen and I decided that if I were captured I would commit suicide. I even went so far as to consider how I would place the grenade under my body so that the pin would stay open.

Yet our departure was to prove unnecessary. We received word over our radio that Arab soldiers were seen fleeing the area around Katamon. This news, despite the steady pressure from the Arab assault, greatly lifted our spirits and provided us with the psychological boost we needed. By mid-afternoon the Arab offensive was over and the shooting had stopped. Reinforcements from the Fifth Company arrived by sunset and the wounded of Companies A and B were evacuated.

I was hospitalized in Sha'are Tzedek Hospital in Jerusalem. My x-rays showed I had shrapnel in my head, but the large number of wounded meant I would have to wait to have it removed. I was finally operated on in Afula during the first cease-fire. By the time the fighting resumed, I was back with my platoon.

My company was engaged in training exercises at a base near the center of Israel called Tzrefin. When I returned I noticed that we had received additional shipments of rifles and light machine guns from Czechoslovakia and that almost each soldier carried his own weapon. The only supply problem we still faced was a lack of motor vehicles. We often solved our dilemma by borrowing the jeeps belonging to the United Nations forces for prolonged periods of time. So as to avoid any misunderstanding, the jeeps were often painted different colors and officially transformed into Palmach vehicles. Our desperation for vehicles was so extreme that we would often travel into Tel Aviv and borrow jeeps parked on the streets.

Once our training period was over we resumed our fighting in the lower corridor of Jerusalem. We were based in Abu Ghosh and replaced the Yiftach Brigade of the Palmach in Bab el-Wad. My unit took up positions on a hill called Khirbet Hatulah overlooking the village of Deir Ayyoub, which is located at what is today the Sha'ar Hagai intersection. It was here that our comapny commander, Efrati, was killed. He and I were friends and it was he who had given me the scarf I had bled so heavily on during the battle for Katamon.

By this stage of the war we were a much better army. We operated according to well prepared battle plans and executed our tasks with greater coordination and organization. Over a short period of time our company participated in a series of successful assaults on Hartuv (including the fortified police station), Beit Jamal (including the monastery), Beit Natif, Beit Zekharya, Hassan, the area that is today Mevo Beitar, and the villages on the outskirts of Bethlehem.

After this series of successful assaults, a second cease fire was put into effect. The Palmach decided to use the lull in the fighting to once again improve our fighting abilities. As part of this campaign many men were sent to take various courses. I was sent to a base near the town of Netanya, half an hour north of Tel Aviv, to participate in the Class C officers' training course.

The first day of the course consisted of registration and orientation. The cadets were from a variety of different units and many had arrived at the course directly from the battlefront. We were assigned to large sheds, with forty men per shed. Each man was given a webbing and a weapon and we were ordered to be prepared to stand for inspection at four o'clock the next morning.

The next morning as we stood for inspection we were given the command to turn right and begin running. Without warning or explanations we kept running until noon. The August sun was hot and we ran for eight hours without rest or water. At noon we had a lunch consisting of a sardine sandwich and half a canteen of water. After a short rest, we resumed our running until sundown. After sixteen hours of running we were led back into our base near Netanya. As we stood before the commanding officer, we were told that the run we had just completed was our entry exam into the officers course and that 120 men had failed to complete the run. The course was modeled after the British officers course, but was altered to include key elements of the Haganah and Palmach fighting ideologies. It was physically difficult and an iron discipline was maintained, but I had little trouble getting through the course. I was highly motivated and enjoyed the rigorous training.

At the conclusion of the course I was promoted to the rank of lieutenant and assigned to the position of Deputy Company Com-

mander at the training base Mahaneh Yisrael, near Lod. Based not
far from our camp, in Beit Shemen, was Strike Battalion 89. The
commander of this unit was a man whose name and reputation were
already regarded as legendary, Moshe Dayan. For new recruits who
grew up on Moshavim in the Jezreel Valley, the name of Moshe
Dayan and his glory-crowned unit were part of the Zionist folklore.
I had many young soldiers from the north, from Kfar Vitkin and
even Nahalal where Dayan was raised, who were anxious to join
Dayan's unit. When these young men announced to me that they
were going to Beit Shemesh to join Dayan's battalion, I did not stop
them. In those days, the army was loosely structured and transferring to another unit did not entail filling out forms and waiting for
an official response. Rather, if a soldier wanted to switch his unit,
he often simply packed his bags and went to the unit he wanted to
join.

Ultimately, these young recruits would be the cause of my
transfer to the Tenth Battalion. Although I did not see anything
wrong with their joining Dayan's unit, Dado, our company commander, looked upon their action as an act of desertion. He had
them arrested and placed in detention at the Fifth Battalion. When
I heard what had happened I went to Dado to plead their case. I
conceded that they had left their unit without proper authorization,
but argued that they did so to join one of the most combat active
units in the Palmach. How could he call them deserters? When my
plea did little to change Dado's mind, I decided to take matters into
my own hands. I recruited some of my soldiers and physically
removed the detainees from the stockade at the Fifth Battalion.
Once they were free I reported directly to the battalion commander,
Yosef Tabenkin, and informed him of my actions. We agreed that
after defying Dado I could not remain in my unit. I requested the
Tenth Battalion because it was in the process of being organized into
a mobile brigade, with jeeps and armored cars. Tabenkin authorized
my transfer and I reported to Ramleh, where I was to serve as the
lieutenant of the company commander, Gavrosh.

The Tenth Battalion took part in a number of battles north of the Lachish region, on the border of the Negev Desert. Later, we were sent further south to Beersheba for Operation Horeb, a concentrated effort to strike at the Egyptian forces which were already being pushed southward from Nitzanim. The Egyptians were holding strong in the Faluja pocket and our task was to oust them. The plan was for the Palmach, which was situated to the north in Nitzana, to push southward toward Rafiah, while other units, including the Golani Brigade, attacked the strip from east to west. During the battle, we witnessed the rise of the young Israeli Air Force, as our brave pilots shot down five British Spitfires flown by British pilots, supposedly the world's best.

After the time I forcibly released the men Dado had placed in the stockade, relations between the two of us were spoiled. Many friends, who knew how close we had been before the disagreement, tried in vain to repair our friendship. Although we did not speak, my reconnaissance unit and Dado's Fourth Battalion worked closely together. When our units reached the Rafiah intersection, Dado requested to join a reconnaissance mission that was setting out to determine how far the Egyptian positions extended. Realizing this was an opportunity to mend our friendship, I offered to lead the mission, and invited Dado to ride in my jeep. There was a great sandstorm blowing and we were blinded by the wind and sand. We were able to find our way only due to our familiarity with the region from previous patrols. Our driver, Simcha, negotiated the roads while I took up position at the spandau machine gun. Dado was concerned that the sandstorm would cause the gun mechanisms to jam, but I assured him that it would not. Dado remained skeptical until we arrived at a fenced-in Egyptian position. Seeing the Egyptian forces closed in was an opportunity too good to let pass and I opened fire, causing a great amount of chaos in the Egyptian camp. We drove away under the cover of the sandstorm and on the way back to our base Dado offered me a slice of cheese and a cracker, his way of telling me that the frozen relations between us were fully thawed out.

Our next mission was to block the Rafiah-El Arish road, the route

Egyptian convoys used to carry supplies to their fighting troops. We set up ambushes and waited for an Egyptian convoy and we opened fire as it approached, causing Egyptian vehicles to turn over and catch fire. The Egyptian soldiers responded by firing on our position. Although we were aware of the dangers presented by the Egyptian response, our sights were set on a new Willy pick-up truck we had spotted at the head of the Egyptian convoy. For our unit, this was the same as an Air Force pilot spotting a brand new jet fighter. We had to have it. Our driver, Simcha, Gavrosh, and myself, inched toward the vehicle, and under the cover of my shooting, we managed to drive it to our position. We were all very proud. A Willy pick-up was a status symbol and units that successfully captured one were looked upon by others with a mixture of pride and jealousy.

That night we heard the growling of Egyptian tanks approaching our position. Our dilemma was that we did not have any means of defense against them, having used all the ammunition for our M-2 recoilless rifles in the battle that afternoon. We broke off contact, as the Egyptians siezed the area and removed the artillery that the convoy was hauling. The next day the Fourth Battalion attacked and re-took the area. The Egyptian military intelligence was unaware that our Fourth Battalion was armed with a six pound anti-tank cannon that was able to greatly damage their American-built 13-ton Locust tanks. The tanks returned and suffered complete defeat. We had managed to hold the area.

In the spring of 1949 a new cease-fire was being rumored. Our unit was sent back to the base at Mahaneh Yisrael and assumed positions for the decisive battle for Samaria. We were assigned the task of advancing east toward Kfar Kassem. However, before the battle began, Jordan announced it was joining the cease-fire talks in Rhodes. The War of Independence was over.

Our leaders believed that the cease-fire would be the first step on the way to a lasting peace. I also thought that there would not be another war and returned to the farm at Tel Adashim. When I arrived I learned that five men from the Moshav had given their lives for our new Jewish State, including Shlomo Granov who had helped me join the Palmach and who had served with Dayan in Strike Battalion 89.

After a year, I was assigned to reserve duty as a lieutenant in a company in the Ninth Battalion of the Northern Brigade. My commanders were eager for me to serve and share with new recruits my rich battle experience. I was called often for reserve duty and served with great satisfaction and purpose. After fifteen months, the brigade commander, Yehezkel Panet, suggested that I enlist in the standing army as operations officer for the Ninth Battalion. Panet and my father were friends from their days together in the Haganah, and he succeeded in gaining my father's consent to once again allow me to leave my duties on the farm.

I was promoted to the rank of Captain and entrusted with the task of preventing terrorist infiltrations along a long strip of the Israeli border from Hedera, through northern Samaria and along the northern valleys up to the Beit She'an Valley. Our mission was complicated by a lack of manpower and we supplemented our defenses with settlers from the Jezreel Valley, who guarded their settlements and provided assistance whenever called upon.

We were a young nation just over a difficult and often traumatic War of Independence. We had fought with valor, intelligence, bravery, and great courage. Yet, the war for our Jewish country was only beginning.

4

Airplanes
and Gliders

In the late fall of 1949, a short time after I returned to the Moshav from the War of Independence, I was enchanted by the notion of learning to fly an airplane and decided I wanted to be a pilot. A woman in our village was a clerk with the Air Force staff in Jaffa and she provided me with advice on how to get an interview with her commander. At the interview I boldly outlined my virtues as a fighter in the Palmach, hoping this would prove my abilities and motivation. The commander, who spoke with the accent of a native English speaker and had the wit and sarcasm of the English, was not impressed. He told me so by inquiring how long the bus ride from the Moshav to Jaffa had taken me. When I responded approximately two hours, he replied "Excellent. Then it will not be any problem for you to get back on the bus again and go home."

This first encounter with the Air Force dampened my enthusiasm for flying, but only temporarily. My only other contact in the Air Force was a cousin who served as a squadron adjunct officer in Ramat David, an airbase near my village. I pleaded with her, arguing that if I was talented enough to be an officer in the Palmach, I was also capable of flying an airplane. After considering my plea, and sensing how badly I wanted to learn to fly, she invited me to come to Ramat David.

The commander of the squadron was a man named Ezer Wiezman, who went on to command the Air Force and later served as Minister of Defense in the late 1970's. Ezer welcomed me with his

mischievous smile and introduced me to the pilot that was to "take
me up" as Adah's cousin. He then whispered something to the pilot
in English, which I did not exactly understand, but proved to be
"shake him up a bit." We got into a small Piper and, hoping to
squelch my enthusiasm for flying forever, the pilot did as Ezer had
requested of him. Once we were in the air we turned so forcefully
that I felt as if the air had been taken out of my lungs and I vomited
almost immediately.

This encounter succeeded in curbing my will to fly, but again
only for a short period. When I began my service as operations
officer in the Ninth Brigade, I took advantage of aerial patrols along
the border and had the pilot, an enthusiastic South African named
Bernie Luria, give me flying lessons.

In later years, when I served as company commander in the
paratroops, I finally got the opportunity to learn to fly. That year it
became customary for senior officers in the Army to take a course
in parachute jumping, and selected officers also learned to fly light
planes. This agreement came about when the Air Force commander,
Dan Tolkowsky, was in the parachuting course and proposed to the
commander of the Parashoot School that he learn to fly. The
commander then passed on this entitlement to me. I was determined
not to miss this chance to finally learn to pilot a plane. As a company
commander in the standing army, I found the time necessary for the
theoretical and practical studies taught at a squadron based at an
airforce base near Ramleh. My progress was not bad and I per-
severed in training long enough to finish the course, despite an
absence due to my being wounded in the Sea of Galilee action.

After completing the course, I requested and received permission
to continue to train as a pilot. The next course of study was the
Steerman plane, which was the basic aircraft in the flying school.
My instructor was Shai Egozi from nearby Kibbutz Ginegar. My
first lesson consisted of my sticking to the tail of another Steerman,
that was unaware of my purpose in following him. The pilot of the
other plane kept trying to lose us, but Shai continued shouting,
"Stick close to him." I had practiced pattern flying in the Piper

squadron but was not used to an airplane like this. And this was on my first lesson! But an instructor's command is an order that is to be obeyed and I stuck fast to the other plane, the whole time with Shai roaring, "Stick close, stick close." When the time for my second lesson approached I was not surprised when Shai told me that it was not really going to be a lesson, but rather a test. He instructed me to fly in the direction of Kibbutz Hulda at a very low altitude. When we reached the kibbutz, he instructed me to fly the airplane under a line of high tension wires that roped the kibbutz. I was a bit apprehensive and was thinking to myself that surely Shai was as interested in living as I was and that he certainly was not asking me to do something he thought I was incapable of doing. I concentrated on the ground and lowered the plane so that the wheels almost touched the ground. We passed under the power lines safely and Shai signaled to me to go back to the base for a landing. After we landed Shai informed me that I had passed the course and I was certified as a pilot for the Steerman. I enjoyed flying this plane as I found it to be responsive and aerobatic, and over the years I flew many hours with it.

A few years later I was overtaken by the gliding craze. I unintentionally entered a base that was involved in energetic gliding activity. I requested permission to try and was gladly accepted. Gliding totally captivated me. This was real flying — going up on air currents in the company of the birds, and staying in the air without the benefit of a motor.

We always dreamed of "long distance" flights, that is, leaving the area of the base for a distant destination. There were four types of flight options: the "small triangle" of 50 kilometers, the "big triangle" of 100 kilometers, a straight-line flight, or a round trip flight. Our level of gliding was not high enough to perform all of these, but we were persistent in our attempts. Eventually we succeeded in performing a triangle flight, increasing our confidence and encouraging us to continue seeking new adventures. My goal was a flight to the far south. I thought that perhaps in the skies of the Negev I would find what every glider pilot hopes for: strong, rising air currents, high altitude, distance, and speed.

My first attempt brought me as far south as Mitzpeh Ramon. I landed on a dirt track late in the afternoon. People passing by looked at me curiously and refused to believe that I had traveled so far without a motor. One family's disbelief was such that they settled down near the glider and didn't leave until a plane arrived to tow me back north.

My second try was more successful. I decided to attempt to reach Eilat, Israel's most southern point. The take-off was ordinary as I was towed to an altitude of 2,000 feet. At this altitude the world seemed quiet, still, with only the murmur of the wind around the closed, comfortable cockpit. Air currents started to flow and I went to work trying to tackle my first challenge of the journey, crossing the mountains of Ephraim. With endless patience and constant turning, in order to locate the center of the rising current, I crossed the mountains of Ephraim and began to glide southward. I located the rising currents by following clouds, or copying migrating birds, who were gliding as I was and could be trusted to find the strong wind currents.

I ran into difficulty near Tel Nof, north of Beersheba as my altitude sank due to no air currents. I steered towards the airfield with the intention to land. Suddenly I felt the wind push me upward in my seat. I glanced at the instrument panel, noticed I was gaining altitude, turned into the air current and forgot all thoughts of landing. I gained altitude to 5,000 feet and continued my journey southward. As I was approaching Beersheba I once again began to lose altitude and once again was rescued by a sudden burst of wind, bringing me this time to the very high altitude of 8,000 feet. From this altitude I easily glided to Sdeh Boker in the heart of the Negev Desert. When I reached the Meyshar my situation again took a turn for the worse. It was noon and my altitude was very low. The road on the Meyshar was very straight as if built to serve as a landing field. With my altitude at only 1,500 feet I checked to see if the road was empty of cars and straightened out the glider on the axis of the road. Then, just as I was placing my hand on the air brake, I heard a huge gust of wind and was lifted from a height of just 900 feet to 6,000 feet in a matter of moments. I reached Grofit on the edge of the Arava with no further difficulty.

I glided into Eilat on a steady northeast wind after a hard push near the lower slopes of the mountains bordering the Arava. These winds created what pilots call a steady, dynamic rising current and it permitted me to fly without losing even a foot of altitude until landing in Eilat.

When I landed there was not a soul at the airfield. When an older man finally appeared, he was confused at the sight of the glider. He questioned where I had come from and why my plane had no propellers. At first I was quiet and did not answer his many questions. Finally I looked him straight in the eyes and answered in English that I had come from Jordan and wanted to go back. When he heard Jordan, the old man panicked and began stammering in his broken English about Israel, passports, and the police. He made hand motions indicating that I would be placed in handcuffs and kept making a gun out of his fingers and repeating "boom, boom." I was quite amused, as I had not expected him to believe that I was from Jordan because my clothing was very Israeli and my glider was marked with the Star of David. As the man's excitement grew and I saw that his confusion might bring him to do something unpredictable, I said to him in Hebrew: "You might want to kiss me." A look of relief passed over his face and he laughed loudly. He helped me tie the glider to the edge of the runway and I then went to get myself a place to sleep in the Soldiers' House and to report my location to the base up north.

I arrived in Eilat at three o'clock in the afternoon after seven and a half hours of flying. I was hungry and thirsty and was anxious to celebrate my successful flight at a restaurant called the Blue Fish, which served the sea delicacies that I loved so much. I went to the restaurant directly after securing myself a place to sleep. As I sat on the terrace a young newspaper reporter asked if I was the pilot who had arrived on the airplane with no motor and requested an interview with me. I agreed in exchange for a cold beer and a sandwich.

A short while later another reporter approached me and a similar agreement was reached. With my hunger and thirst satisfied, I retired to my sleeping quarters.

The next day I was towed north in two hours. When I landed at my base, I attracted glances of astonishment and doubt. To this day no one else has ever succeeded in reaching Eilat in a glider.

I had many other flights and made other attempts at reaching the south. One of them ended in a real adventure as I was forced to land in a field occupied by a herd of goats as I lost altitude over the mountains of Ephraim. I was close to the border and there was very little flat land suitable for a landing. My only option was to gather speed on the descent and drop the glider's speed to zero as I approached the landing plot. The goats scattered and I was very lucky not to have been injured. The glider also escaped without damage.

As my responsibilities in the army grew, I had less time for gliding. As compensation, I was able to continue flying in the Air Force and took training courses for additional planes including the Cessna, the Dror, the Agur (a two-motored plane), and the Fouga, a training plane for jet pilots. I was also taught aerobatic exercises, navigation, pattern flying, instruments, and many other aspects of aviation.

The Fouga was an absolutely different kind of flying experience from any I had known before. I was allowed a solo flight after only three flights with an instructor, but once I was in the air alone, I had realized a dream; I was alone in the air, piloting a jet.

My passion for jets notwithstanding, my true love is gliding. Gliding can be achieved even in planes with motors. Once I was sent from the squadron in a Dror aircraft to Jerusalem so that I could gain some flying hours. In Jerusalem I was asked to take two separate groups of pupils in a radio officers' course in the air as part of a training exercise. I was told that after two hours of flying I could refuel on the field. On the first take-off I caught a strong rising current at the end of the runway and lowered the flaps, shut off the motor and allowed the wind to provide us with altitude. When we reached 6,000 feet I straightened the plane out and allowed the cadets to complete their exercise. I landed the plane without the plane's motors. I continued to use the Dror as a glider with the second group and proceeded to return to the squadron in Tel Aviv. In filing my flight report I wrote "negative" to the question concerning refueling. I was quizzed as to how I flew the plane for three hours on less than a quarter tank of fuel. My answers resulted in my being certified as a gliding instructor and I was pleased to have the opportunity to teach this wonderful skill to many young Israeli pilots. One such pilot who learned to love gliding was my son, a fighter pilot in the Air Force. His love for gliding and flying was cut short when he was killed in combat.

5

Ben-Gurion Decides

During the beginning of 1950 I was working on the Moshav and served in the military reserve. Although I found both of these activities rewarding, I was anxious to engage in activities I felt would directly contribute to our budding Jewish State. My opportunity came when I was requested to assist the large numbers of immigrants who were entering Israel from the European displaced persons camps and the Arab countries. These people were being encouraged to settle in the Negev Desert to revive the wasteland, but they had no agricultural experience or equipment. In an effort to assist these new Israelis, a group of young farmers from the Moshavim and Kibbutzim Mizra, Ginegar, Sarid, Merhavya, and Tel Adashim brought our tractors and plows to the south and taught them the art of farming. We set up a small camp of shacks for ourselves in Moshav Patish and worked with the immigrants side by side. We worked hard but got a tremendous amount of satisfaction from working and laughing with these courageous people. It was not long until we were able to look out at the rows of plowed desert earth, confident that soon our labor would reap fruits and vegetables.

My adventures in the Negev ended in the summer of 1951 when I was called upon to return to the regular standing army and serve as operations officer for the Ninth Brigade. The decision to return was difficult, as I had to weigh my responsibilities to the farm and the contribution I was making with the new immigrants against the wishes of my commanding officer and the knowledge that I would contribute a great deal by re-enlisting. In the end, I decided to enlist for two years.

During this time three events took place which permanently altered my life. The first was my marriage to Miriam. Marrying Miriam was a very natural thing for me. Her family had come to Israel from Germany in 1936 and settled on the Moshav in 1937. We first became friends when I was eight years old and she was six and a half. We were considered a couple even before we knew what being a couple meant. In January 1952, we made the link between us official.

The second event was my successful completion of the parachuting course in the spring of 1952. It was a difficult course which required a great deal of physical effort. The third influential happening was my learning to fly.

My first meeting with Ariel "Arik" Sharon was also an important event for me. We met during one of the many shooting incidents with the Jordanians in the region of the split village of Barta'a in northwestern Samaria. Arik was the intelligence officer of the Northern Command and our paths crossed during our respective official duties. It was a quick acquaintance that I did not attach much importance to at the time. In later years, however, my relationship with Arik Sharon would have a decisive influence on my life.

After a short while as operations officer I was sent to the battalion commanders' course, which I successfully completed. The course was the sixth such course in the history of the modern Jewish State and was commanded by Zvika Zamir. After the course I was assigned the post of commander of a reserve paratroop company and in mid-1953, at the end of my two year commitment, I was released from the army. I returned to the farm and once again began a routine of farm work and prolonged reserve military service, continuing to serve as company commander in the paratroop brigade. This was during the time Arik Sharon was setting up his famous and glorious anti-terrorist squad, Unit 101, which was later merged with the paratroop brigade.

I was serving reserve duty in the winter of 1955 when a parachuting exercise for the commanders' cadre was postponed due to inclement weather. Taking advantage of the free time, my friends and I went to a movie. During the movie my name was called over the loudspeaker telling me to report outside immediately. Once outside, I was informed that a company commander and his lieutenant had been killed by a mine on the border of the Gaza Strip. I was instructed to take my lieutenant and report immediately to the Egyptian border to take command of the company.

I took command in Sa'ad at midnight the same night. I was met by a group of young officers and a company that had been called up only a year before. Most of my soldiers were from farms and the few I saw that night worried me. The officers were bearded and it appeared to me that discipline was lax. My first act as commander was to issue an order that every soldier, both officers and enlisted men, was to report for inspection the next morning clean-shaven. My order did not make them very happy. They straightened their backs and looked in amazement at their strange new commander.

I felt that I had enough authority and experience to demand discipline from my men. I had my ways and beliefs about how soldiers, particularly officers, should conduct themselves. In later years, this company was the best in the battalion and I was their commander throughout the whole tense and active period of reprisal actions.

My unit was engaged primarily in patrols along the Egyptian border, surveillance, lying in ambush, and routine security procedures. Our challenge arose when we were selected to carry out the Khan Yunis action, the capture of a fortified Egyptian installation. The majority of my soldiers had no prior experience in this kind of difficult fighting and when the mission was imposed on my company, Company E, we spent many hours practicing tactics to be used in fighting against a fortified objective.

We set out at night on foot. We deployed south of the Egyptian position and when we reached the fences, we placed Bangalore torpedoes to break through. There were mines between the fences and we had to walk a narrow path. Our only loss occurred when a

young soldier, Lavi from Kibbutz Sarid, went off the path and
stepped on a mine. The Egyptians were totally surprised and didn't
have time to fight. Backed by artillery support, we overcame them
quite easily.

The Khan Yunis attack began the period of reprisal actions on
the Egyptian border. Our aim was to convince the Egyptians that
we would exact a heavy price for the many border penetrations from
their territory that resulted in military attacks on Israelis, often
civilians. These infiltrations took place not only with the knowledge
of the Egyptians, but also at their explicit initiative.

At the beginning of this period, I was under a great deal of
pressure from two competing directions. My wife and my family
wanted me to return to the farm, while the army argued that it would
be wrong for me to leave my company, particularly when the border
was heating up. I settled for a peculiar compromise that required
that I neither join the regular army nor return to the farm. I simply
signed a new agreement for reserve service every month. In this way
I served an additional year.

My company's next mission was to take over Tel Nitzana, where
United Nations troops were stationed. The battalion's mission was
to capture the whole Nitzana demilitarized zone. As we expected,
there was no battle in Tel Nitzana. We passed the United Nations
troops and proceeded to round up the Egyptian troops that were
there. In the morning, we took the Egyptians and told them they
were free to cross back into Egypt. They became panic-stricken,
sure that we were going to shoot them as they walked away. They
didn't believe that we were simply letting them go and did not move
until I swore to them on my word of honor as an officer that nothing
would happen to them. They began to move towards their border
at a hesitant pace. They were suspicious until they reached the
border. Our letting them go free did not fit the behavioral norms
they were used to.

Our next action was not conducted very smoothly. It was a
comprehensive action which included a variety of different units.
The objective was to attack the Egyptian positions in the region of

Sabha Be'erotayim. My company was ordered to take the central position which controlled the lower ground leading up to the Israeli border. We started at Mount Harif and travelled on foot. We walked in a deep flanking movement and attacked the Egyptians from behind. There was no real resistance and we overran the position in a quick night attack. Yet, despite the lack of resistance, the attack was one of our company's most challenging. Our difficulty had nothing to do with the Egyptians, but rather an error made by our cook that caused the whole company to be stricken with a severe case of diarrhea. We had no choice but to continue fighting, but we were very uncomfortable and dirty when the fighting ceased.

I was called to report on this action to the Prime Minister and Defense Minister, David Ben-Gurion. The exact reasons I was honored with the opportunity to report directly to Ben-Gurion I still do not know. Perhaps it was because the results of the action diverged from the original goal in that there were many Egyptians killed and taken prisoners. Whatever the reason, the jokers in the army rumored that Ben-Gurion, who saw how dirty I was, generously offered me his underpants. Of course this never happened as I had enough time to wash up and change clothes, but the idea was enough to allow us to make a joke out of what was a very bad memory.

I had met Ben-Gurion once before in the winter of 1953. He had resigned from the government and was living in the Negev on Kibbutz Sdeh Boker. It was he who had summoned me, among the group of young northern farmers, to the Negev to persuade us to move to the south to assist the newly arrived immigrants. In his cabin in Sdeh Boker, Ben-Gurion spoke to each of us, and with his air of authority he raised a finger toward us and told each of us what we were to do and where each of us would be of greatest benefit. He told me I was to serve in the army and stay in the army. After he spoke to us, as far as he was concerned, the matter was closed to discussion; Ben-Gurion had decided.

Another boy who had been there that day was Zorik Lev from Kfar Bilu. He was killed in the Yom Kippur War leading Skyhawks in an attack on Suez. His body has not been found to this day. Zorik commanded the Air Force base in Ramat David. He missed being my in-law when my son, many years later, married his orphan daughter. I didn't have time to be a father to his daughter because my son, who was a fighter pilot, was killed while flying two weeks after the wedding. In 1953 Zorik was in exile from the Air Force because many years earlier he had hit the roof of a car with the propeller of a Mosquito aircraft. The car belonged to a Rothschild and Zorik was expelled from the Air Force. At our meeting with Ben-Gurion he explained the accident and requested to be allowed to return to the Air Force. Ben-Gurion arranged for Zorik to return to active service.

Our detail on the Egyptian border served as an excellent training mechanism for my forces and we continued to grow into an excellent fighting unit. We were always on alert and ready to be called into action. One morning we got an order to raid Kuntilla that same night. The plan was to ride from Camp Natan near Beersheba, over the Sdeh Boker road, through Mitzpeh Ramon and Nahal Paran and up to the Egyptian border. We were to raid Kuntilla across the border and come back to the base the same night. Preparing for an action of this kind was already routine. We worked out the minutest details while traveling from the camp to the Egyptian border. We got out of our vehicles at ten o'clock at night and began to march the fourteen kilometers to Kuntilla. My company was joined by another reprisals unit led by Meir Har-Tsion, a man who was to become a legend because of his bravery and leadership. A third company was also involved and it put up roadblocks on an access road to block Egyptian patrols. The night was well lit from the light of a bright moon and Meir and I feared that we would be spotted too early. When we noticed Bedouin tents ahead of us, we decided to change the direction of our attack and had the troops exercise a right flanking action, instead of a left flanking action as was planned. We attacked from west to east and quickly took the two central buildings of the Kuntilla police fortress which stood on high Tel Kuntilla. Our attack was a total surprise and our speed did not allow the Egyptian forces enough time to organize a credible response. We even had the opportunity to seize two Egyptian units, as a replacement of units was taking place on the evening of our attack.

I received a merit citation for this action from the chief of staff of the army. The citation was later changed to the "Medal for Bravery." I was cited because during this action I and two other soldiers stormed a heavy machine gun post and succeeded in neutralizing it with our Uzi sub-machine guns. We left Kuntilla before dawn carrying one dead, several wounded, and a great deal of equipment. We also led a caravan of Egyptian prisoners back. From a physical point of view, this was one of the most difficult actions I had ever experienced. It was an important example of the ability to act quickly in difficult and extraordinary conditions, and to perform an action in its entirety. It illustrated the prevailing spirit in the paratroopers that it was important to complete a mission in its entirety, under all conditions and without limits.

The actions of those days developed combat doctrines and methods of combat still in use in the Israel Defense Forces today. The ideas were revolutionary and innovative. We developed ways to penetrate mine fields, break through fences and fight in trenches and built-up areas. We trained in land-sea maneuvers and engaged in special parachuting exercises. We reached a high level of cooperation and coordination with the Air Force and Navy. The great sense of readiness we felt as a result of our skills contributed to the ability of each soldier to dare bravely and believe that the capability of each soldier has no bounds.

At this time Arik Sharon had risen to paratroop commander. He made a great contribution to the fighting spirit and development of methods of combat. He was avid for operational activity and hurried to the Chief of Staff, Moshe Dayan, to urge him to allow us launch a reprisal action after every terrorist attack. His zeal and the strength of his influence led us to perform actions in quick succession with each action having its own character and merit.

6

Wounded on the
Sea of Galilee

In December 1955 my company had its status changed to a squad
leaders' course. Our camp was set up the mountains of Ephraim.
One Friday afternoon we received an order to prepare for an assault
we would be launching against the Syrians who were constantly
harassing the Israeli fishermen on the Sea of Galilee with motar
assaults and sniper fire. It was felt that a vigorous response was
necessary. The next morning, the Sabbath, we gathered in our
commanding officer's tent for a planning session. The action was
set for Sunday night.

We came together in Filon, an assembly area. On Saturday and
Sunday we were feverishly busy with preparations and planning. We
conducted surveillance missions, reviewed the mission with the
soldiers and readied the equipment we needed to cross the Jordan
River. Our company's mission was to cross the Jordan north of the
Syrian position, which was situated at the river's mouth. We were
to attack the Syrian platoon position and maintain our control over
the site. Attention was given to every detail. We observed the Syrian
position from very early morning, so that we would be able to detect
their nighttime deployment.

Many units took part in the assault. Additional forces crossed the
Jordan at the same point as my unit. One company was heading for
the Bey's House, while another went to block the upper custom
house road in Taha. A fifth unit stood by in reserve.

The night of the attack was cold and rainy and the skies were completely dark. We carried the rubber boats for crossing the Jordan River on our shoulders. On the bank of the Jordan we began to blow up the boats with containers of compressed air. The inflating process was noisy and we feared we would be discovered by the Syrians. We decided to abandon the boats and instead marched through the cold water.

My company crossed first. We approached the eastern wing of the Syrian position while other units were crossing behind us. Suddenly soldiers from our unit were fired upon by a group of Syrian soldiers who had crossed the Jordan to the west and met up with the last of our soldiers crossing the river. Two of our soldiers were killed. The shots woke up the Syrians in our target position, but we knew it was doubtful that they understood that a large Israeli force had crossed the Jordan.

Our company split up into three sub-sections. The northern unit was to penetrate under the fence and capture the communications trench. The central unit, under my direct command, was to penetrate the entrance and the third unit was to penetrate under the fence to the southern trench. This unit encountered an obstacle, in that the trench under the fence was sealed with fishing nets and they could not pass under as the other two units had done. I ordered that the other two units, the northern and the central, begin fighting, while the southern unit blew up the fence and penetrate the trench.

The Syrians were surprised. Approximately ten seconds after we began the assault, we heard an explosion which indicated to us that the southern unit had succeeded in penetrating into the trench. The process of taking the position ended quickly. While we were still reorganizing within the position, heavy fire was directed toward us from an outside post about ninety feet away from us, at the northeast corner of the position. A machine gun and three rifles were firing upon us and placing us under heavy pressure. We jumped into a shallow trench behind a mound of dirt and spread out with the dirt in front of us. We returned fire in the direction of the Syrians and then, facing heavy fire, charged them. A Syrian bullet hit officer Itzik Ben Akiba in the hand and I was struck by three bullets, two in the foot and one in the chest, not far from my heart. I felt as if someone had caught me by both legs and was pulling me to the ground. I fell heavily and was pulled back to the trench. My unit then destroyed the Syrian position that was firing on us.

The medic quickly bandaged me, and although it would not be easy, it was decided that I should be evacuated. Several blankets from the Syrian position were wrapped around me as I was very cold from the strong rains. My troops found a fishing boat anchored in the Jordan next to the position and I was placed in the boat on a stretcher. My troops then began to push the boat with their hands down the river into Lake Tiberias towards Kfar Nahum.

I sailed in the lake along the northern shore. The water was above the height of those pushing me and the boat shifted about and filled with water, despite the desperate attempts to keep the boat stable. I was cold and wet and had the sad thought in my blurred mind that this was the last time I would ever sail on the Sea of Galilee.

Finally we arrived at the ambulance. A military policeman was with the ambulance and insisted I give him my personal details such as my military ID number. Next to my number he wrote "Reg" for regular army, to which I informed him that he needed to write "Res" because I was a reserve soldier. He disregarded my statement and informed me I was in a state of shock and therefore perhaps confused. I insisted he write "Res" and pointed out the absurdity of his arguing with a wounded man. Finally, he did as I requested.

It was nice in the Poriyah Hospital in Tiberias. I was operated on to remove the bullets in my foot and chest. They cleaned and sutured my wounds and I recuperated. I left the hospital in January 1956 and was promoted to the rank of major. I was temporarily prohibited from parachuting because of the wound in my chest and therefore was appointed deputy commander of Battalion 890. After a short time, preparations began to send a delegation of paratroopers to the free-jumping competition in the Soviet Union. I received official status in the delegation and waited impatiently for the opportunity to jump once again.

7

An Emotional
Encounter in Moscow

Our group traveled in July 1956 to the Soviet Union to compete in an international skyjumping competition. The trip to Moscow was the first time in my life I had left the borders of Israel for peaceful purposes. In fact, only two people in our group had ever been abroad. They were born in Europe, but they too had not left Israel since their early childhood.

As first-time tourists we had many humorous situations arise. Perhaps the funniest concerns a stopover we had in Brussels for one night on the way to the Soviet Union. We were placed two to a room, and I was rooming with my friend Micah Kapusta. That evening we were impressed that the Belgians had thought to place two toilets in the room and as it was in the army, it was natural for us to go to the bathroom together, to converse while tending to nature. To our dismay, and initial alarm, when we were finished and flushed, one toilet performed as we were accustomed, while the other sent sprays of water forward into the air. It was then that we learned what a bidet was, this having been overlooked in the education we received on the farm and in the Palmach.

After a brief stopover in Prague, an Aeroflot airplane flew us to Vilna, where we had a heavy meal before continuing on to Moscow. When we arrived in Moscow we were placed in the Moskva Hotel. I was again rooming with Micah and we were relieved to see that the room did not have a bidet.

Every morning we trained at Toshino airfield. We had a Russian

N-2 airplane at our disposal, complete with pilot. We also had an older Russian man attached to our contingent, who would bring his motorcycle with a sidecar to where we had landed and drive us back from the far reaches of the base. I enjoyed this man's company and by the time three weeks had passed I was able to remember enough of the Russian I had heard as a child to speak with him comfortably.

After our daily training session we would return to the hotel to shower and eat. The Russians would then take us on organized trips in Moscow and the surrounding areas. We were very pleased with the way the Russian government and people were treating us. We were the benefactors of their gracious hospitality and their warm greetings. The hotel also provided a gesture of hospitality in that there was an old "babushka," a sweet, kind woman, on each floor to care for our needs.

One of the funniest sights was the courtyard near our hotel where the police used to gather the drunks. We were able to hear the arguments and misunderstandings as the drunks attempted to negotiate their release. Finally, we watched as the police and drunks made peace by sharing bottles of volka and getting drunk together.

We were assigned a small bus with a cheerful Ukranian driver named Mikhail Stepanovich. He used to amuse us by pressing the clutch down when traveling downhill. Although we advised him that he would ruin his clutch if he continued to drive in this manner, he persisted, explaining that it saved gas, which was his own expense, while a replacement clutch would be the problem of the government.

We also had a permanent escort, a friendly college student named Anya, who shared with us many stories about life in Russia. She quietly explained to us that the clean and comfortable Moscow we were being shown was not the same Moscow the residents knew. She described poverty and fear of government agents, as well as food shortages and poor housing.

The day of the parachuting competition we noticed that the Toshino airfield did not have a control tower. Instead, pilots communicated with a woman seated at the end of the runway by signaling her with a wave of a scarf. We did not do well in the competition, finishing last out of eleven teams, but this did not dampen our trip.

The uncontested highlight of the trip for me was completing a task my father had requested of me, a visit to a relative of his that he had not seen since he left Russia in 1904.

One afternoon I left the hotel determined to find my father's relative. I had his address, but no idea where his house was or how to get there. As I left the hotel a man I assumed was being friendly approached me and asked if I needed assistance. I showed him the address and he immediately offered to show me how to get to my destination. He hailed a taxi and together we rode out of the Moscow I had been shown and into the Russia Anya had described. We passed old, broken down houses and traveled on dirt roads and after a short while we arrived at the address I needed.

My escort, whom I still considered to be no more than a kind soul, told the taxi driver to wait for us and accompanied me to the house. The door to the house was made of a heavy wood and I knocked hard for fear that a soft knock would not be heard. After a few moments of silence, the door opened and an old man, with wrinkled skin and sad eyes, stood before me.

I addressed him in Hebrew, having been told by my father that this old man before me was once a brilliant doctor and ardent Zionist. I told him that I was from the Land of Israel and watched as his sad eyes became bright and full of joy. He invited us into his one room apartment and I was saddened by his poverty. He had once been the chief surgeon at Moscow's central hospital, but at the time of the infamous "Doctor's Plot" campaign, he was sent to Siberia, the effects of which doomed him to live out his life in squalor and filth.

As we sat and talked I was told, in Hebrew, that the kind man who had so graciously escorted me was a Soviet government agent and that I should take caution in what I said. Despite this, I was anxious to make this poor relative of mine happy, and spoke at length about Israel, the War of Independence, the Palmach and anything else he was curious to know. Every place I mentioned in Israel lit another spark in his eyes and I knew he was receiving much joy from my visit.

When the time came for us leave, he escorted us to the door and, placing his hand on my shoulder, told me that he would never have the opportunity to make aliyah, but that he was with us in his mind and soul. I will never forget his final words as I left his home, as he stood by the doorway, an old and broken man. "Israel is ours," he said, "Guard our treasure."

After my return to Israel I would often think of my old relative when times were difficult, because his memory served as an inspiration and renewed my sense of obligation and commitment.

Interestingly, during the course of our conversation he had mentioned that he had two daughters living outside Moscow. While I was there I did not succeed in finding them, as I had no address. After I left the army in 1985 I was giving a lecture in Haifa, after which a woman approached me and placed a note in my hand. I was accustomed to receiving such notes, which usually requested my assistance in some personal matter, and was about to explain to this woman that I was no longer in a position to assist her, when instead I decided first to read what she had written. Her note was simple, it read, "It was my father you visited in Moscow in 1956." I was very happy to finally meet her and chided her for waiting all those years before contacting me. She informed me that her sister was also in Israel and that they both had children. I was pleased that my old friend's family had made it to Israel, so that through them his dream was being fulfilled.

On the way home from Moscow we stopped in Warsaw and toured the Ghetto. I was very moved, filled with a mixture of anger at what had been done to my people, and pride at the strong Jewish army I represented. From Warsaw we continued on to France, where we stayed for a few days as official guests. Afterwards, we returned home to Israel.

Upon my return I was appointed commander of Paratroop Battalion 890. In the first few months we carried out numerous reprisal attacks against Jordanian police forts in retaliation for attacks perpetrated by Arab terrorist gangs operating out of Jordan. We attacked forts in such places as Grandel, R'ava, Husan, and Kalkilya. Our strikes were well organized and executed.

During our raid on the R'ava police fort, situated on the Beer-sheba - Dahariya highway, Meir Har-Tzion was badly wounded. The doctor accompanying us, Dr. Ankelevitz, operated immediately, under extremely tense and dangerous conditions. He saved Har-Tzion's life and was honored with a merit citation for his bravery. In a twist of sad irony, the attack on the Husan fort claimed the life of Musa Efron, the man who had commanded Battalion 890 just prior to me. He had been assigned to another position, but voluntarily joined our unit for the Husan mission.

The attack on Kalkilya was the most difficult of all. Our battalion was to serve as a reserve unit, and was stationed on the slopes of Kibbutz Eyal. A Nahal unit was assigned the task of capturing the police fort. Their reconnaissance platoon had the task of blocking off access to the fort and positioned themselves at the foot of Camp Azub, east of Kalkilya. They came under heavy Jordanian fire, and it was feared that they would be cut off from the rest of our forces. My unit, traveling on foot, went to assist the beleagured platoon, as did an armored vehicle unit commanded by the Deputy Brigade Commander Hofi. This unit suffered losses as it approached the Jordanian position, Sufin.

In all, the brigade lost eighteen soldiers that night. It was a difficult time for me, and one of the many that caused me to think of my old relative in Moscow, with his sad eyes that glowed at the mention of Israel. "Israel is ours. Guard our treasure," he had told me, and I knew that he was right and that we also had no choice.

8

Operation Kadesh — The Sinai Campaign

The Kalkilya assault was the last reprisal action against a Jordanian police fort for my unit. Yet, the experience we obtained through the assault, and from so many others like it, was to be put to the test when hostilities with Egypt intensified and Operation Kadesh was launched.

Two days prior to the initiation of hostilities, on October 27, 1956, I was advised of the pending assault in our brigade operations room. The walls of the room were covered with aerial photographs of the Israeli-Egyptian border and the Sinai Peninsula up to the Mitla Pass, approximately thirty miles from the Suez Canal. I studied the photos, taking special note of the road access, while listening to the role my battalion was to play.

On Monday, October 29, my brigade was to parachute into the heart of the Sinai. Our mission was to establish a defensive position around the crosroads near the eastern outlet of the Mitla Pass. We were to maintain this position until another paratroop unit, which would be traveling by vehicle and was going to cross the Egyptian border near Kuntilla, met up with us.

The task was formidable. We were going to jump only a short distance away from the Egyptian border without knowing how long we would be totally isolated. The unit assigned to meet up with us was going to have to travel a great distance, successfully overcome Egyptian resistance, and build the roads they were to travel on as they advanced.

After being given the order to prepare the battalion for the jump, my unit had the difficult task of determining which equipment and what quantities to bring along. Naturally, on a parachute jump, the amount of supplies that can be brought along are limited. Therefore, our priorities had to be clarified. Would we need water more than bullets? Should we bring more machine guns or hand grenades? Our problem was alleviated the next morning when we were informed that a French cargo plane would be dropping equipment to us during the night of October 29. The plane had recoilless rifles, jeeps, 120mm mortars, food rations, water, ammunition, and fuel. The 106mm recoilless rifles were unfamiliar to us and a last minute decision was made to assign a platoon to train on these effective weapons immediately. They would train until the rifles were dropped and would parachute with the supplies.

As is always the case with an operation of this magnitude, there were last minute changes. Although we had first planned to jump at the western end of the Mitla Pass, the discovery of a small tent village housing road workers on the site forced us to shift our jump to the eastern end.

In the afternoon of October 29, we boarded sixteen Dakota transport airplanes and began our flight to the center of the Sinai. As our planes flew above the Kuntilla border crossing we saw clouds of smoke and dust below. We understood this to be our brigade crossing into Egypt on its way to meet us at Mitla.

As the plane approached the drop site I stood by the door, first in line. I had a feeling of great excitement, despite having jumped many times before. This jump was part of a wide-ranging military operation and was far from the Israeli border. When I got the go-ahead I jumped and drifted slowly down toward the Mitla crossroads. It was five o'clock in the afternoon and the sun was beginning to set. There was a stillness interrupted only by the sounds of our planes and isolated gunfire.

After freeing ourselves from our parachutes, we quickly regrouped and unloaded our weapons. We spread out and assumed positions in the staging area. The sun had already set as we began to set up roadblocks, lay mines, and dig in. The task of fortifying our positions was made easy by the bunkers and communication trenches that were still standing from the days of the Turks. After positioning two units at the Parker monument to the west, we completed our days work by marking the area the French planes would need to drop our supplies.

Not long after completing our position, we had our first encounter with Egyptian forces. They were traveling past us, unaware of our presence, when we took them by surprise. We captured several of their vehicles and were lucky to find a generous supply of drinking water as well. After the French completed their drop, we were confident that we were well supplied.

Late that night I prepared to sleep. Sleeping the night before a battle is always difficult because there is great tension and excitement. Yet, I dug myself a foxhole, upholstered it with cardboard, cushioned it with parachutes, and went to sleep.

At dawn I awoke and examined the area. Our troops were engaging in minor clashes with Egyptian forces that were passing through the Mitla Pass as they fled our advancing troops. As I was inspecting the area I noticed some of my troops engaged in what appeared to be a very strange ritual. They were examining each package of battle rations the French had dropped to us the night before, throwing some aside and opening others. My inquiry revealed that the French had prepared two kinds of rations, one for Moslem soldiers, which were without alcoholic drinks, and others for Christian soldiers, which had small bottles of cognac. My troops were searching for the preferred Christian rations.

We had some men who had been wounded in the jump and we called for a Piper plane to come and evacuate them. As the plane arrived we were attacked by two Egyptian MIG-15 planes and our Piper was set ablaze. We placed our wounded, and the Piper pilot who was wounded by the Egyptians, in a makeshift infirmary which we placed in the center of our encampment.

We were under slight pressure from the Egyptian Air Force. Luckily, a light fog had fallen over our position and the Egyptian pilots had difficulty locating us. The Israel Air Force was also very active in defending us from air strikes and successfully shot down four Egyptian Vampires who were harassing our battalion.

We received reports from our pilots that Egyptian forces had entered the Mitla Pass and in the early afternoon of October 30 our unit at the Parker monument was attacked. A mortar exchange ensued and we were successful in stifling the Egyptian assault.

Toward midnight of Tuesday, October 30, we spotted the distant headlights of our brigade as they advanced. When they arrived we greeted them with great joy, our shouts and screams breaking the pastoral ambience of the still desert.

As dawn approached on October 31, the newly arrived brigade was resting before resuming its advance west toward the Suez Canal. As I reviewed the area, I again spotted soldiers involved in what appeared to be strange behavior. They were carry huge pieces of frozen sheep meat on their shoulders. It was explained to me that the soldiers from Nahal had acquired the meat from the Egyptian refrigerated storerooms and had given my soldiers some of their prized booty. Unfortunately for them, I ordered them to return the meat, explaining to them that in my battalion what was not available for all my men would not be available to any of them. Although disappointed, they understood my position and willingly complied with my order.

At noon the Nahal unit, commanded by Motta Gur, began its drive toward the Suez Canal. With their departure came the beginning of the battle for the Mitla Pass, as they were soon to encounter the equivalent of two Egyptian battalions. Our pilots had reported that there were no Egyptian forces in the area, but they had failed to spot those Egyptians that were positioned in sand holes and the caves among the rocks in the Pass.

The Egyptians allowed the Nahal unit to pass their first position and then opened fire on them from both the front and rear, effectively trapping our forces. In the mid-afternoon I was ordered to travel the four miles to the Pass to check the situation. Upon my arrival, I met up with the paratroop unit command by Aharon

Davidi, which had not yet entered the Egyptian-controlled area.

Although there was enough of a link with the trapped Israeli unit to know that their situation was severe, we did not have any data concerning the deployment and strength of the Egyptian forces. We sent a reconnaissance unit on a flanking maneuver to link up with the trapped force, but it returned unsuccessful, having taken heavy fire and suffered losses.

Davidi and I held an impromptu strategy session to determine how we would discover the Egyptian positions and strength. It was decided to send a volunteer to the besieged unit to gather a full account and update of the battle. Although I personally volunteered, Davidi did not agree to my going, and we accepted Davidi's driver's offer to volunteer. As Ken-Dror's jeep traveled west around a curve we heard heavy gunfire and a loud explosion and we understood that his jeep had exploded.

We were now a larger force, as units commanded by Oved Ladjinski and Levi Hofesh arrived from the base area. The Egyptian air force was harassing us and inflicting damage and injuries, as we were without the protection of our airplanes, that had gone to refuel.

We finally decided to send in a group of fighters in a half-track. This unit was to be commanded by Dan Ziv. While Ziv's unit was reaching Motta Gur's trapped soldiers, we succeeded in locating three Egyptian units situated on the cliffs and initiated fire with our recoilless rifles. When Ziv's group returned with detailed information concerning the exact Egyptian positions, we immediately began planning a night assault to free the besieged unit.

That night the unit, commanded by Oved Ladjinski, attacked to the left, while Levi Hofesh's unit attacked to the right. Within two hours the two units had successfully destroyed the Egyptian positions and linked up with the Nahal unit. The next day my unit continued the action by mopping up the remaining small number of Egyptian forces in the area.

The battle for the Mitla Pass cost us a great deal in blood. Thirty-six soldiers were killed, including commander Oved Ladjinski, and many more were wounded. We suffered these losses due to a severe error on the part of our intelligence division and because we were excessively confident in our belief that the area was free of Egyptians.

When we returned to our base area we immediately improvised a runway and called in Dakotas to evacuate the dead and wounded. Gur's battalion was evacuated to the north.

On Thursday, November 1, my unit received orders to advance to Ras-Sudr. We gathered our equipment and painted our vehicles with the air-ground identification markings which were being used by Israeli, British, and French forces, to prevent our aircraft from mistakenly firing on our infantry and artillery troops. At nightfall we began our move toward Ras-Sudr, navigating our way through the ink-dark night with poor maps and by trial and error. By daybreak we reached our destination and entered without resistance, since Ras-Sudr was completely empty. There were no soldiers and no civilians.

We took positions and awaited our next orders, which arrived the night of November 2. A Dakota flying overhead instructed me to move south to At-Tur. I ordered one platoon to stay behind and hold Ras-Sudr and began the 150 mile trip to At-Tur with the rest of my battalion. Although navigation was no problem because there was only one road along the coast, we were concerned that we had no intelligence data regarding the military formations we might encounter along the way.

As we entered the village of Abu-Zneima we were surprised to be greeted by cheering residents. After a brief inquiry we learned that the villagers mistook us for Syrian soldiers, who they believed had arrived to save them from the advancing Israeli army. When we informed them that we were the advancing Israeli army the streets cleared out quicker than anything I had ever seen. We refueled our vehicles and continued on to Abu-Rodeis, where we also stopped to refuel.

Our encounters with Egyptian forces were increasing as they were withdrawing in our direction from Israeli troops advancing on Sharm el Sheikh and At-Tur. When we arrived in At-Tur in the late afternoon our forces had already captured it without encountering any resistance. We were ordered to rest and await our next orders.

The men in my battalion were tired and hungry. We had not eaten since we passed Abu-Zneima and were out of rations. The commanding officer at At-Tur informed me that rations would not be arriving, but that there was a general store in the center of town. I immediately drove to the store and startled the Egyptian merchant by announcing that I was buying all the canned goods in the store. I had a burlap sack of Egyptian currency that we had captured during the initial battle at the Mitla Pass and emptied the sack onto the counter. I asked the merchant to take what the merchandise was worth and he carefully picked seven pounds out of the pile. I did not know the value of what I was taking, but trusted that the Egyptian was so startled and frightened that he would not cheat me. I then loaded the cans, which had very colorful labels, into the jeep and returned to base, anxious to give my troops the good meal I knew they deserved.

When I returned to my battalion I divided the cans evenly among my men, giving each platoon ten purple cans, twelve yellow cans and eight green ones. My men enthusiastically gathered driftwood from the sea and began campfires, anticipating the warm food awaiting them in the cans. After a few moments I heard a series of disappointed moans coming from all directions. I heard one group shout that the purple cans contained only jam, another shout that the yellow cans contained only jam and yet another confirm that the green cans were also jam. I had bought seven pounds worth of jam. My men were hungry and they ate, although I am not sure many of them were able to eat jam ever again.

Before we retired for the night, a runner brought me a note with our orders for the next day. Without any briefing or commanding officer to consult, the note simply read that we were to take Sharm el Sheikh the next morning.

At dawn we embarked on our 40 mile drive to Sharm el Sheikh. The tires on our half-tracks were ruined and we were traveling on the rims. As we entered the mountain passes between At-Tur and

Sharm el Sheikh our encounters with Egyptian forces intensified. As we drew closer to our destination we discovered a variety of obstacles blocking our way, including mine fields and sections of the road so damaged we could hardly pass over them.

Once we arrived at Sharm el Sheikh we encountered no resistance. We took many Egyptians prisoner, including officers, and one soldier who looked familiar to me. I later discovered he had fallen prisoner to us a year earlier during an assault we had carried out in the Nitzana demilitarized zone.

We were hungry and thirsty and took advantage of the abundance of provisions we found in the storage room. There were canned meats and vegetables, and for the first time in my life, I drank Coca-Cola.

Once we had finished eating we interrogated the senior Egyptian officer and other ranking officers. We were particularly interested in the whereabouts of the Israeli pilot Yonatan Atkess, whose dog tags and flying certificate we found while searching the area. The officers told us that Atkess was shot down over Ras-Nasrani and transferred to an Egyptian boat. We had no independent means of verification, but we later learned that we had been told the truth.

After a short time the Ninth Brigade, commanded by Avraham Yaffe, reached our position. We had been responsible for the southern district of Sharm el Sheikh and the Ninth Brigade had taken the northern sector. Many young men from Tel Adashim were assigned to the Ninth Brigade and we greeted one another with great enthusiasm. I was saddened to learn that one resident, Max Fisher, was killed at Sharm el Sheikh.

Upon his arrival, Yaffe surveyed the area and ordered my unit to return to At-Tur. Although we were disappointed to be leaving the plentiful rations we had discovered in the Egyptian army warehouses, we had no choice but to obey his direct order. We gathered our belongings and left Sharm el Sheikh for the journey south. As we were traveling, we spotted an Egyptian car coming toward us. Immediately we jumped to the side of the road and prepared to fire. Only at the last minute did we realize that the car was carrying Moshe Dayan, the Israeli Chief of Staff and other top Generals. I was so relieved that we caught ourselves before firing that I gave Moshe Dayan the Egyptian flag from Sharm el Sheikh, that I had taken as a souvenir.

We arrived in At-Tur in the evening and were told that we were being evacuated to the north on the following night. Prior to our evacuation the General of the Southern Command, Assaf Simhoni, landed at At-Tur in a small Piper. After his plane refueled, he took off never to be seen again. He and his men died in a plane crash and I was the last person to see them alive. I learned of the accident only after we had been evacuated to the base Tel Nof.

Prior to the Israeli evacuation of the Sinai I too came very close to death in an airplane. We were flying over the Kuntilla area on a patrol flight when we spotted a group of men waving their shirts rather desperately. We immediately landed close to them and to our horror learned that they had stumbled into a mine field and that we too were inside its parameters. It was a miracle that our plane had not been blown up as we landed. We told the group that they should stay exactly where they were and that we would go and call for help. Our dilemma, of course, was how to take off without blowing ourselves up. After discussing it with my co-pilot, I decided the only thing to do was to take the chance that there were no mines directly around the airplane. I took the nose of the plane, which was facing south, and walked it around so that it was facing the north. Once this was successfully accomplished, I rode the plane on the tracks we had made while landing. Although miracles are not in the habit of occurring twice in a matter of moments, our luck stayed with us and we took off safely.

After the withdrawal from the Sinai, my unit went back to our base near Kfar Yonah and Kibbutz Nirim. We spent a good deal of our time engaging in operational activity such as ambushes, patrols, and preventing terrorist incursions along the Gaza Strip and south of Mount Hebron.

The base was more than a military installation. Since almost all of our military activity was performed during the nighttime, the daytime was spent training and patrolling. Our base was also the site of many school visits from Kibbutz Nirim because we had five camels on base that had been confiscated from Bedouins who had been smuggling hashish into Israel. The children loved to play with the camels and we had no objections until one day one of the camels became angry and charged the small children. I was passing by at the time this potentially dangerous incident occurred and immediately picked up a big stick and positioned myself between the angry camel and the frightened children. The children managed to retreat to a nearby tent and I managed to distance myself from the enraged animal. After a short time, the camel calmed down and strolled away. During this whole episode, however, many of my soldiers had gathered, watching their commander play with this camel. In fact, the troops roared with laughter when, at the height of the tension, my deputy, Marcel Tobias, dryly commented, "So, our commanding officer plays with camels. Beautiful." I later returned the humor when I was taking off in a small plane and I noticed him walking through a series of puddles. I lowered my altitude just enough to give him a scare and he responded by throwing himself to the ground. I laughed heartily as I watched his wet body rise from the ground. Later, we laughed together, agreeing that the score was even.

In 1958 I took a break from the constant operational activity and attended a command and staff course. I enjoyed the year's course and returned to my brigade as deputy commander. In this capacity I had the honor to serve under three distinguished brigade commanders; Yitzchak "Hakka" Hofi, Eli Ze'era and Menachem "Men" Aviram.

During this year I also received my Pilot's Certificate and Wings. I had completed the course officially in 1957, but missed the graduation ceremony because my unit was called upon to bring home Israeli weapons that had been left near Hen-Duwar, where Kibbutz Sanir now stands in the north. A year later I was on a patrol flight in the south and accidentally crossed the border into the Sinai. Although I returned to the Israeli side of the border immediately, the United Nations forces below took note of my airplane identification number and reported the crossing. I was a bit apprehensive when I was called before the Chief of Staff, Chaim Laskov, and Commander of the Air Force Ezer Wiezman to report on the incident. I explained what had happened with absolute honesty and was commended by Laskov for doing so. He then informed me that Weizman was present to give me my pilot's wings.

Pinning pilot's wings on a soldier is usually not a very complicated task. However, in this case it proved to be. When Weizman asked if he could pin the wings above my left chest pocket I refused, noting that my red paratrooper wings were there and that I was extremely proud of them. After Weizman demanded that I remove the paratrooper wings and I again refused, we decided we would pin the pilot's wings above the paratrooper wings. This, however, was not acceptable to Laskov, who reminded us that two sets of wings could not be worn on the same side. Finally, it was agreed that although it was a departure from normal procedure, the pilot's wings would be worn above my right chest pocket.

Thus, as the Sixties approached, I proudly displayed my pilot's wings and paratrooper's wings as I tended to my daily responsibilities as deputy brigade commander, and as my unit continued in its rigorous routine of military activity.

9

With the
U.S. Marines

After I completed the Command and Staff course in 1958, the army wanted to send me to France for advanced courses. In an effort to prepare myself for my studies, I began to learn French. My strong suit, however, has never been the study of foreign languages, and it was not long before I realized that my French would not be sufficient to allow me to completely benefit from the course of study, so I gracefully declined to attend the course. Then, in 1960 I issued a request to Commander Laskov that I be sent to the Command and Staff school of the United States Marines. Although no Israeli soldier had ever studied there before, Laskov agreed.

I was less concerned with this language barrier because I had a foundation in English and was able to understand most of what was said to me. However, I did take a series of lessons to prepare for an informal English test the United States Naval Attaché in Israel was going to give me over lunch. My admittance was dependent on this exam.

As I faced the Naval Attaché in the resturant I was aware that I was with an American war hero who had commanded a submarine during World War Two and had seen a great deal of action against the Japanese. As we spoke, only in English, it was clear that I was not passing the exam. I did not understand much of what he was saying and he had no idea what I was trying to say. To my amazement, as our meal arrived he spoke to me in perfect Hebrew, telling me that we would never finish our meal if we continued to speak

English and that it was better if I learned English in the United States, while attending the Marine Command and Staff course. I was so happy I wanted to kiss him. Despite my poor English, he was willing to take a chance with me, and in the process he was offering me a wonderful opportunity.

In June 1960 I arrived in the United States with my family. I was met by the Israeli military attaché, who drove me to Quantico where I registered for the course. My family found a small house, called Parker House, which was damp and humid and had toilets that frequently stopped up. It looked good from the outside and we tried to make a home out of it. After living in the dampness of the Parker House for a few months, we decided to move into an apartment which was in a two-family house occupied by a sergeant from the base. The house was a wooden cabin and was situated in the heart of a forest. It was very beautiful there and we stayed there until the year course ended.

My first adventure in America was the purchase of a used car. I had never bought a car before and did not understand the importance of bargaining with the salesman. I had carefully allotted two hundred dollars for the car and made the mistake of telling this to the salesman, who happened to have a car for two hundred dollars. It was clean and the engine ran well and so I bought it. It was only later that I learned that the same car could have been mine for one hundred dollars.

There were sixteen foreign students in the course, from South American, Far Eastern, and Western European nations. I was the only representative from the Middle East. For the first two weeks we studied English, local customs, the structure of the Marine Corps. and modes of behavior. The Marines have a fascinating history and I was intrigued by their structure, in that they are unlike other military organizations. A marine is trained in many different areas and can perform well as a platoon leader one day and as a pilot the next. The variety is tremendous, the quality is impressive, and the "esprit de corps" is high. Most of the Americans at the course had the rank of major or lower. At this time I was already a lieutenant colonel, but I temporarily demoted myself so that I would not be isolated from the others.

I was very much accepted by the American students and instructors and a close friendship developed between the school commander and myself. Later on in his career he was a candidate for commander of the Marine Corps., but was not chosen for the post and retired from the military. Sadly, a few days after his retirement he suffered a heart attack and died. To this day my wife and I are in contact with his widow.

The course of study was extremely interesting to me. We studied military tactics and strategies and even explored matters involving nuclear warfare. The course also included many tours throughout the United States, which gave me the opportunity to see this country in all its grandeur. During much of the course I felt at ease and at home because a great deal of the behavior and thinking patterns were similar to those I had encountered and learned in the Israeli paratroopers. Both they and the United States Marines have a special readiness to bear any burden and believe in the unlimited potential of every soldier.

At the beginning of the course I had difficulties with English and often recalled the words of the American Naval Attaché during our lunch in Tel Aviv. He had expressed confidence in my ability to learn English while at the course and I was not going to let him or myself down. In a short time I was able to lecture the class, as was required, on the central security issues of my country. My real integration came about through a tactical exercise the school held whereupon each student was to prepare an American Marine landing in Israel to help defend it from an Arab attack. For several days all the students in the course turned to me for assistance and advice. I was asked where a base should be positioned, where the best site for launching a counter attack was and what were the best routes for the transporting of supplies.

Naturally I could not be in the United States for a whole year without putting myself in near death situations at least a few times. The most frightening of these was the time my wife and I took the children for a six hundred mile drive to visit some of my wife's relatives in Constantine, Michigan. We loaded the kids into "Carl," as we called our car, and set out for what was to be a nightmare. Coming from Israel's warm climate I did not know that the car needed anti-freeze in the gas tank. It was the middle of winter and the snow was as high as sixteen inches. On the ride to Michigan we broke down numerous times. We'd pull over to the side of the road, place a white handkerchief on the car antenna and wait for assistance to arrive. While waiting we wrapped our freezing bodies in blankets, newspapers, and rags.

Once we arrived in Michigan I learned that my wife's cousin had married an amateur pilot. Despite the cold, I suggested we rent an airplane and hit the skies. We took off with the snow white ground below us and the sunset above us. It was very beautiful, peaceful and quiet. We decided to fly to Kalamazoo and then turn back to Constantine. After completing the round trip we arrived at what we thought was Constantine, but could not be sure because the snow had covered the ground and there were no clear ground markings. We could not distinguish the runway and Constantine had no control tower or radio operator. With little else to do, we decided to fly back to Kalamazoo and calculate our exact flying time. We would then turn around and, through this calculation, hopefully find Constantine. Neither of us was particularly happy with the situation, because, aside from the possibility of running out of gas, we also knew that as the night grew darker, our landing would be more difficult. In addition, we knew we ran the risk of not finding the Constantine airport, in which case we would have to make a forced landing. Luckily, our calculations on our trip to Kalamazoo were extremely helpful and on the way back we spotted the runway lines in Constantine and successfully landed the airplane.

The whole year I was in the United States my town, Tel Adashim, was never far away. On one occasion, as I was touring a base of the American Special Forces, I was introduced to two Hebrew speaking sergeants. One of these sergeants told me that he had been an illegal immigrant in Israel in the 1930s, that he had arrived from Czechoslovakia and that while in Israel he stayed on a Moshav not far from Haifa. While the sergeant spoke I recalled that when I was a child my Moshav had hosted a group of illegal Czech immigrants. My suspicions that he had in fact stayed at Tel Adashim were confirmed when he told the story of a farmer named Eitan who worked with a pipe in his mouth and always looked after the immigrants' needs. I told this sergeant that I was that farmer Eitan's son and we laughed and hugged each other warmly.

A similar incident occurred while being flown to Canada for a tour of a Canadian military base. My guide shared with me some of his experiences as a member of the British Special Police during the days of the British mandate. He recalled that once a group of illegal Jewish immigrants were embarking at a beach near Tel Aviv from a boat called "Shabtai Ludinsky" and that he and others had arrested many of the Palmach troops that were on the site. As he spoke I listened with a slight grin on my face, and after he completed the story I informed him that I was one of the Palmach soldiers that had succeeded in escaping that night.

After the year in the United States was completed, my family and I eagerly awaited our return to Israel. On the way back we made a stopover in Germany and our hosts were very cordial, although I must confess that I felt a barrier between us, as if none of us could completely overcome the Nazi murder of six million of my people. I knew that those with me were too young to have been involved in the war of twenty years before; however, the wall could not be removed.

Upon my return to Israel I was appointed to the position of Chief of the Operations Department of the General Staff. During my two years in this capacity I was a participant in a great many planning and strategy sessions on the general staff level. I maintained my connection to the paratroopers, taking part in jumping exercises, but also learned a great deal about the many other branches of the Israel Defense Forces. During these two years I also studied general history, military history, and Middle Eastern geography at Tel Aviv University. These studies, my combat experiences, and my studies at the United States Marine Command and Staff course greatly assisted me in the successful execution of my duties.

10

A Dangerous
Lion in Ethiopia

Following my studies at Tel Aviv University, my thirst for knowledge intensified. As a child I had not had the opportunity to continue my studies at Tel Adashim, so I was now eager to take advantage of every opportunity. Thus, although it was clear that upon completion of my tour of duty as Chief of the Operations Department I would be appointed to follow Motta Gur as Commander of the Golani Brigade, I instead requested to attend the first class of the Israeli National Security College. My request was approved and a tacit understanding was reached that after my course of study I would serve as Commander of the Paratroop Brigade.

Prior to my entering the Security College I took two trips overseas. The first trip, to Argentina, was in February 1963. I was the head of Israel's delegation to an international gliding competion. Part of our time was spent in Buenos Aires, but the competition was held in a small town in the heart of the Pampas flat plains called Junin. Our stay in Argentina was extremely uncomfortable, as it was consistently marred by acts of anti-semitism such as the painting of Nazi swastikas and desecrated Israeli flags on the walls. Our hosts were for the most part apathetic and would do little more than have the walls painted over.

The second trip was to Ethiopia. An Israeli military delegation was to tour this African nation and despite my request not to go, the Chief of Staff, Yitzchak Rabin, assigned me to the delegation.

After we landed at Addis Ababa and registered at a small

European style hotel, I set out to find my brother, who was in
Ethiopia instructing and helping to organize the border guard. To
my delight, we were staying at the same hotel and we took advantage
of the opportunity to spend some time together.

The Ethiopians received us graciously and generously. We were
taken on many tours and hosted at many receptions. Often we were
faced with a dilemma because they would go to great lengths to
prepare a feast for us, complete with their delicacies, and we would
not find much of the food appetizing.

Our first reception was at a military base not far from Addis
Ababa. The Ethiopian military had cleaned the base and set out a
variety of sliced and cubed meats. The meats were all half-cooked
and certainly were not kosher. Also on the table was a big, round,
flat bread they call "injeera." To my taste, the injeera seemed to be
made of straw and mud, and together with the meats, seemed to
present a frightening culinary adventure. Yet, we were all conscious
of the feelings of our hosts. Luckily, the Ethiopians also placed a hot
sauce on the table that was used to spice the meats and injeera. We
used this sauce generously; it was so hot that it made you forget what
you were eating and where you were eating it.

From Addis Ababa we flew to Harar. From there we accompanied Ethiopian officers on a jeep ride to Jijiga in the Ogaden
desert. The ride was fascinating for me as I had the opportunity to
see the African wildlife: apes, deer, and a wide variety of birds. While
in Jijiga we also had the chance to visit local tribesmen, who were
not always on friendly terms with the Ethiopian government. The
village we visited, in the Ogaden desert, was cooperative and even
allowed us to take some spears, arrows and swords. This was an
incredible gesture because usually the tribes hid their weapons from
the Ethiopian authorities.

Continuing our tour of the country's beautiful landscape, we
visited Lake Tana, the source of the Blue Nile. At a magnificently
beautiful oasis called Agrodath, near the Sudanese border, we had
yet another close call when our Ethiopian guides wanted to shoot
some wild baboons, so we could enjoy a "special lunch." Our

dilemma was stopping them without insulting them, which we achieved by firing a rifle and scaring the baboons away. What was most fascinating about this whole episode was that after we fired the rifle we watched as a few large baboons made frightening sounds and chased the smaller ones away. Interestingly, these large baboons did not run away themselves until all the smaller ones had left. For us, Israeli soldiers with a tradition that calls for leaders to take responsibility and accept danger, it was an incredible sight.

Our trip to Ethiopia ended earlier than expected. Although the others in the delegation knew the reason for our early departure, they did not reveal anything to me. When I returned to Israel I greatly appreciated their self-control, as I was met by my wife who informed me that our oldest son, Yohanan, who was only ten and a half years old, had died of asthma at our home in Tel Adashim.

Upon my return, it seemed hard to imagine that only a few weeks before I had been standing in the courtyard of Haile Selassie's palace where there were caged lions on display. Since I have always loved animals I approached the cage of the largest beast and placing my hand in, began to pet him behind the ear. Although I did not think I was doing anything extraordinary, I later learned that my lion friend was considered the most dangerous lion they had ever caught in Ethiopia. The irony that I could pet a ferocious lion and survive, yet, my little boy lost his life to an asthma attack did not escape me.

11

Pranks and the National Security College

In 1964 the National Security College opened in Jerusalem. For me, this was a very interesting year of study that greatly broadened my horizons. Our courses included problems of the state from the national aspect, the civilian system, the Jewish-Arab conflict, economics and security, and the impact of these on national security.

The year at the College, however, was not all study. There were plenty of pranks too. We were not able to devote ourselves to our studies only, although our practical jokes did not detract from the seriousness of our courses or our diligence as students.

The best example of our dedication to the practical joke is the time we played a great prank on our fellow student, Bar-Giora. One dark, cold, very rainy night, a group of students were guests at the home of the course commander, Uzi Narkiss. Those of us who did not go stayed at the College, and with little else to do, planned a joke on our friend. Bar-Giora was hopelessly obsessed with his car and we decided that the best joke would be one that revolved around his car. Among our group was a friend who could adapt his voice to imitate different dialects and he telephoned Narkiss' house and pretended to be a neighbor. He explained to Narkiss that he unfortunately had to confess to hitting a car with military plates parked in front of his house and asked if perhaps the owner would be at the

Narkiss residence. He then apologized, noting that in the darkness he simply had not seen the car. Uzi asked those present if their car was parked outside, at which time Bar-Giora became very anxious. He was sure it was his car that had been hit and, as we later heard from those present, he stormed outside and felt his way around the car's every side while getting soaking wet in the rain. When he came back to the party he told Uzi that we fixed him pretty good and that he would be seeking his revenge.

His revenge came later that night when he called us where we were gathered in the College. I lifted up the receiver and Bar-Giora told me that although the joke was funny, something unpleasant had happened as a result. He told me that Narkiss had also run out of the house and had slipped and fallen on the wet pavement. I was told that our course commander was injured and very angry. This news deflated our celebration over our successful joke and caused us all great concern. Each of us went to sleep while in our imaginations we saw the commander coming to the College in the morning, resting on a cane, injured and angry and asking just one question, "Who was it?" Bar-Giora's practical joke had an effect which lasted far longer than ours did.

Another interesting and fun part of the course was a series of hidden camera films we made for our graduation celebration. Perhaps the funniest of these is the one in which the hidden camera is aimed at the front door of the home of the commander, Uzi Narkiss. The door opens and Uzi and his young daughter go out to their car. Two "street cleaners" are standing next to the car and have placed a cardboard box stuffed with wet trash on the car's gleaming hood. The camera focuses on Uzi's face, which reveals rage. Uzi is speechless and then barely manages to scream, "What's going on here?" One of the "workmen" innocently responds that they work for the city and are cleaning the street. Uzi continues to protest about his car, but instead of answering, one of the cleaners puts his hand in the pile of trash on the street and spreads it over the box on the hood.

Uzi decides to act and tries to grab the filthy box and push it off the hood, but one of the cleaners gets in the way. Uzi is now terribly angry and he grasps the two ends of the box and lifts, only to discover that the box has no bottom. The trash spreads all over the hood and sprays the windshield. Uzi, nearly out of his mind, tries to grab a broom from one of the cleaners to brush off the hood and the windshield, but is told that the broom is city property and only they are authorized to use it. After an argument with terrifying shouts and threats, Uzi opens the door and pushes his confused daughter into the car. While one of the workmen cleans off the car, Uzi starts the engine and then drives away in a hurry. The film ends with one of the workers shouting toward the car, as it drives away, "Why are you so nervous? We're only cleaning the street."

Another great hidden camera film was centered on Rafael Vardi, an instructor in the College, who was a former Commander of Military Police. Vardi is a man of law and order, of limits and discipline. He is precise about small things and believes that in the massive army system, precision in small endeavors decides the fate of the bigger, overall system.

One evening a "military policeman" knocks on Vardi's door and asks him to come outside. The policeman explains to him that there is a suspicion that Vardi's car has been involved in an accident with the Prime Minister's car. Vardi is told by the young policeman that his car must be checked and that he, the policeman, was sent to investigate. Vardi is surprised, but understands and tells the young military policeman to carry out his orders.

The policeman drives Vardi's car and suddenly brakes, doing this three or four times. Vardi watches quietly, while the hidden camera picks up signs of tension on his face. After the policeman returns he points out to Vardi that his military police emblem is really that of the National Security College and the camera focuses in on Vardi's wide smile as he realizes the practical joke.

The year at the Security College was a great deal of fun. More importantly, however, I learned a great deal and I brought the lessons with me to my new assignment as Commander of the Paratroop Brigade.

12

Commander of the Paratroop Brigade

As was promised, upon my graduation from the National Security College I was promoted and assigned to the position of Commander of the Paratroop Brigade. For me personally this was the fulfillment of a personal aspiration and I entered my new task with great enthusiasm. I believed in the quality and ability of our young, brave paratroopers, and was proud to be their commander.

We placed special emphasis on training. We engaged in airborne amd sea landing exercises and cultivated resourcefulness under conditions of complete isolation. We focused on these aspects of warfare because we recognized them as the unique fate of a paratroop unit. By definition they would be parachuting or landing by sea, often behind enemy lines. Under these circumstances, they would always be in risk of being cut off from food and other essential supplies.

In attempting to simulate the conditions of warfare, we often brought our soldiers to isolated areas, as we did when the whole brigade participated in Maneuver Avraham at Sdeh Avraham, near Uvda. What made this maneuver memorable was that due to winter weather conditions we were truly cut off from supplies for two full days, making the exercise very genuine.

We trained in different terrains and under a variety of weather conditions. We planned every training session so that it would be diiferent from the one before it in duration and objective. Our emphasis on training brought about a high operational level and increased our organizational structure.

The airborne exercises are the most difficult, in that they require a great deal of coordination. In addition, every paratrooper is aware that on occasion a chute fails to open. This frightening experience happened to me four times during my military career. The first and most frightening time was two days before I left for the United States for the Marine Command and Staff Course. We were engaged in a night jump exercise near Hedera. The first to jump was the brigade commander Yitzchak Hofi, and I jumped immediately after him. As I was falling into the absolute darkness I realized that my chute had not opened. Before I could pull my reserve chute open I fell into the canopy of an open chute beneath me. Realizing that I had fallen into Hofi's chute, and that we were rapidly falling together, I moved my body in every direction so as to free myself. The darkness was so heavy that I was not able to see and did not know how long it would be until I reached the ground. Thus the moment I was free from Hofi's chute, I pulled my reserve chute open. From the moment my chute opened, it was only a few seconds before I hit the ground.

We spent a good portion of our time on routine security patrols along the borders and performing retaliatory raids in response to terrorist attacks. We struck at the flour mill and police force in Jenin and blew up eleven wells in Kalkilya. We were active in the south, in Jerusalem, along the Syrian and Jordanian borders, and in the north. I often led assaults personally. Others were led by my deputy commander, Arik Regev.

A constant area of concern was south of Mount Hebron, a zone of action for Arab fedayeen harassing Israel. In response to a series of Arab actions we were ordered to enter the town of Rifaat, on the southern edge of Mount Hebron. Our mission was to destroy ten homes indicated in aerial photographs. We evacuated all the residents of these homes prior to blowing them up, and in a move that was to become famous in Israel, we distibuted candy to the Arab children, so that they would not be frightened.

Our biggest reprisal action south of Mount Hebron was in reponse to a mine that was planted by fedayeen on the road along the Israeli border. One of our vehicles rode over the mine and some of our soldiers were killed and wounded. Within two days of the incident we planned a broad reprisal action including paratroop and tank units. Our target was a town called Samu'a.

We crossed the Jordanian border at six o'clock on a Sunday morning and captured and surrounded Samu'a. Once in control of the town we destroyed certain installations and retreated back to the Israeli border. During our disengagement we encountered Jordanian troops and inflicted heavy casualties. Our price was also heavy however, as we lost battalion commander Yoav Shaham and suffered several wounded.

I served in this manner for two and a half years and toward the end of 1966 I began to hear talk of a change in post, as is customary in the Israel Defense Forces. At this time there was a great deal of tension between Israel and our Arab neighbors and I felt that war was on the horizon. Under these circumstances I wanted to remain the commander of the Paratroop Brigade. I met with the Chief of Staff, Yitzchak Rabin, and requested a six month extension of my duties. He agreed to my request, thus securing me a role in Israel's remarkable defeat of the combined Arab armies of Egypt, Syria, and Jordan in June 1967.

Part Two:
THE SIX-DAY WAR

13

Waiting

The first reports of an Egyptian concentration of forces in the Sinai reached our Prime Minister and Defense Minister, Levi Eshkol, and the Chief of Staff, Yitzchak Rabin, while they were reviewing the Independence Day parade in Jerusalem in mid-May 1967. Shortly after being appraised of the situation, Rabin remarked to me that we "are entering a period of tension," which was confirmation of the fears I had expressed to him several months earlier.

The Egyptian actions were cause for great concern, and the crisis intensified when the Egyptian leader, Nasser, expelled the United Nations forces which had been stationed in Sinai after the 1956 war. While the political echelon was struggling with the crisis, our brigade was shifted about from division to division, in accordance with the nature of our missions, which changed completely from day to day. Finally, we were permanently assigned to the division commanded by General Tal.

A few days before the war broke out we were given orders to proceed south. As a gesture of unity, we decided to partake in a farewell jump on the sands of Palmachim. The whole staff was to jump, including the female clerks, sergeants, and unit commanders. The first person to jump was a female clerk, who also happened to be my sister's daughter. I jumped third, following my personal clerk, and all the others jumped after me. While I was happily gliding under the canopy of my parachute and slowly approaching the sand, I heard terrifying screams from the girls who had jumped seconds before me. As I landed I immediately freed myself of my parachute and rushed to them. When I reached them I found them upset and pale because they had landed next to a huge viper which had taken shelter under a bush on a mound of sand.

I glanced at the snake and was surprised to see a reptile so large that it would surely endanger the life of anyone landing near it. Fearful that the snake might cause someone great harm, I decided it would have to be killed. Unfortunately we had jumped without any weapons, and so I was forced to improvise. I decided to shake the snake out of the bush by banging on the bush with the helmet of one of the clerks. Once out in the open I was hopeful that I would succeed in tiring the snake. Once tired, I planned to seize his tail, turn him in the air, and knock his head on the ground until he was dead.

As the snake fell from the bush he slithered around the ground and shook his formidable tail. Forty-five minutes later both I and the snake were worn out. I remained calm and patient, however. This was a war of attrition. There could be no frontal assault here. I simply had to wait him out. I noticed his reactions slowing down and that he was becoming less alert. These are the decisive seconds in any battle and I increased my concentration. I resumed my banging of the helmet until the snake finally stopped reacting. He did not shake his tail and he did not slither anymore. He had come to terms with his defeat. Suddenly I saw that the end of his tail was projecting outward and I seized it. My heart grew faint at its length and thickness as I grasped it with both hands, turning it in the air and knocking his big head on the sand. After a few moments it was clear that this massive reptile was dead and that we had won this small battle before the big war.

As we headed south our tasks were still undefined, although the smell of war was looming in the air. We wandered from zone to zone as our assignments were constantly changed. Finally we settled down, helping settlements on the border of the Gaza Strip to dig trenches and to fortify themselves.

With the war only a few days away, I had great problems keeping my brigade whole. The brigade originally contained three battalions and four other units. At first the army reassigned our armored car company which we had just set up. Later, despite my efforts to resist, the brigade reconnaissance company was also reassigned. When they notified me that I must give up one battalion, I felt besieged and burdened in a way I had never felt before. The task of choosing which battalion would leave the brigade, and fight the war alongside another unit, was very complex. I had trained each of my battalion commanders and woven warm and special ties with them in preparation for the day we would fight a war together.

Yet a decision had to be made, and finally I chose to send the battalion commanded by a strong leader named Barzani, who later rose to the post of commander of the Border Guard. In making my decision my main considerations were which unit I felt could act more independently than the other battalions, which commander would be less insulted if I sent him out of the brigade, and, quite honestly, which brigade was I least committed to have fighting beside me during the war. There is no final, unambiguous answer to any of these considerations and none of the battalions supplied a complete answer to the three criteria. I was quite tormented until I actually settled upon my decision.

After reviewing the assault plan for the attack my brigade was to participate in should war break out, I felt uneasy with the direction we were being told to attack from. A day before the war began, I went to General Tal's HQ truck, spread out my maps, and explained to him my apprehensions. I offered a counter-proposal, which to my relief he readily accepted. The next day, as war broke out I was very confident as to the quality and motivation of our forces.

The morning of the war we assembled at the Tse'elim base at

around eight o'clock. In the skies we already saw our airplanes flying toward their targets in Egypt and the Sinai. The commanders gathered under the camouflage netting to review the battle plans. There was radio silence and at nine in the morning, I received the order to move out. The plan was to outflank the Egyptian positions defending Rafiah from the south, and to then turn north and fight them along their narrow axis, until we arrived at the Rafiah intersection.

We proceeded in a horseshoe format with the tanks taking the lead in two columns, the paratroopers on half-tracks in the rear, and my command group in the middle. The engineers advanced between the tanks, linking the two columns of the brigade.

As we crossed the border the steep dunes and deep sand made movement very difficult. The tanks had a better capability of advancing over such ground conditions than the half-tracks and they moved ahead faster, leaving a gap. After a short while they encountered fire at the southern end of a Egyptian position, but it proved inconsequential.

We crossed the Rafiah-Nitzana road, which had been destroyed in Operation Kadesh in 1956, and turned north. Further ahead we were able to see a Nahal battalion, which had gone straight up to the edge of an Egyptian position, preparing for their assault on the position. My unit continued forward and I was puzzled as we passed a group of Stalin tanks, some of which seemed whole, while others had been blown up. One tank was still burning, which indicated that a great deal of time had not passed since our forces had destroyed them. Still, I didn't understand where these tanks had come from and it was only later that I learned that a rare conjuncture of events had saved us from a very severe blow. As is often the case in warfare, many times you escape injury only because, it would seem, an angel was sitting above and directing harm away from you. The tanks, destroyed and still burning in the middle of the desert was one such time that the angel was watching.

When the Egyptians noticed our flanking movement to the south, the commander of their southern brigade ordered his Stalin tank company to move southward and deploy against us. There they were to wait for our arrival. Had they succeeded, they could have devastated us. Their Stalin tanks are the heaviest tank in the world and are equipped with a terrifying 122 mm cannon. Luckily, the tank unit with us, commanded by Danny Shani, had gone ahead of us a great distance and spotted the Egyptian column. At the short range of under one thousand feet Danny's tanks destroyed the Stalin tanks one by one. The encounter cannot even be referred to as a battle because the Stalins did not have time to shoot even one shell. The danger we faced from the Stalin tanks was so great because we did not have any weapons that would have been able to confront the tanks. Quite simply, if Shani and his men had not been alert, we would have been destroyed.

As we continued our advance north, the war was raging along the whole width of our advancing front. The area was saturated with Egyptian soldiers, their artillery batteries, and command posts. We also spotted many Egyptian soldiers fleeing from our advance and running from the war. We were fighting over a wide area with the battalion on the left fighting in the area of Kfar Sh'an, the brigade command group in the center, and the Nahal battalion at the Egyptian position on the right. As we passed a series of eucalyptus trees, I shared with the young men in my half-track the history of the site they were passing. I told them that we had fought right at that same spot during the War of Independence and that we had set up an ambush of an Egyptian artillery convoy. Such were the realities of being an Israeli soldier. The political climate and international inclination has always been not to allow Israel to win decisive military victories. Thus, there are many Israelis who have been forced to return to the same battlefields to fight another war.

In the area of the 1948 ambush the command group, consisting of my half-track and two additional half-tracks, got bogged down by Egyptian fire. We had been fighting for hours against a variety of Egyptian positions, bunkers, artillery positions, and infantry and were tired of running, jumping, diving to lie down, and firing while sitting. To make matters worse, our ammunition was running out and the war was still at its height. The Nahal battalion, to our right, was involved in a very intense battle and I could not order it to detach a unit to come and assist the command group. I therefore ordered the other battalion, the one on the left, to send us a company. Reinforced, we continued fighting and turned from south to east toward our objective, the Rafiah intersection. On our way, we encountered Egyptians and were forced to engage in hand-to-hand combat, in which the brigade commander, officers, sergeants, and soldiers all took part. In the battle for the Rafiah intersection we were fighting for our lives. We were under heavy fire and I responded by shooting my Uzi sub-machine gun virtually without pause. In the midst of the fighting, I was conscious of another sort of shooting going on behind me, the shooting of photographs, as our brigade intelligence officer, Mula Shaham, with whom I had been raised in the paratroopers, immortalized the fighting with his camera. I must confess he took some very unusual photos.

Our first Egyptian prisoner of the battle was captured by the command staff of my half-track. He was a smiling Egyptian sergeant who watched the day's heavy fighting from the relative safety of our position and passed the time chewing cookies and sucking candies he had taken from our battle rations. I even caught him gulping down some water from our canteens. Naturally, with supplies low and the war raging before us, food and water had to be rationed out carefully. I explained this to our friendly prisoner.

With the battle exploding around me, I received a request from General Talik for a report on the progress of our advance. The microphone was placed outside the half-track and I was practically screaming so as to be heard above the noise of the constant fire. Hearing the shots, Talik ordered Gorodish to rush a unit to assist us. I told him that we were progressing nicely, albeit under heavy fire, but that we would manage by ourselves and did not need any help.

As we fought on, the operations officer stationed in my half-track was wounded. As he was being evacuated he requested that we save him a Kalashnikov, a Soviet-manufactured automatic rifle that the

Russians had supplied to the Egyptians. At the time a Kalashnikov was a rare find and all the soldiers longed for one.

As we reached the Rafiah intersection I met Talik and provided him with a total debriefing. He in turn advised me of the overall situation and the advances being made throughout the Sinai.

The Nahal battalion, which was supposed to meet us at the Rafiah intersection, contacted me by radio and informed me that their battalion commander had been wounded, and that they had suffered many more wounded as well. They were unable to continue their advance and would not be able to link up with our units at the Rafiah intersection. I understood that they were in desperate need of immediate assistance.

I got into the tank of the tank battalion commander and ordered him to move, together with other tanks, from the Rafiah intersection southward in the direction of the Nahal battalion. Although he protested that he had little fuel and no ammunition, I insisted that he join in doing all that could be done to save the battalion.

A quarter of a mile south of the intersection we made contact with the northern edge of the same Egyptian position that the Nahal battalion was fighting from the south. Our tanks charged with their very last drops of fuel and their cannons paralyzed for lack of shells. We opened the turrets and shot with our Uzis and machine guns at the dense Egyptian position. We advanced southward to the Nahal battalion, with the aid of the mortar battalion of the brigade, which was laying down fire at the maximum rate. As the sun was beginning to set and, rather suddenly, as if by magic (our friend the angel was still working for us, examining events and ready to help) masses of Egyptian soldiers began fleeing and the battle turned in our favor. Once the battle was over, a strange stillness prevailed over the zone. The transition from the chaos of battle, the noise of explosions and the shouts of fighting men, to absolute silence once the battle is over is an experience genuinely astonishing in its power.

With the Egyptians fleeing westward we were able to connect with the boys from the Nahal battalion. Their relief and gratitude was expressed through hugs and kisses. This too was an extremely powerful moment.

We returned to the Rafiah intersection together with the soldiers of the Nahal battalion, Battalion 50, carrying with us their dead and wounded. As we arrived, the battalion that was fighting in Kfar Sh'an (Battalion 890) linked up with us. We proceeded to evacuate all the wounded and gather what was left of our ammunition supply. I found refuge from the bone-chilling cold upon the hood of a half-track that was giving off some precious heat. While I was on the half-track, an officer from Battalion 890 came up to me, obviously distressed. Although it was difficult for him to speak, he informed me that my nephew, my brother's son, who was the commander of a company in Battalion 890, had fallen in the battle for Kfar Sh'an.

The news of his death greatly saddened me. The morning before the war had begun, while we were waiting for the order to cross into the Sinai, he had come to me under the camouflage netting to bring me a bottle of liquor. We were very close and I loved him. Despite the intense feelings of loss, I knew I had to cut myself off from the pain and could not occupy myself with the task of mourning his death. I had a responsibility to a great many other young men. I had to reorganize the brigade so that we would be best prepared for the tasks to come. After all, we were only at the beginning of the war.

The battalion that had fought in Kfar Sh'an was ordered to remain in Rafiah to remove any Egyptian soldiers that were still in the area. The rest of the brigade's units, including my battalion, moved northward, as we were ordered to assist in the taking of the Gaza Strip. We rode along the railway tracks and entered Khan Yunis from the south. As we entered, our lead tank went over a "sandwich of mines" and was severely damaged, forcing us to leave it in place. Yet, we had not heard the last from this tank, or some of its amazing crew.

We entered the main street of Gaza under the command of Barzani, whom I had been forced to give up before the war began. We advanced within Gaza up to the beach lining the Mediterranean

Sea. Encountering no significant resistance, we turned south and came back to the outskirts of Khan Yunis.

As we approached the tank that we had left disabled on the outskirts of Gaza just the day before, we saw an astonishing sight. It seems that after the tank had been disabled from the mines, we had not succeeded in removing all the soldiers that were in it. One lone fighting man had been left inside the tank. Amazingly, this one courageous man had resisted wave after wave of Egyptian and Palestinian Arabs, who assaulted the tank from their Khan Yunis encampment. He bravely fought for his life, alternately firing with the tank's cannon and the machine gun. This solitary tankman devastated the enemy and survived until we came back the next day from Gaza and rescued him from the field. This single fighter inside a lone tank in enemy territory was yet one more example, among many, of the power of a stubborn, brave fighter and served as a motivating force for us all.

The last company to arrive at Gaza was a group of cadets from a training camp who were attached to the Nahal battalion. They got lost on their way to Gaza and met heavy fire in the northern suburbs of Khan Yunis. We were dispatched to rescue them, after which the whole brigade encamped on the main road on the eastern outskirts of Khan Yunis. We gathered our equipment and prepared for our assignment for the next day, which was the mopping up of Khan Yunis.

With the lull in active fighting, hunger descended upon us. We were out of battle rations and no supplies had reached us since the war began thirty-six hours earlier. During battle there is no feeling of hunger, basically because there is no time. All attention must be paid to the more concrete dangers, closer perils, that are confronting the soldier. However, when the battle falls silent, it is not unusual for the stomach to begin making noise. This time, however, we had nothing to calm our hunger. We were simply out of food and every unit took upon themselves the task of searching for food in any place they could. Finally, somebody succeeded in finding two stray ducks, but he didn't know what to do with them and nobody else appeared very enthusiastic. After watching the "city boys" struggle with the ducks, I explained to them that a "farm boy" like myself would solve the problem. "Let the brigade commander from Tel Adashim show you how to cook a duck" I told them as I proceeded to slaughter, pluck, clean, cut and roast them. Only when presented with the end result, delicious duck meat, did the men of the staff join me for the celebration.

That night was one of restless sleep. In the early morning hours I was awakened by a feeling of pressure on my chest. As I opened my eyes I realized a big drake was standing on my chest, blowing into my face, as if asking: "Where is my duck?" The shots coming from the direction of Khan Yunis interrupted my encounter with the bird, as I rose to evaluate the situation.

In the morning while we were preparing to go off on our assignment in Khan Yunis, two stray tanks that had become separated from their brigade asked to join us. Since I do not accept just any tank crew into the paratroop brigade, I told them that they would be permitted to join us only if they were able to hit, with their first shot, a water tank that was situated approximately one thousand feet away. They were visibly tense as they positioned the barrels of their cannons, and I was impressed as each tank proceeded to strike accurate hits with their first shells. I welcomed the crews to our brigade and they stayed with us until the end of the war. Reinforced by the two tanks, we attacked Khan Yunis and overcame with relative ease, all the obstacles and barriers that the Egyptian and Palestinian Arabs set up inside the city.

All communications between us and headquarters were conducted in a strange, inefficient manner. We had no direct line with headquarters and could not receive instructions from it or report on the brigade's advances without the use of an intermediate radio station which transmitted instructions to us and even responded to our questions, after communicating with the divisional command. Naturally, this is not the ideal communications system to employ during wartime. It was a source of regrets, misunderstandings, and the waste of valuable time. On one occasion it was almost the cause of a near disaster.

We reached the beach of Khan Yunis by noon and found there a considerable amount of Egyptian equipment, including new trucks loaded with weapons. While I was considering what to do with the Egyptian equipment, the radio liaison contacted me with a directive from headquarters instructing us to cut off and destroy Egyptian tanks that were seen fleeing Gaza and moving south. I was a bit confused by the order because only the day before we had been in Gaza and had not seen even one Egyptian tank. When I imparted this information to the liaison, he responded that he was simply a "go-between" and was giving us the message he had been instructed to relay. I understood his situation and told him to inform headquarters that we had received the order and were commencing our drive toward Gaza.

We moved north with a reduced number of tanks, traveling along the shore and with jeeps riding on the dunes on the ridges over the coastal strip. Anticipating a confrontation with the enemy, and in an effort to avoid surprise, I constantly examined the area with a telescope. Suddenly I noticed a tank in Deir al-Balakh that had its cannon projecting towards us. I ordered our tanks to stop, indicated the target to them, then brought the telescope back to my eyes. Realizing what I was seeing, I suddenly cried out "Don't shoot! Don't shoot!" for I had no doubt that the tank which was aiming its cannon at us was one of ours. Its cannon was slowly moving towards us and I knew its muzzle would eject the first shell in only another few seconds. I noticed other tanks and realized that according to their movements and the angle of their cannons, they considered us enemy tanks and were waiting for the right moment to destroy us. It was a terrible dilemma, for I could prevent a shot from our side, but how could I prevent a shot from their side? My mind was racing with an effort to find a way out of this situation. Should we move backward, or would that serve as confirmation for the tanks confronting us that we were Egyptian tanks trying to flee? If so, they would surely send their deadly shells after us. Should we move forward in the hope that they too would come to realize we were on the same side? Doing so would run the risk of inviting a terrible slaughter at the hands of brothers.

I tried to make radio contact, but was unsuccessful. Finally, I decided to place our fate in the hands of the commander of the tanks facing us. I ordered that the cannons of our tanks be turned aside. The assumption, or perhaps better said, the hope, was that the Israeli commander would see that our cannons were turned to the side and either understand that Israeli tanks were in his sights or, in the worst case, he would continue to think that Egyptian tanks were in front of him but were not looking for a fight. Luckily, the commander noticed this and gave the order to hold fire. Our meeting was a moving experience as we all felt a great deal of relief at the disaster we had managed to avoid.

This close call was with an MX tank unit from the same brigade that we had met the day before at the entrance to Khan Yunis. They had received a report that the Egyptians, in an effort to link up to the Gaza Strip, were preparing for a tank counterattack along the shore. They were ordered to prevent the linkup and our movement exactly fit the information they had received. Similarly, we had received information that there were Egyptian tanks there and had orders to destroy them. The inaccurate information, and the potential tragedy that was luckily averted, were both due to the poor and disorganized communications system. That evening we returned to our encampment of the previous night near the Khan Yunis road, and awaited new instructions.

The next morning I requested and was granted permission to return to the Rafiah intersection in order to reorganize my battalion. When we arrived I noticed the supply officers of Tal's division were there and immediately requested new supplies. We also reattached our mortar battalion to our brigade. At dawn we received instructions to proceed on the El-Arish-Ismailia-Qantara axis to link up with our forces in the Roumani area, after which I was to take these forces under my command, and to continue to the Suez Canal.

As we were moving southward on the El-Arish-Roumani-Balouza-Qantara road a squadron of Egyptian MIG-21 jets dove over us, missing us with their bombs. They flew off without causing us any damage. My unit's radio password was "Acid." Before the war began I had told a friend of mine, a squadron commander from Tel Nof, that if he heard the code "Red Acid" over the ground-to-air radio, he would know that my unit was in trouble. After the MIG attack, I radioed my friend, using the "Red Acid" code, and to my delight, received the response that he was in the area and would confront the MIGs.

As we advanced southward, we linked up with our forces before we reached Balouza. As I stood in front of my half-track, speaking by radio with the forces that were coming under my command, I again heard the voice of the squadron commander. I explained to him that I was standing next to the half-track and asked him if he could identify me. When he responded that he could, I told him that the MIGs had been circling above us and asked if he would fly west, along the road axis, and advise me of the concentration of enemy forces from here to the Canal.

Joking that I was requesting "private service," he did as I requested and informed me that there was an Egyptian tank unit ahead of us. He had managed to hit them and then reported that he was short of fuel and had to return to his base. We ended our exchange with my requesting that he call my home and tell my wife that he had seen me by the half-track and that I was doing fine.

We moved in the direction of Balouza, Qantara, and the Canal in the early afternoon. One tank platoon was traveling to the right of the road and a second one was to the left. The command group was on the road at the head of the column. Behind us was another tank platoon and behind a Nahal battalion. On our left, in an area of marshy, soft soil, was the brigade recoilless rifle unit.

As we traveled, out of the corner of my eye, I noticed Shamal anti-tank missiles being shot at us on the right. I looked through the telescope and determined that the first missile would pass over us, which it did. I called the second one, which passed to our left, and even accurately judged the danger of one that exploded only a few yards from my half-track. We directed our artillery at the Egyptian missiles and continued moving.

As we continued, I noticed Egyptians in trenches in front of us, blocking the axis of our advance. They began shooting at us with automatic rifles. At the moment I noticed them, and it always happens at a certain moment, and this becomes the one critical moment among the millions of moments of the war, a brown screen came down in front of my eyes and I fell into the half-track. I gripped the round iron rod over the driver and tried to get up. I felt as if I were hanging high up on one arm, while being pulled forcefully downward. Sinking into the half-track, I was thinking that I must still be alive. It is certain that I'm alive, I thought, for I feel a brown screen over my eyes, and if I were dead, the screen would be black.

14

Raful Is Wounded

"**R**aful is wounded. Raful is wounded," I heard the men in the half-track shouting. One officer stayed in the half-track, shooting with a machine-gun at the Egyptian positions, while several other officers brought me out of the half-track and dragged me into the vehicle's shadow. I could utter only one word, "Israel." Although this appears to be an extremely noble and nationalistic statement to make upon being gravely wounded in battle, what I meant was that Yisrael Granit should take command. After all, he was the senior officer.

I understood everything that was happening around me. I had taken a bullet in the head and I felt it when they were bandaging me. I could not react or speak. The sun was beating down on my eyes and by using hand motions I asked that they move me out of the sun's rays. I was evacuated to the rear, where I was to be removed by helicopter. When the helicopter landed, they carried the stretcher to its door. Although the pilot was a good friend of mine, I was unable to wave my hand to him or even whisper hello. I was conscious, but incapable of doing anything. I was evacuated to El-Arish and from there to the hospital in Beersheba.

The hospital was staffed in part by high school boys too young to be fighting the war, but serving the country by replacing those who had gone to the front. As they were wheeling me into the hospital I was amused to hear them whisper excitedly that they were pushing a colonel. I wanted to talk to them, but I simply couldn't. This was on the fourth day of the war and I was very filthy. I had not changed my uniform since the war began, and had only gotten rid of my underwear, without replacing it. In the emergency room I felt the nurses undressing me and as they progressed, I heard them remark with surprise that I had no socks...no undershirt...no underpants.

In the operating room I noticed everything was green. The last thought I had before receiving the anesthesia was that my friend the pilot most likely had already contacted my wife to tell her that I was well. In fact, this is exactly what had happened, as he called her and told her that he had seen me next to my half-track and that I had waved to him. Shortly after she received his call, she was informed by the military that I had been wounded and was in the hospital.

After I awoke from the operation, a doctor entered my room and showed me five bullet fragments that he had removed from my head. In a voice that did not disguise his surprise, he remarked that these fragments could not have come from this wound and inquired as to where I might have picked them up. His surprise turned to shock when I casually informed him that the fragments must be from the wound I received during the War of Independence, nineteen years earlier. I explained to the young doctor that during that war there simply was not enough time to operate on me and remove the bullets. To which he replied that they had removed an additional bullet, my souvenir from this war, and that it had pierced the upper part of my skull, only about two millimeters above the brain membrane. "Luckily I am a short man," I remarked. "If I were even two millimeters taller, I would not alive."

Not every man was as lucky. My most difficult experience in the hospital, more difficult than the wound itself and everything involved with it, was watching a good friend die. One morning, the nurses brought a badly wounded, unconscious man into my room. He was wrapped in blankets and bandages and I was not able to recognize who it was. I was saddened and shocked when the nurses told me it was my good friend, Colonel Shlomo Alton. The nurses asked me to speak with him, as the voice of a good friend sometimes helps draw a comatose individual out of his unconscious state. And talk to him I did! I had so many things to speak with him about, so many things to tell him. "Shlomo, it's me, Raful," I shouted repeatedly, and told him about the war and our mutual friends. To my great sorrow, it was to no avail, and my good friend died, in my room, before my eyes, a few days later.

I recovered quickly and by the fourth or fifth day I was already walking around. Nine days after being wounded I told the doctors that my treatment process was over and I was ready to go home. By the end of the month, I was already fully active.

I returned to the army in time to participate in the Southern Command's discussions, summing up the war and analyzing its lessons. In the middle of July, I transferred command of the brigade to Danny Mat and was assigned the function of compiling the lessons of the war for the General Staff. The post was not to my taste because I wanted to go back to activity in the field, but I fulfilled my task to the best of my ability.

After my release from the hospital in Beersheba, I was pleased to discover that a very dear friend from my days at the United States Marine Command and Staff School was in Israel. Shortly after arriving home, I received a letter from Jan, a Norwegian, who informed me that he had volunteered to serve as a United Nations observer. I immediately tried to track him down, and heard rumors that he was stationed in the Golan Heights. Although the fighting had not completely ceased there, my son and I drove to the Golan and found my good friend at a United Nations observation post near Quneitra.

Our meeting was very emotional. We had been very close in the United States and immediately began reminiscing about the good times we had shared. Jan pressed me to share a drink with him and although the doctors had advised me to refrain from alcoholic beverages, the mood of the meeting was so joyous that I knew I had to bend the doctors' rules a little bit.

Jan told me that his search for my whereabouts ended when he met a friend of mine, an Israeli liaison officer, and was informed that I had been wounded in the head. Anxious about my condition, he had driven to Tel Adashim, but did not enter, for fear of discovering the worst. His anxiety remained until I showed up in Quneitra and he was able to see for himself that I was recovering nicely.

Now that we had found one another again, we made a special effort to remain in touch. Our families got together in Tiberias and Tel Adashim on a regular basis, and when he was posted as an observer on the Syrian side, he would drive through Lebanon so as to visit. When his official duty as an observer was over, Jan and his family set up their house-trailer on the lawn at our house and lived with us until Jan decided that the time had come to go home. They left Israel in their trailer and drove through Syria, Turkey, and Europe on the way back to Norway.

I saw Jan again in 1968 when I took part in a military delegation to Europe. Between tours of the military installations of various Western European nations, I took a break and flew to Norway. There I was his guest in the tiny town he lived in south of Oslo. It was October and the long, cold nights were spent in front of the television watching the Olympics being held in Mexico. We drank whiskey and ate shrimp. As our glasses got lower, the pile of shrimp shells grew higher. It was a simple pleasure, and I marveled at the ease they enjoyed living in a war-free zone.

My relaxation was broken by a call from the Embassy explaining that I was to return to Israel immediately, as the plan I had worked on to assault a Jordanian village was about to be carried out. I said goodbye to Jan and his warm-hearted family, goodbye to the whiskey, and goodbye to the shrimp. I told my good friend Jan not to feel bad for me. I wasn't complaining. Every nation has its own fate.

Part Three:
TERRORISTS IN THE JORDAN VALLEY, ATTRITION AT SUEZ

15

A Chill Down My Spine

At an officers' meeting at the end of October 1967, I overheard Arik Sharon and Deputy Chief of Staff Bar Lev discussing the worsening security situation in the Jordan Valley. I approached Bar Lev and requested to be appointed sector commander and commander of the reserve paratroop brigade. My request was granted and I was appointed on November 3, 1967.

On my first visit in the field I realized that the sector was in a very disorganized state. There was no organization of forces, no command posts, no tactical positions and no communications infrastructure. In addition, I found a unit of paratroopers from my brigade performing routine security functions in which their actions were random and unsystematic. I reported to my commanders that I needed two months to organize and build a headquarters, structure a security line, and format the operational activity in the field. My efforts were to be aimed at stopping the infiltration attempts of terrorists crossing the Jordan River into the areas we had captured in the Six-Day War.

My task was such that I had to begin literally from scratch. Reorganizing was difficult and the winter rains and flooding did little to make the task easier. Throughout the period of reorganization we also had to contend with repeated infiltration attempts and constant clashes with terrorists and Jordanian forces. Yet, when the two month period had passed, I was able to see, with a great deal of personal satisfaction, that the sector was in top form and functioning properly. In fact, that very night, two months after I assumed command, we had a clash with a terrorist band of nine or ten Arabs. Although most of them were killed, several succeeded in escaping. We pursued them up to the river and found on the Jordan's banks clothing, ropes, weapons, and food. We assumed that the remnants of the terrorist gang had left these supplies behind as they crossed the river and that they had succeeded in re-entering Jordan. A few days later we learned an important lesson. In another clash a terrorist was captured and revealed to us that he was a member of the gang that we had confronted a few days before. He informed us that they had not crossed the Jordan, but had thrown down their equipment to give the appearance that they had, and that they had actually hidden in the thick vegetation along the river. So, while we were standing at the water's edge telling each other that the terrorists had crossed into Jordan, they were in fact only a few meters away from us. We realized what could have been the result of our actions when the terrorist stated, "If we had not thrown down our weapons, we could have killed all of you in one short burst of fire." I felt a chill down my spine as he spoke. On the water's edge that night stood the general of the Command, the commander of the brigade, other high-ranking officers and a number of soldiers. The thought that they might have been in a position to ambush us was truly frightening. We learned our lesson. I instructed my forces never to act on the basis of assumptions. In all situations, they were ordered to behave as if the terrorists were located in every possible hiding place, threatening their lives. The mark of a good soldier is never needing to be taught the same lesson twice and we took concrete steps so that this valuable lesson was incorporated into our strategies in fighting the difficult war in the Jordan Valley.

We entered a period of protracted fighting along the Jordan River. As we built defensive positions, blocked infiltration attempts, and engaged in an increasing number of pursuits, we also initiated actions across the Jordan River to the east aimed at harassing the terrorists on their own turf. We soon learned that the terrorists could be tempted into assisting us in their own destruction and we proceeded to boobytrap various objects that would be of interest to them and leave them on our side of the Jordan. We often sat in ambush and watched as the terrorists discovered what they thought were supplies, only to have them explode in their faces. Once, we placed shoe mines along the border and a truck used by the terrorists blew up the mines, damaging its tires. A group of terrorists, called to check what was behind the explosion, found out when another explosion was detonated. Those still alive ran to hide in a small house not far from where the truck blew up. Anticipating their action, we had a tank hidden nearby, and when all the terrorists reached the house, our tank destroyed the structure. We continued this policy for many months, as it provided us with a vehicle for neutralizing the terrorists while allowing us to minimize the danger to our own soldiers.

This was a war of cunning and surprise and could not be conducted in a routine way. In that period not one gang succeeded in carrying through its objective. Most attempts at infiltration were successfully blocked, and those terrorists who succeeded in crossing the Jordan were liquidated during chases. An unlimited quantity of stubbornness, perseverance, decisiveness, and a simple refusal to yield was required by our troops as we withstood the tests and ensured that the terrorists would not sow death among our population.

Although there was no security fence, we had various methods developed at that time to inform us when and where a gang of terrorists had crossed the Jordan. When we did not succeed in stopping a penetration, we pursued them by all means at our disposal and we performed about one-hundred pursuits in the Jordan Valley in the period immediately following the war.

In one incident, a gang of armed smugglers succeeded in crossing the river and encountered one of our night ambushes. Our troops did not wound any of the terrorists and they fled, not to the east and back to Jordan, but to the west, where they disappeared into the mountains. At dawn, another officer and I took a light plane and began combing the area until we discovered them, walking with their mules on a steep slope, looking for a way to reach a nearby Arab village. We alerted our forces, which were not in the vicinity, and we slowed their progress by making sharp diving motions toward them. The speed of our plunges frightened the mules and they fell down the slope. The smugglers, equally frightened, sought to hide in the clefts of the rocks, but were easily caught by a unit of our forces that had arrived by helicopter.

An interesting situation arose when suspicion of collaborating with terrorists was cast upon a monk from the Qasr-el-Yahud Monastery, on the bank of the Jordan River near Jericho. It was alleged that he would house the terrorists after they crossed the border, provide them with clothing and equipment and help them penetrate the areas west of Jericho. These charges were no simple matter and we had to find a way to either verify or refute our suspicions.

We decided to send a Bedouin scout and an officer into the

monastery, posing as terrorists. A group of soldiers and officers, under my command, would lie in wait outside the monastery, ready to intervene if necessary. Our only problem was that we did not have an officer who was dark skinned enough to pass for an Arab or who spoke Arabic. We solved our dilemma by wrapping the officer's head in an Arab keffiyeh and instructed the Bedouin scout to explain to the monk that his companion was silent due to a terrible toothache.

The night they entered the monastery was rainy and unusually cold. We all waited in anticipation, lying silently in the mud and rain, as the scout and the officer knocked on the monk's door. After two full hours passed, my concern for the safety of the two men inside resulted in my ordering a unit to forcibly enter the monastery. As our forces rose to execute my order, the monastery door opened and our two men left. With my teeth chattering from cold and anger, I demanded an explanation for the amount of time that had passed. I was informed that the monk had honored his guests with a fabulous meal, the likes of which they had never seen before, and that they felt it necessary to partake of the meal so as to draw the trust and confidence of the suspect. Naturally, their enthusiasm for the delicacies caused the monk to comment on the officer's appetite, despite his toothache, but did not raise his suspicions, as was evidenced by the success of their visit.

The monk had implicated himself by agreeing with our men on their plans for a supposed penetration into Jericho. He told my men of a pit next to a nearby road and instructed them to hide there for the night. He explained that the next morning he would ride his bicycle into Jericho and arrange a meeting for them with others who would also provide assistance. On his way back from Jericho, he would pass their pit and ring his bicycle bell. At that point the men were to leave the pit and await a car that would come to pick them up.

We requested the assistance of a unit from the reconnaissance platoon and posted them and others in hiding places around the pit. We put two soldiers in the pit who were not involved in the original sting operation, and informed them that they were to act only on direct orders. With this in place, we settled in and waited for the monk to make his move.

The following morning the monk did as he had promised and made his way on his bike to Jericho. After a short time he returned and stopped by the pit and rang his bell. When there was no response, he rang the bell a few more times and then returned to the monastery. At the monastery, he was met by our troops who placed him under arrest.

The car that was supposed to pick the two men up never arrived, which of course disappointed us, as we had hoped to arrest all those who were involved in the terror ring. However, we were ultimately successful as the monk came to understand that we had enough to convict him solely on the evidence provided by the officer and the Bedouin scout. With this in mind, he willingly shared with us all the details of the operation and the names and locations of all involved. All of these individuals were arrested and their terror ring was effectively destroyed.

This was the most difficult period in my life. I almost never slept at home, and when I did I did not sleep well for fear that an important action was taking place while I was spoiling myself with the comforts of home. There was tension twenty-four hours a day and I was required to be everywhere and take part in almost every pursuit. I participated in blocking incursions and joined pursuits in all circumstances, without regard for distances I would have to run or the weather conditions of rain or intense heat. I was determined to set a living example for my troops and often included myself in actions when it was not necessary. Thus, if I met up with a unit checking tracks to determine whether they were fresh or not, I would wait for the final determination before continuing on my way. If it was determined that the tracks were fresh, more often than not I would participate in the pursuit. We never had the luxury of waiting before initiating a pursuit procedure because we knew that the terrorists were heading toward our farms and kibbutzim with the sole objective of killing our civilians. We could not wait for reinforcements or vehicles to help us in our pursuit. Every unit that was in the field and discovered tracks of a penetration began an immediate hunt. Time was of supreme importance, and the key to preventing a slaughter at the hands of the terrorists was staying on their trail, making contact with them, discovering their exact position and neutralizing them. While a pursuit was in progress, reinforcement forces at times were able to join in, but each unit had to have the ability to discover a border violation and track down the terrorists independent of all outside assistance.

One particular morning, as I was on my way back to the Jordan Valley, I joined a unit in pursuit of a terrorist gang that had penetrated the border a short time before. We were a small group of men and we stayed on the trail of the terrorists from the Jordan Valley road as they worked their way to the west. We had excellent Bedouin scouts with us and we followed the terrorists over a difficult slope. The noon sun was nearing and I felt the oppressive effects of the sun as it rose higher in the sky. I hiked next to a scout who examined the clues the terrorists left behind them, such as a cigarette butt and a chewing gum wrapper. Our scout studied the earth and remarked that the marks on the ground indicated that the terrorists were walking differently, and we could assume that they were getting tired. With this in mind, we increased our speed of pursuit, as we were anxious to catch them before they managed to reach the not so distant Arab villages of Samaria. We understood that if they succeeded in reaching the villages we would never find them, as they would be hidden and protected by the local residents. As we completed the difficult ascent from the Jordan Valley road, other forces met us and joined in the chase. As we approached the flat area before us, we saw a series of small hills with caves and tombs carved of stone in the immediate distance. I glanced through my binoculars, but saw no real signs of activity. Using my considerable experience and attempting to think like a terrorist who was running for my life, I isolated one hill that seemed to me to be the ideal hiding spot. I ordered the hill surrounded and took another unit around the hill and up its far side. When we spotted a pit below us, we threw a hand grenade in and were relieved to see a keffiyah waving surrender pop out. We immediately descended on the pit and arrested all six men inside. They were all very well armed and had a considerable amount of explosives with them. We did not know what tragedy we had prevented, but we all understood that the weapons they carried and the amount of explosives they had indicated that they would have brought great sorrow to the people of Israel had we not been there to stop them.

It should be noted that in many cases the terrorists who infiltrated Israel were not very physically fit and were inclined to tire quickly. Also, their morale was not very high, most likely being hindered by their dismal rate of success against our forces. Although these elements assisted us in our war against the terror they sought to sow, nothing can diminish the bravery and endurance displayed by our forces during this period. We maintained our forces with the assumption that we would be fighting against formidable enemies and conditions were often difficult and dangerous.

Their incompetence did not prevent them from fooling us on occasion. One of our most unusual pursuits involved a group of terrorists that had successfully infiltrated our border and managed to erase their tracks.

The commander of the reconnaissance platoon and a few other men joined me in a helicopter as we attempted to locate the terrorist gang. I asked the pilot to fly in a particular path and I noticed what appeared to be a natural hiding place — a pit on a hill covered by thick bush. I instructed the pilot to land on the hill and we approached the pit cautiously. As I began to pull on the bush covering the pit, a burst of fire was directed at me from within the pit. We responded with several grenades, killing five of the six men inside. The lone survivor immediately surrendered. These men were dressed in shiny, new Dacron uniforms and equipped with good weapons. Their downfall was that their combat level was low.

At a later stage, after a long series of failures, the terrorists enlarged their penetrating units from six men to twelve and at times up to fourteen men. Although their assumption that larger units would fight better was inherently faulty, the larger units did present us with a greater risk.

One of the first large gangs we encountered penetrated our border north of Jericho. We pursued them on foot and determined, from the signs on the ground, that they had not left the area. I joined a helicopter patrol and we discovered them hiding in a dry canyon. As our forces surrounded them, the terrorists shot at the helicopter and hit it, damaging our steering mechanism. The pilot informed me that we had little choice but to land where we were.

Our forces surrounding the terrorists opened fire and killed them, making way for us to land on the hill. But while we were in the air, I had noticed that the group had split up and that two terrorists, the ones who had actually hit the helicopter, were still alive and hiding about two hundred feet from where we landed. The battalion commander, the two soldiers who were with us in the helicopter, and I began chasing the two terrorists southward, in the direction of the refugee camps north of Jericho. Despite our use of additional forces and roadblocks, our findings of a Kalashnikov and traces of blood, and an extensive search of the refugee camps, we simply failed to locate them. Their success in evading us was in some ways a direct result of the fact that they had been part of such a large group.

The country celebrated Independence Day in 1968, as we always have, with a large Israeli Army parade in Jerusalem. After the splendid victory of 1967, and the increase in terrorist attacks following the war, security was tightened so as to ensure that the parade went smoothly. As a result of our security procedures a terrorist incursion in the northern part of the Jordan Valley was spotted and three of the terrorists were immediately killed. Knowing that the terrorist gangs never consist of only three men, we understood that at least three of them had succeeded in evading us. We went back over their tracks to the Jordan River and noticed suspicious movement on a very steep cliff on the other side of the Jordan. We opened fire on the cliff and one terrorist rolled down into the river. We provided cover for a small detail of our soldiers that crossed the river and killed the other two terrorists. We simply could not take the chance that they would try to re-cross our border at a different location or at a later time. The parade in Jerusalem was too great a security risk and too important a symbol of our freedom and liberty. We could not allow the terrorists to spoil our day of pride and glory. Once the terrorist gang had been completely neutralized, I rang up the parade-reviewing platform in Jerusalem and informed the General of the Central Command that we had wiped out the terrorist gang. He responded that the parade was set to begin, and that now he could relax and enjoy it.

In addition to our struggles with the terrorists, every day we had additional incidents with the Jordanians. There were artillery firings, mines planted on our roads, and occasional sniper attacks. This war of attrition required of our troops a great deal of mental and physical stamina. We were not allowed a second of weakness, a moment of rest.

In March 1968, we carried out the Karamah action. The task of the force under my command was to take the Jordanian positions across the Jordan River and block the axis of the Jordan Valley on the Jordanian side at the Al-Masri intersection, east of Damiya. Another unit was to cross the Jordan on the Allenby Bridge and attack the Karamah refugee camp, the central location of the terrorists and the point of departure for most of the terrorist penetrations of our border.

In preparing for this operation we were most concerned with the large numbers of Palestinian civilians living in the refugee camp. In an effort to avoid casualties among their population, we dropped leaflets prior to the operation, warning the civilians of our pending operation and asking them to temporarily leave Karamah. This was a noble, but foolish error, as it served to warn the terrorists as well. Many of their leaders took the warning as an opportunity to flee, while many others organized the terrorists to resist our assault.

My plan to take the Jordanian positions included the exploitation of the element of surprise. I wanted to launch the assault in broad daylight, and using no preparatory fire, break through across the Damiya Bridge with an armored, mechanized force, which would bypass the Jordanian positions and attack them from behind.

Unlike today, at the time there was no agreed upon system of open bridges between Israel and Jordan. All agreements were still secret and provisional. Thus, at night the Jordanians would lay mines on the Damiya Bridge and at dawn they would remove them so that trucks loaded with vegetables and other goods could cross the bridge to the east. The day of the assault we waited until the mines were removed and quickly crossed the river. We took the Jordanian forces by total surprise and captured our objectives. Once our positions were secure, another of our units passed by the positions and blocked the Jordanian Jordan Valley highway. Unfortunately, tank and artillery exchanges with the Jordanians inflicted some losses on our forces.

Our major difficulty was that the Sherman tanks we were using were outdated and slow and could not stand up in battle to the new Jordanian Patton tanks, which were hitting us from long distances. By afternoon our problems were solved as a regular tank platoon came up from Karamah and joined up with us, using their cannons to hit and destroy the Jordanian tanks.

The operation was over by early evening, and after nightfall we returned to our side of the border. Upon our return, we discovered that in addition to the three dead we had suffered, the unit fighting in the main battle sector, Karamah, had lost twenty-eight men. Clearly, there was a need for evaluation, for there were many lessons to be learned. In reviewing my unit's role and performance in the operation, we concluded that we did not properly foresee the development of the battle with the Jordanians, nor did we anticipate that they would fight as forcefully and bravely as they had. The unit fighting at Karamah similarly underestimated the enemy and also suffered from not having the benefit of the element of surprise, taken away by the leaflets warning the village's residents of our attack.

I commanded our forces in the Jordan Valley for nine months, from November 1967 to July 1968. Although it was a short stretch of time, it was an extremely stormy period. Our strategy of mine-laying, blocking actions, bunkers along the border, constant, around

the clock, alertness, and our ability to effectively cover the whole
length of the border succeeded in preventing every terror gang that
crossed our border from achieving their objectives. Personally, I was
able to leave the Jordan Valley pleased with the personal example I
had set for my soldiers, with my willingness, indeed insistence, to
join most missions and the high level of dedication and motivation
I had tried to instill in them.

I left the Jordan Valley to assume the post of Chief Paratrooper
Officer. I served in this position for four years and spent most of my
time dealing with two very important, but very different, areas of
concern. My first task, and general focus, involved a long series of
military reprisal actions, mainly against Egypt. I was quite experienced in reprisal assaults and approached this task with a great
deal of confidence. My second task was much different, and one in
which I had little personal experience. The Israel Defense Forces
were undergoing major changes after the 1967 War and an attitude
of scorn had developed within the IDF which mocked the infantry
and the paratroopers. The new focus of attention and the bulk of
financial and human resources were being directed toward
strengthening the tank corps, whose newfound prestige was derived
from the decisive role it played in the Six-Day War. This resulted
in an inclination to minimize the value of the Chief Paratrooper
Officer and cut his authority. In fact, I would say that it was not until
the Yom Kippur war, with its many victims, that the General Staff
came to realize the mistake involved in promoting the tank corps to
the neglect and detriment of the infantry.

Despite the difficulties, and the occasional feelings of estrange-
ment, I spared no effort in my attempts to advance the interests of
the paratroopers and the infantry, and to argue their value. After a
while my authority was slightly expanded, when the Chief Paratroop
Officer became Chief Paratroop and Infantry Officer, and my
command was expanded to include other infantry brigades. However, I understood that the only concrete way to restore the infantry
to its former glory was to provide the Israel Defense Forces with
the best infantry possible. I worked to train the soldiers, improve

their professional level, and inspire them with a spirit of pride as brave fighting men. Perhaps the greatest remedy for the lack of self-confidence and pride many of our soldiers were feeling as a direct result of the atmosphere of scorn was the series of bold and daring successful military actions we engaged in along the Egyptian border. Not even the greatest scorners of the infantry soldier were able to ignore these successes.

16

Raid on Green Island

Following the 1967 war, Egyptian President Nasser embarked on a War of Attrition with Israel along the Suez Canal. This war was a central aspect of Nasser's strategy, as he did not have the necessary military strength to remove the Israeli Army from the Sinai Desert. Nasser feared that a long period of quiet in the Sinai would result in a lack of international attention, and would lead to acceptance of Israeli control of the area. Israel had made it clear that it would consider withdrawing from the Sinai only in exchange for a stable peace agreement and security arrangements. A peace agreement with Israel was not an option Nasser was willing to consider. Thus, he chose to maintain an active state of war along the Suez Canal border. For Israel, it was vitally important to extract a high price from Nasser for his attacks on Israeli positions along the Canal, so as to convince him that the policy he had chosen was paved with dangers for Egypt, and therefore not in his best interests. To this end, it was not enough for the Israeli Air Force to execute deeply penetrating and massive attacks on Egyptian military targets. Although effective, and despite the complete supremacy of the skies enjoyed by the IAF, these assaults were not daring enough to frighten the Egyptians. Furthermore, the ease with which the Air Force inflicted its will on Egyptian targets was somewhat limited after the Soviet Union set up ground-to-air missiles and decided to assume the responsibility of protecting the air space of Cairo and the zone along the Canal. In considering these developments, it became clear to the General staff that infantry actions were vital for the successful implementation of our policy of deterrence and punishment.

I personally took part in several actions, but quite often had to be content with planning raids and instructing troops. Our raids were always based on the element of surprise and speed. We wanted the Egyptians to understand that they had no control over when and where we would hit them next. We wanted them to understand that they were completely vulnerable. The Najji Hamdi action saw our forces blow up the high tension lines the Egyptians used for conducting electricity. Although the wires were forty yards high we blew them up by placing demolition charges at the base of each foundation. The power transforming station at Najji Hamdi was destroyed and we left without even firing a shot. In another assault, designed to show the Egyptians our ability to penetrate deep into their territory, an Egyptian military base deep inside Egypt was bombarded by a mortar unit which landed in helicopters and flew back to its base before the Egyptians even recovered from their shock. Many times we landed forces deep in the Egyptian rear so as to execute demolition actions and lay ambushes for Egyptian supply convoys heading for the Canal zone and the Gulf of Suez.

One of the unique approaches I initiated was the introduction of the naval commando unit into the operational routine in our strikes against Egypt. One of the most daring raids combining infantry and naval commando forces was the complicated raid on Green Island, at the entrance to the Suez Canal. This was a tiny, rocky island forty yards long and eight yards wide. It was the sight of a major strategic Egyptian anti-aircraft position, which was solidly fortified with concrete. The island was carefully guarded by Egyptian forces. We chose Green Island as a target because of the anti-aircraft position stationed there, but also because of the Egyptian perception that it was virtually impossible to penetrate the island.

We set out on a very dark night in rubber boats from Ras-Sudr. We navigated our way in the darkness to the buoy in the middle of the Gulf. From there the naval commando unit swam to the edges of the island. Our plan called for the commando unit to reach the edges of the target and climb into the fortification at an area that had been determined through intelligence reports to be the most vulnerable. The rest of the strike force would arrive in rubber boats and join the attackers on the island. The plan was executed with great precision, the navigation was exact and the timetable was executed fully, without deviation.

During the attack stage, while the island was still partly under Egyptian control, the Egyptians began a heavy bombardment of the island from their coast. Six of our soldiers were killed in the battle that ensued. Once the operation was completed, our forces evacuated the island under extremely difficult conditions. The Egyptians were sending up flares and subjecting the island, and the surrounding waters, to an extremely heavy artillery bombardment. Our troops gathered in rubber boats and headed for our bases in Sinai. By dawn we were out of range of the Egyptian artillery; however, we had lost contact with several of our boats and feared for the fate of their men. Only later did we learn that they did not turn southward in the heart of the Gulf, but sailed due east and landed on the beaches north of Ras Sudr. Although the action was a great success, both in military terms, and in the psychological effect it had on both our troops and Egypt, the high casualty rate of six dead detracted greatly from our celebrations. None of our other raids in Egypt required that we pay so dear a price.

Another difficult and daring action involved our attack on Shadwan island, which I planned painstakingly. This island has unique elements that required special attention and a great deal of thought. Shadwan island, a small piece of land with steep terrain, lies halfway between Ras Muhammad and Rardakah, and blocks the entrance to the Gulf of Suez from the north. The areas that would provide access for an assault unit were limited and defended by Egyptians forces. Using aerial photographs, we noticed a small ground surface, on top of the mountain, that was situated approximately 500 yards from the island's Egyptian position. We determined that the area would allow for the landing of one helicopter, and that, under such conditions, the assault would be best executed at night. It recognized the need to apply measures that would enable the helicopter to land such a short distance from enemy positions without being hit. We also knew we had to develop a plan that would grant the landing force the ability to regroup after landing so it could begin fighting effectively.

Although the difficulties were formidable, we solved them by including a smokescreen in the form of an Air Force attack. The plan called for the helicopters to land on the designated surface while the Egyptians were tending to their chores of confronting our air assault. These aspects of the plan went extremely well and our soldiers successfully disembarked and opened combat on the slopes of the mountain and across the island. The action proceeded according to plan and achieved its objectives. We lost one officer who was killed near the lighthouse at the island's far end and suffered several wounded.

During the night Egyptian IL-28 planes tried to bomb our positions. They were repelled by our Air Force, as were the Egyptian torpedo boats that tried to approach the island. We remained on the island until the next day and brought back to the Sinai with us the Egyptian radar apparatus and other supplies. We also brought a number of Egyptian prisoners who were to remain captive until after the Yom Kippur War, in late 1973.

In addition to harassing the Egyptians and spoiling their procedures and operational plans, our actions across the Suez allowed our forces to set high standards for special operational actions, gain valuable combat experience, and improve combat procedures.

There are times that a military action ignites the imagination and brings worldwide prestige to those who execute it, not necessarily because of the difficulty in carrying it out or the brilliance of the plan, but because of the uniqueness and resourcefulness involved in the execution. This was no doubt the case with the Israeli raid on the Soviet radar station, during which we dismantled the station in Egypt and brought it, in its entirety, home to Israel.

This operation was made necessary because of the inability of our planes to cross the Gulf undetected. Air Force raids deep into Egypt were an essential component of our strategy, so the Egyptian means of detection on the shores of the Gulf had to be removed. Our only problem was that the exact location of the radar installation was unknown.

Our aerial photographs revealed an Egyptian position along the coast and we assumed that this was the position that was reporting the crossing of our planes to the Egyptian anti-aircraft system operated by the Soviets. We knew we had to destroy the installation and began planning ways to raid the position. However, after the raid had been authorized by the General Staff, a young officer, who had closely scrutinized the aerial photographs, discovered a Soviet radar station well-hidden, not on the coast itself, but in Egypt, about two miles west of the position on the coast. It was clear that this was the radar station that had been reporting the penetrations by our planes. Armed with the aerial photos, I reported to our Chief of Staff, Lieutenant-General Chaim Bar-Lev, and requested authorization to change the target of the raid. I explained that the new mission would not aim to destroy the radar station, but rather to bring it back to Israel. With his authorization secured, we began to plan and prepare for the mission.

Luckily we had plenty of captured Soviet war equipment to assist us in our preparatory exercises. On the basis of the aerial photographs we identified the various pieces of equipment we would need and began a long series of exercises to practice dismantling a steel carriage from the framework of the vehicle to which it was attached, and then attaching it to a helicopter. We used a framework similar to our target in Egypt and we practiced until we had accumulated the experience and increased our speed so as to perform at an acceptable level of execution.

The operation was executed with near perfection. Our unit landed and reached the radar station undetected. To our amazement, the steel carriages and vehicle frameworks at the site were exactly like those we had practiced on and the separation of the equipment and the attachment to the helicopters was relatively simple. The only potential problem occurred when one of our helicopters, carrying the carriage of a radar apparatus which weighed several tons, suffered a severe breakdown in its hydraulic system while over the waters of the Gulf. By all the rules and standing orders, the pilot should have released the heavy load and let it drop into the water, saving himself, and the aircraft. Only the circumstances weren't typical and the pilot felt that the challenge was monumental and the potential too great. He decided to take a risk and not drop the carriage into the Gulf. He continued flying to his base of departure, landed the radar carriage on the ground and landed next to it.

A rainy morning greeted us back in Israel as we landed at an Air Force base. Only upon landing did we fully comprehend that we had successfully brought a Soviet radar station, with its leg struts and all its parts, back to Israel. The Commander of Military Intelligence and the Chief of Staff greeted us at the air base and I learned that other Israelis, as well, had been out "thieving" that night. I was told that some missile boats Israel had ordered and paid for in France, but had never been delivered due to an unfair French arms embargo, had "disappeared" from the French port at Cherbourg. I did not feel like a thief. The missile boats were ours and there was no reason for us to allow the French to keep them. Although the Soviet radar station was not technically ours, we had an obligation to our pilots to remove the threat the Egyptians and Soviets were posing to their safety.

During my tenure as Chief Officer of the Paratrooper and Infantry additional actions were carried out by foot soldiers in Jordan and Syria. One of the most complicated was the destruction of three bridges in southern Jordan, between Aqaba, Ma'an, and Kerak. The three independent actions, which were very sophisticated and required special training and a high level of skill, called for the placement of an explosive charge at the base of each bridge. Before the charge was detonated and the bridge destroyed, the troops were instructed to make sure that no Jordanian civilian vehicles were on or around the bridge. A civilian vehicle would disrupt the operation and risk injury to innocent people. Therefore, the plans required our troops to enter Jordan in all directions and set off smoke grenades to deter travelers from approaching the bridge. Further precautions were taken by having troops place triangular nails on the roads leading up to the bridges, so as to cause flat tires in any car that continued despite the smoke grenades.

Operations designed to harass and disrupt, like those executed in Egypt, were also directed toward Syria. The methods employed were always similar in that each action would call for the landing of troops by helicopter deep into Syrian territory, where they would open fire with mortars and artillery at Syrian military installations and positions. Each action had a pre-determined number of shells that were to be fired, after which the attack force would reload its equipment and return to Israel. In almost all cases, the Syrians never had time to launch a response.

These attacks on Syrian and Jordanian positions, despite the fact that they had not officially joined Nasser in his War of Attrition strategy, were due to constant violations of Israel's borders by the armies of these two countries and their continued use of tanks and artillery against our forces. Thus, although not as intense, the borders with Jordan and Syria also required the attention of our Air Force and special infantry units.

In addition to these special actions, a new challenge that was posed by the new tactic of hijacking airplanes began to occupy our attention. In fact, when an El-Al plane was seized and flown to Algiers, the possibility was considered of flying a strike force to Algiers to free the plane and its passengers. The plan was not implemented due to difficulty in overcoming the flight distance. However, we knew that this new method of terrorism was going to pose another threat to our freedom, and we began preparing methods of confronting it.

17

Raid on Beirut

I was eager to do my part against the threat presented by the wave of hijackings by Arab terrorists, and was encouraged by the aggressive posture assumed by my government. One Thursday evening I was called to a meeting of the General Staff and presented with an assignment unlike any other I had done to date. My commanders had instructed me to raid Beirut International Airport and destroy all the airplanes there carrying Arab markings. This action was to be in retaliation for the specific targeting of El Al airplanes by the terrorists, which were supported and given tactical assistance by the Arab governments. I was told I had to carry out my orders no later than that coming Saturday, giving me less than forty-eight hours.

I immediately got to work gathering the necessary information and planning the logistics of the assault. I looked over the intelligence aerial photographs of the airport, interviewed Israelis who had been at the airport, looked over jumbo jets at Ben-Gurion Airport and reviewed maps. I designated three units for the operation and decided that the total operation, from landing to evacuation, could not take more than half an hour. I discussed with explosive experts exactly where to place the explosives so as to guarantee to destroy the planes, and determined that our best chances involved two explosives per plane, one situated in the forward wheel compartment and the other in the landing gear mounting. These would ensure that the pilot's cabin and the fuel tank would explode, leaving the remainder of the plane virtually useless.

The three units involved would land on the airstrip by helicopter and immediately begin to set the explosives. Another helicopter would drop smoke grenades and triangular nails on the sole two-lane road leading up to the airport, so as to prevent Arab forces from reaching the airfield. Once the explosives were set, they would be detonated, and the units would board the helicopters and return to home base.

On the day of the assault we took off under the cover of darkness. The Jewish sabbath had ended only fifteen minutes earlier and there was a pleasant stillness as we flew over Haifa Bay. Once at sea, we turned north and flying at a very low altitude, went up the Lebanese coastline. Once our pilots spotted the bright lights of Beirut's airport, we turned east over Lebanon. Our men landed at their designated locations and the helicopters took off and returned to Israel. We had other helicopters waiting off the Lebanese coast that were to come and retrieve our troops at a pre-arranged time. We felt this was a safer procedure to follow than risk having the helicopters wait at the airport to bring us home. The danger, of course, was that they could be destroyed while on the ground, leaving us stranded.

The airport was stirring with activity as small tractors moved cargo, carts transported passenger luggage and food, maintenance crews worked on planes, and passengers moved toward their aircraft. Avoiding all of this activity, our forces began their demolition operations immediately upon landing. I set up my command post next to a building that housed the fire station and the Red Crescent and was facing the terminal at the end of a broad plaza where most of the planes were parked. I allowed the firemen, drivers, and other civilians that were on the field to leave, and they went up to the second floor to watch as we destroyed the two fire trucks and our troops went from plane to plane attaching explosives and detonating them.

After only twenty-nine minutes on the ground we had completed our mission. The airfield was ablaze with airplanes burning like giant bonfires. A DC-10 exploded and covered the tarmac with pieces of metal like a carpet. When our helicopters arrived, our troops boarded first, and officers followed. My helicopter was delayed a moment as one of my officers returned to the field to pick up a piece of metal as a souvenir.

On the way home I reported to Chief of Staff Bar-Lev that we had destroyed fourteen planes and that all of them had carried Arab markings. I was later to learn that my initial report was erroneous. We had, in fact, placed explosives on fourteen planes, but in final count, only thirteen had exploded. Luckily, the fourteenth, an old piston engine plane that was parked in a hangar, did not explode. Many frightened people had taken to hiding in the hangar and the explosion would have caused a great loss of life. In planning the mission I had done all I could to avoid the loss of innocent life, and would have been sorry if this had happened. As it was, the explosives did not go off, and the mission was a total success.

Unfortunately, the feeling of elation that often follows the completion of a successful, daring raid was short-lived. As we landed at our base of departure we were greeted by Chief of Staff Bar-Lev and the Minister of Defense, Moshe Dayan. Although Bar-Lev expressed praise, I noticed Dayan was silent and that he appeared to be holding back anger. Finally he lashed out at me with scolding criticism, expressing anger that we had not destroyed the airfield. Although my relations with Dayan were always shaky, I was surprised that he would condemn me for following orders. I responded that destroying the airfield was not part of the mission as explained to me, and Bar-Lev came to my aid, also stating that I had no orders to destroy the airfield and that we had performed our mission exactly as it was ordered. I knew that it was very characteristic of Dayan to find a pretext to strike out at officers, but his outburst left me with a very heavy feeling.

18

With the Kurdish Fighters in Iraq

Early in the 1970s I traveled to another war area, to assist other fighting men. Israel was providing support to the Kurdish warriors in their war for independence against Iraq and I was sent to examine the opportunities for increasing our assistance. My mission was preceded by a visit to Israel by the Kurdish leader, Mullah Mustafa Barzani, and his sons. They had been trained by the Israeli army, as Israel had long been sending the Kurds weapons and instructors, almost all of them paratroopers. During his visit Barzani voiced his desire to broaden his war against the Iraqis and to change its character from that of a guerrilla war to a war of open attacks by his forces against the Iraqi army. My mission was to check the battle conditions for such a bold new initiative.

I flew to Teheran and proceeded, on a civilian flight, westward to the town of Khaneh on the Iraq-Iranian border. At nightfall, we drove Landrovers across the border into Iraq, and arrived at Barzani's headquarters. I was tired, but excited and was pleased when the first man to approach me was an Israeli, a doctor who was attached to the Israeli group assigned to Barzani's headquarters. This man was also named Eitan and he joked with me that there being two Eitans (Eitan meaning firm in Hebrew) could only be a good sign. I expressed my hope that he was correct.

A three-man team was assembled consisting of a Persian who was the representative of the Iranian regime, an Israeli who had experience serving with Barzani, and myself. The service we received was excellent. They provided us with a spacious tent and assigned Kurdish soldiers to watch over our security. In addition, they spared no effort to meet our special requests and needs. After a few days, our goods were loaded onto two Landrovers and we crossed back over the Iranian border, traveling south for a full day to a place called Sar Dasht. From there we crossed back into Iraq and arrived at Qal'at Diza, a part of Iraq situated along the Dukan River that was controlled by the Kurds. The road in this area twisted through the mountains and our vehicles groaned as they moved around the curves. I noticed the signs of war everywhere and spotted dead mules ripped open by air attacks, and burned equipment strewn about the area.

We stayed overnight in an abandoned town that played host to only a few inhabitants. Many towns had few men, as every able-body male, from ten years of age until old age was mobilized into the Kurdish army. The women and younger children were kept far from the combat zone, leaving many towns in the combat area virtually empty. The following morning we set out on foot, crossed the river, and walked along its banks in the direction of the Dukan Dam, toward Iraqi positions.

Iraqi Sukhoi planes were bombing targets not far from the path we were walking on. When we approached the Iraqi positions, situated on the top of a mountain, we were spotted and the Iraqis shelled us with artillery. I took shelter in the shadow of a boulder, but did not stop taking pictures. I photographed the shells coming down and caught some amusing shots of the Persian quivering with fear. The Kurdish fighters, used to bombardments, took shelter under large boulders and waited quietly until the shelling ended. Once it was over we returned to the village.

The whole situation was new to me, and not necessarily to my liking. I was being asked to set out on long walks, but was never told the purpose of our journey or its final destination. I was in the company of men I did not know and had never fought with. We were different from one another, to say the least, and the way we saw things were different. After our episode with the Iraqi artillery,

I urged the Kurds accompanying us to share our destination with me, but would only receive vague answers like "toward the mountains." When I asked how long we would be walking, I was told "we shall see."

I had little choice but to adjust to the circumstances. If my companions decided to walk silently, then I too would be silent. I didn't ask questions, I didn't advise. I simply walked. If they wanted to go for a week, I would go for a week. If they didn't care about having an operational plan, so be it. If they did have a plan and simply didn't care to share it with me, that was okay too. I was with them, and that's all there was to it.

Apparently they had a plan and were just not interested in sharing it with the dubious foreigner. We walked and climbed up the mountain trail. My Kurdish companions carried old-fashioned Czech rifles that they called "Brno," which were about two yards long from barrel to stock. They placed special status on the length of the barrel, as if this was more important than accuracy, firepower, range, and modern technology. I noticed they were very poor and wore all the clothing they had, two pairs of pants and two shirts, one on top of the other. The wealthier ones had four pairs of pants and four shirts, but they too, wore them all at the same time.

Although I had promised myself I would walk in silence and not ask questions, my curiosity overtook me and I began to inquire into their dressing habits. In jest I asked if they wore all their clothing because they were cold, but received an answer so sad and serious that I felt ill at ease that I had joked with them. They wore all their clothing, I was told, because they had no homes and no place to put their belongings. Thus, they carried all they owned with them at all times.

During the course of our walk we spotted a valley with a herd of horses being watched by two small Kurdish boys. We walked into the valley and the Kurds requisitioned the horses. They saddled them up and we were transformed into a caravan of riders. One of the two boys accompanied us on foot as we rode through beautiful mountainous country and passed through forests of mulberry and wild pear trees. There were many water springs on the way and I noticed that there was a metal cup with a stone in it at the opening of each spring. The cups were there to allow all who passed an opportunity to drink. The stone was placed inside the cup so that it stayed in its place for the next thirsty person. At many of the springs we took advantage of this old Kurdish tradition.

We had no battle rations and no other food supplies. At times we stopped the horses next to a tree laden with wild pears and enjoyed the fresh fruit so much we almost forgot about the war. Yet, we would ride for long hours. Our bottoms were sore and our bones were aching. Our only relief was to stop from time to time, stretch our sore limbs, and continue our journey for the next few hours on foot.

When we reached a small village with small, destitute huts, I did not say anything, but was sure that we had come to obtain food. The manner with which we were to receive our food was quite alien to me, and I must confess, not all to my liking. My Kurdish companions began to discuss among themselves which hut to target and sat down at the entrance to the chosen home. They did not knock at the door or call out. They made no verbal request, but rather sat in a circle before the home and rolled cigarettes. When the woman living in the hut glanced outside her door and saw us sitting there she entered her home, also without speaking a word. When she opened the door a second time she presented us with a tray of warm flat loaves of bread. Still not a word was spoken. The woman continued to return with trays of cheese, eggs, and vegetables, and still not one word was spoken. We ate quietly and diligently and completed our meal with a splendid tea. As we left my shock at the silence was only compounded by the fact that we offered this generous woman no money and not so much as an expression of gratitude. As we rode on I was not able to hold my tongue any longer and asked my companions why we took food from a poor woman without offering to pay for it. Their response was simple. She has a goat, and therefore she has cheese. She has a chicken and therefore she has eggs. She has land and therefore she has wheat for bread and can grow vegetables. She has no need for money, and her food was her contribution to the war effort.

Around midnight we reached a relatively large town, with even a paved road leading up to it. The boy from whom we had requisitioned the horses had plodded along behind us since the morning, but returned to the mountains after we returned his horses to him. He left without a word of protest, without questioning the long journey he still had before him.

I was told we were to wait for a car that would come to take us to Barzani's headquarters. While waiting we feasted on roast meat and cheese and I found the food to be particularly tasty. When the cars arrived, we immediately set out for camp and entered our tents broken and exhausted. I was asleep before my head hit my pillow.

The morning brought great excitement as, so I was told, Barzani was preparing to visit me in my tent, an honor he rarely bestowed upon a guest. I requested time to prepare myself for his visit and bathed and shaved at a stream outside my tent. I dressed in Kurdish garb, which to me was the most comfortable clothing I had ever worn, and awaited the leader's visit.

My tent mates and I greeted the Kurdish leader at the entrance to our tent. Barzani marched before us, slowly, with a walk full of the pageantry of leadership and authority. His sons were at his side and his bodyguards stood behind him. When he approached me we embraced, and Barzani presented me with a curved sword set with gold engraving. The interpreter translated his words as he spoke, saying to me, "I give you this sword, because we honor you a great deal and know that you have helped us. I also give you this ancient sword as a sign of admiration. Your escorts told me how you conducted yourself during the Iraqi bombardment at Qal'at Diza."

After his presentation we embraced again and exchanged words of kindness and blessing, while amateur photographers immortalized the scene. As we parted, I knew that the magnificent sword, as well as the warm words, were not meant only to reward me for my good deeds, but rather to turn my heart toward the brave leader's wishes. He was asking me to return to Israel and recommend that my leaders honor his requests for additional aid.

After leaving the Kurdish headquarters I was taken on the main part of my tour, a scouting mission along the main road in northern Kurdistan. Down the slope of this road was the town of Rawanduz, where an Iraqi division was stationed. It was the Kurd's request to attack this Iraqi force that had brought me to Kurdistan. We advanced cautiously toward the last in a series of Kurdish barriers, this one located not far from the Iraqi force. It was a "barrier" in all respects, made up of a log and a eucalyptus branch that were laid across the road. A Kurdish fighter armed with a long-barreled Brno rifle sat in a hiding place, behind a large rock. From this position we watched the Iraqi troops for a short while before leaving by horseback for a Kurdish camp in the north.

We spent the night on the side of a tall mountain with a very steep slope. We slept with our heads uphill and our feet resting on a log, facing downhill. The night required cautious sleeping. One wrong move an inch in either direction and it was unlikely I'd be able to stop rolling downhill. In the morning I awoke to the scent of eggs and bread being cooked on an open fire. The air was clean and the mountains were beautiful. Everything was so pastoral I almost forgot there was a war going on.

My next stop was another Kurdish encampment. Also situated in the middle of a beautiful, natural site, the conditions were simple. I also found the people to be very nice. They were simple in their needs, tough, handsome, self-respecting and blunt. They were proud and highly motivated and I did not doubt that each of them was ready to sacrifice his life in the war they were waging for their right to independence. They were a people that aroused in me immediate affection, without the need for prolonged ceremonies.

An example of the light innocent fun we shared can be seen in the time we decided to have an international marksmanship competition, with the Iranian, a Kurd, and myself each representing our respective peoples. We set our target, a chewing gum wrapper slipped into the edge of a stick, at a distance of twenty-five yards and chose the long Czech rifle we wanted to use. The Kurd missed, to the mocking hiss of his peers. The Persian missed, to the joy of the spectators, since Iranians were not very well liked despite the assistance they provided. I hit the target and watched the status of Israel, the IDF, and Jews everywhere rise dramatically.

I had an emotional experience at the campfire that night. I had made a point of paying special attention to the admirable young Kurdish fighters, who were only boys of ten or eleven years old. They were strikingly silent, and I had witnessed them bearing a tremendous amount of suffering. To these children there was nothing too hard, nothing that was impossible. One handsome little boy with a determined look had particularly captured my attention. He sat by the fire and listened carefully, absorbed in what the older men were saying. In my rucksack I had a Swiss pocketknife with blades and keys and various other instruments. This knife was perceived by the average Israeli boy as a wonderful gift. I thought my young friend deserved it, and when the campfire was over and the songs had been sung, I presented him with my gift. He initially glanced at me with happiness, but caught himself and pulled his hand away, not accepting my gift. A Kurdish boy is taught to avoid all temptation, particularly those presented by a stranger. I requested the assistance of some of the elders, who urged the boy to accept my gift. For hours this young, brave, proud boy refused. As the morning neared, the boy conceded and took my gift, turning away immediately so that I would not see him in his weakness or defeat. That little boy taught me more about the Kurds, their nature and their character than I could have learned from reading a thousand books.

I returned home through Teheran. I was the official guest of the Iranians and the unofficial guest of the Israeli instructors who were teaching Iranian farmers. I spent my time in Iran struggling with the knowledge that I was going to disappoint all the wonderful Kurds I had just shared so many exciting memories with. They were good men, proud and strong, but I knew that they would not be able to absorb modern combat techniques and effectively engage the Iraqi army in open battle.

When I returned in the spring of 1970, several months before the Israeli-Egyptian cease-fire agreement put an end to the War of Attrition on the Suez Canal, I was surprised to see a large scale raid by the Shaked battalion of the Southern Command was carried out on the western side of the Canal. This operation was broad in scope, in that it was a night raid, conducted solely on foot. The unit crossed the Canal north of Qantara and attacked Egyptian positions and units in a wide sector along the Canal. The result was a mass flight of Egyptians in that zone and a tremendous impression was made on the Egyptians. In effect, it resulted in an end to Egyptian raids and ambushes on the Israeli or eastern side of the Canal.

One interesting aspect of this operation to me was that it had been planned, down to its last detail by the Southern Command with my participation as Chief Paratrooper and Infantry Officer, a relatively long time before it was executed. The delay resulted from basic differences of opinion between members of the top echelons of command. The Chief of Staff, Bar-Lev, opposed carrying out the operation on various operational grounds. Our attempts to convince him that the operation was vital, had a good chance of success, and that its results would be positive did not persuade him. Yet, he was the Chief of Staff and the one responsible for the decision. Obviously, his opinion outweighed those of all others. The height of the dispute took place in Baluza where General of the Southern Command, Arik Sharon, myself, and other senior officers bombarded Bar-Lev with all our arguments and vigorously urged that he authorize this night raid. Bar-Lev did not budge, but in light of our concentrated barrage, he agreed to place the dispute before the Minister of Defense, Moshe Dayan. When Dayan was briefed about the raid he was enthusiastic and in effect cancelled all of Bar-Lev's opposition.

In the middle of 1972, after serving four years as Chief Paratrooper and Infantry Officer I had a full and varied history of battle experience and expertise in the development of new combat methods and weapons. I was therefore a bit surprised when Chief of Staff Bar-Lev sought to put an end to my military career and force my retirement from the Israeli Army. He summoned me to his office and told me with a tone of finality that it was time I "went home," that I was already a Brigadier General and that I would receive a General's pension. He told me this was "the end of my service." His words hit me very hard. I had come unprepared, but I knew I had no intention of resigning. I had aspired to prolonged service, as well as to additional senior positions. I left Bar-Lev without reacting and he did not demand an immediate response. Perhaps he thought I needed time to digest his order. I consulted with the Deputy Chief of Staff and Chief of the General Staff Branch, Ezer Weizman, and he advised me to ignore Bar-Lev's words. I found this good advice and did just that. When Bar-Lev's term came to an end, he was replaced by an old friend, David "Dado" Elazar. I trusted the new Chief of Staff would have more faith in my abilities and experience.

My hopes that Dado's appointment would mark a new era that would end the poor attitude displayed toward the paratroopers and the infantry, and toward me personally, were quickly diminished. Dado supported the primacy of the armored corps and allowed it to continue to dictate its will. The importance of the infantry continued to be overlooked.

Four years as Chief Paratrooper and Infantry Officer were enough for me and I was looking for the opportunity to move on to another position. I wanted to serve as General of the Northern Command, but Motta Gur, the present General of the Command, did not welcome me and opposed my appointment to this position. In one of the meetings of the General Staff I exchanged notes with Elazar in the Cyrillic alphabet, which we often used to pass personal notes. I requested the appointment of the commander of the reserve armored division in the north. Elazar approved my request and the appointment was made. I also asked to be allowed to continue my studies in Political Science at the University of Haifa.

I decided to place my division on a course of training. To this end, I set up a gunnery range for tanks and training courses for all reservists. The old time officers of the armored corps were surprised at my boldness in setting up a gunnery range. I was a paratrooper and it was clear to them that a gunnery range was strictly a matter for the expertise of tank corps. Yet, the facility was good and useful. However, when General Avraham "Bren" Adan, Commander of the Armored Corps, came to visit the range he threw our instruction books down and screamed in a silly, infantile outburst. I was saddened to see a general behave in such a manner, and thought he should have the best interests of his troops at heart, and not the politics of turf. The tankmen who witnessed his outburst were embarrassed. They were angry when a few months later the Yom Kippur War broke out and they realized the training they had received saved their lives. They could have been denied that training, and indeed, in a time when the fate of the State of Israel oscillated on the scale of victory and defeat, they could have lost important battles over an issue as silly as control.

Bren wouldn't let me go. A short while after his outburst at the division gunnery range, he summoned me to the Armor House in Tel Aviv and forced the "battle of the berets" on me. He demanded of me, as a commander of an armored division, that I remove my red paratrooper's beret and put on the black tank man's beret. I refused, explaining to him that I am a paratrooper and remain a paratrooper in any and all positions I assume. I reminded him that I was assigned to my post by the Chief of Staff and that he was fully aware of my history as a paratrooper. Although he was very angry, I got up and left.

In February 1973, the division finished its training. The spring and summer of 1973 were a time of tension. My division was located in new bases in the eastern sector and the large Syrian forces facing us were constantly becoming more powerful. I felt there was going to be a war and I shared my fears with the men of the divisional staff and the commanders of the brigades and battalions. A few months later, I was to learn how right my instincts were.

Part Four:
THE
YOM KIPPUR WAR

19

The Syrians Attack

As early as a week before the war erupted I saw clear signs that indicated to me, without a doubt, that we would very soon be at war. I could not understand how the senior command did not notice the same Syrian actions I did, or how they did not conclude, as I had, that war was imminent. The signs were so clear.

A week before the war, my unit was not prepared for the difficulties I was convinced were approaching. I increased my battalion's exercises, and, in a mobilization exercise for one brigade, I had my forces load the cannons of their tanks. These tanks were removed from storage, where they had been kept without ammunition. I returned the tanks to their depot, but requested and received permission to leave them with their ammunition intact. On the Sunday before the war I brought my concerns to the attention of the general of the Northern Command and implored him to order the laying of thousands of mines along the border on the Golan Heights. With his consent, a broad campaign began and hundreds of mines were laid. Although it was not the quantity or scope I had demanded, they proved to be vital at the outset of the war.

Each day during the week before the war the intelligence officer came to show me the latest developments and changes in the Syrian deployments. Each morning we understood that we were one day closer to war, and there was little we could do about it but wait for it to happen.

When the Seventh Brigade came up north at the end of the week without their tanks they equipped themselves with the tanks from my division, using the loaded Centurions first and deploying the others later. On the eve before Yom Kippur, and the outbreak of the war, the officers of the Seventh Brigade joined my officers in a drink to victory. Simply spoken, but deeply felt, we raised our glasses as I said, "To victory in the war."

Mobilization of our forces was not authorized until the next morning, only hours before the war began. With little choice we rushed to prepare the tanks and equipment and deploy our key forces. My division was assigned to join the Seventh Brigade, and the regular, standing armed forces in the area, in the defense of the Golan Heights from Syrian attack.

At one o'clock in the afternoon on Yom Kippur day, the war had not yet begun. My deputy, Reserve Brigadier General Menachem "Menn" Abiram, who had been my commander in the paratroops, came to see me and jokingly asked why, despite my prediction, was there still no war. I solemnly replied that the war would begin in one hour, at two o'clock, which in fact it did. When the war erupted, Menn probably thought I had shared with him some secret information. In fact, all I had done was offer him my personal opinion. I did not know that the war was set to begin at two o'clock. I was just sure that there would be war. I chose two o'clock because that was when the Jewish army, which was fasting on its holiest day, would be hungriest and weakest.

Thus, at two o'clock on the afternoon of Yom Kippur, Syrian shells from long range 180 mm guns began pouring down on us.

Our troops moved quickly to load their tanks and return fire. We had mobilized our reservists and made special efforts to smoothly and speedily integrate them into the battle plan. Although we did not know anything about the scope of the war, the enemy's intentions, the extent of their attack, or its objectives, we understood that, at a minimum, the Syrians wanted the Golan Heights and our task was to deny it to them. At four o'clock that afternoon the General of the Northern Command, Hakka Hofi, came to survey the area and asked me to join him as he rode up to the top of the Heights to Naffach. I left my deputy and chief of staff in my office to organize the division and carry out the orders that I would send from the Golan and joined General Hofi and his staff.

We were going to Naffach because we had received reports that firing had broken out all along the front and that Syrian tanks were moving toward the Heights in masses. We needed to go there to see for ourselves, to try to get an understanding of the scope of the war and the center of gravity of the Syrian assault. I remained with General Hofi as he managed our war effort, and as he left the scene, slightly after midnight, he transferred responsibility to me.

The division's forces of reservists began to arrive and we directed them to combat sectors where we understood the situation to be most severe. Our major problem was that we were operating without concrete knowledge of the overall picture. We sent forces to the southern sector because we "heard" that the Syrian pressure was greater there than in the northern sector. We were receiving only partial and interrupted reports. We had to operate on fragments of information, that often turned out to be little more than rumors.

Yet the rumors had their purpose as well. I knew the situation was grave, but the morale of our forces would have been severely hindered if they thought we were being beaten. They knew the situation was dangerous, and this knowledge motivated them to fight harder, be braver. Yet they also talked about the landing of Israeli helicopters on Mount Hermon at a time, I was to learn, that Mount Hermon had already fallen to the Syrians.

Upon receiving command from General Hofi, I sent instructions to Ben-Shoham, the commander of Brigade 188 to leave his bunker and move his brigade, which was spread out along the border, to the southern sector. Even in the atmosphere of confusion and lack of clarity, it was obvious that the Syrians were applying the greatest amount of pressure on the southern sector. In fact, prior to relinquishing command, General Hofi had ordered the evacuation of tactical localities and all civilians from this sector. To my dismay, the Jewish settlements in the area were not properly organized or fortified and could not serve the support function many of the border settlements had traditionally served in Israel's wars. This severe failing was corrected only after the war, but had been the topic of heated discussion during the months prior to the war. The concept in the IDF was that the Armored Corps would be able to handle all attacks, and that the Air Force would complete the task of defeating any attacking Arab armies. Thus, the strategy of old-fashioned civilian-based territorial defense, despite the many tests it had withstood, was not worth the time and energy. As it turned out, this concept was extremely faulty. The Armored Corps could not do everything, and the Air Force found itself limited in its activity and ability as it fought in a zone saturated with anti-aircraft missiles. The heavy Syrian assault had precluded any IDF attack on the missile sites to destroy them.

In the hours before dawn I worked feverishly to organize the command post for controlling the entire Golan Heights. I gathered updated reports on the situation from each sector in an orderly and accurate manner, updated maps according to the deployment of the Syrian forces and began directing our forces in response to the staging and assault status of the Syrians. In a hasty decision that turned out to be very lucky, I ordered a tank brigade that had come to replace the tanks given to the Seventh Brigade to take a short cut from the Golani intersection, which was a distance from the front, by using their threads to travel the El-Al axis. It would appear that my friendly angel that accompanied me through all the other wars was still with me in this hour of dire need. The tank battalion, commanded by Yossi Amir, moved up the axis just in time to confront an advancing Syrian unit. The Syrian unit had already passed Ramat Magshimim and was very close to going down to the Sea of Galilee near Giv'at Yo'av. The night before, this Syrian unit had trampled small, dispersed groups from Brigade 188 and had arrived at the Hushaniyah intersection. They were standing at the opening of the Ramat Magshimim-Ein Gev axis without any Israeli forces to face them. Then along came Yossi Amir's tank brigade. They effectively halted the Syrian advance and literally saved the Sea of Galilee from being overrun by the Syrians. I cannot even begin to imagine the consequences of a Syrian advance that succeeded in reaching the Sea of Galilee.

The order to evacuate Ein Gev and Tel-Katzir had been given by someone other than me, but it was an indication of the severity of the situation. We sent additional forces up the Yehudiyeh-Hushaniyeh axis, where they confronted and stemmed a Syrian assault moving west. The deputy brigade commander of the unit fighting this battle, Gideon Tsimbal, was killed. He was from my village, a little younger than I.

By Sunday morning we had a clearer understanding of the situation. We knew Mount Hermon had fallen and that the northern sector was holding out. In the southern and central sectors the Syrians were applying heavy pressure and the area from the Hushaniyeh intersection to Naffach was also controlled by the Syrians. It appeared that they were fortifying their positions in this sector.

Our combat strategy was still overcome by confusion. We had tanks and men arriving at the front at different times, and without the rest of their units. Each time a tank crew with a tank arrived at the reserve base they were sent up to the front without waiting for their combat outfit to be complete. We simply needed all the men and equipment we could get, as soon as it was available. However, the price of the speed was the confusion. Once they arrived at the front we directed them to the critical points. A large portion of them were destroyed in their first fire contact with Syrian forces because they were just thrown at the enemy forces. Nonetheless, they did

weaken the Syrian pressure, which was the most important immediate task. Many of our brave men stood their ground against
overwhelming Syrian forces, causing them losses and further
weakening their effort. Unfortunately, at this juncture, we were still
failing to halt the Syrian advance.

In the morning hours Syrian tanks reached Naffach and effectively surrounded us. We had no weapons to fight them with and it
was clear that they were getting ready to assault the fences. Without
the means of confronting them, we knew their tanks would knock
the fences over within seconds. I had no desire to taken prisoner by
the Syrians, not only because it would personally prove to be a
terrible experience, but also because I had the responsibility of
commanding our forces, a task I could hardly do under Syrian
captivity. Therefore, I gave the order to my staff to evacuate and we
rode our half-tracks northwest to Alikah, where we had a tank
gunnery range. It was the perfect site to be in contact with our forces,
without having to make decisions under direct Syrian pressure.

Our departure from Naffach was very hectic. We had several
half-tracks and one jeep. I knew I would not be comfortable with
myself if I assigned to one of my soldiers the dangerous task of
leaving the area in the jeep. Each of my men should benefit from
the added protection afforded by the half-track. I had always sought
to set a personal example as a commander, and often this translated
into taking the danger upon myself. With Syrian shells chasing after
us as we left, the danger was quite real. As we turned onto the road,
we met a foreign television crew that was filming our departure and
joyfully mocking our bad fortune. Although the press had never
shown a great love for us, and I certainly had no great love for them,
it appeared particularly out of place for them to be taking sides as
the war was still raging. I was angry. These Syrians had attacked us,
and on our holiest day of the year. What had we done to deserve the
spiteful laughter of this camera crew? I exercised all my personal
restraint and avoided the heartfelt temptation to press the trigger
of the jeep's machine gun. Meanwhile, the Syrians were still shooting at us. Some of our tanks, which were immobile due to slipped

or broken treads, were being repaired on the helicopter pad at Naffach, and they began to return the Syrian fire. Although they could not move, they could shoot, and they answered the Syrian bombardment with a significant response of their own. We left Naffach under thick, black smoke, with the smell of war heavy in the air.

We reached Alikah near noon and reorganized our command post, setting up communications with our forces. By mid-afternoon I had received reports not only from my troops fighting on the Golan Heights, but also from the Southern command post fighting the Egyptians in the Sinai. The reports made clear the dimensions of the war, its scope, and the coordination between the Egyptian and Syrian armies. It was clear that this war was to be the most fateful for the State of Israel since the War of Independence, and that this war had been initiated by the Arabs, not to determine boundaries, but in an effort to destroy Israel. Literally, the very existence of Israel, our homes, and our families were being threatened. As I came to this dreadful conclusion, I vowed that I would not leave the Golan Heights until the last Syrian soldier had been driven back. If it was decreed from Above that I be the last Jewish fighter, that I lay down my life, I would fight and die.

The Syrian tanks assaulting the fence at Naffach were defeated and my command post returned to its original place. We stayed only a short time, however, as another Syrian unit, advancing along our oil pipeline through Tel Shipun, applied tremendous pressure on my brigade of reservists. My men fought desperately to check the Syrian advance.

In the afternoon, Dan Laner arrived at the front with his command headquarters and division. We decided to divide the command in two, with Laner taking command of the southern sector, and I remaining in command of the northern sector, beginning at Quneitra. Many of Laner's forces were still being mobilized and I agreed that his command would extend over some of my forces fighting in the south, such as the brigade commanded by Ori Orr who would become Commander of the Northern Command in the late 1980s.

When responsibility was divided between Laner and myself, I decided to relocate my command post near Tel Shiban. I left Naffach and rode north along the oil pipeline. As I traveled I met many tank crews that had been cut off from their units and were traveling toward the front without any clue to the battles in progress or the exact locations they were most needed. I was frustrated by the level of confusion and at times was very forceful as I led these units back to the front and into contact with the advancing enemy.

The situation at Naffach worsened and it was apparent at various points in the fighting that the area was going to fall to the Syrians. In truth, the situation was reversed only by the heroic struggle waged by the brave men led by Ori Orr. Orr set a personal example as he fought gallantly. His unit was assisted by the courageous men manning the tanks of Battalion 82 of the Seventh Brigade. By evening it was clear that the situation had been successfully reversed, as the Syrian pressure continued to fade. Although exchanges of tank fire continued, the situation was stable and we were in control.

On Sunday night Israeli forces failed in an attempt to regain control of Mount Hermon. The assault resulted in many casualties, and although I was not involved in the decision or the execution, I realized that the fault lay with the lack of intelligence data available to the Command center. The assault was undertaken on the basis of erroneous information which indicated that sections of Mount Hermon were still under Israeli control. If the Commanders planning the assault had known that the whole area was controlled by the Syrians, it is doubtful that the attack, as it was planned, would have been implemented. The lack of accurate information led to a faulty appraisal of the situation and the initiation of an ill-fated attack. I was deeply frustrated that the confusion that had hindered us from the outset was still the cause of unnecessary casualties.

During the night, it became clear to me that the Syrian advance in the south had been thwarted, but that there would be an equally aggressive Syrian attack from the east. As reports pouring into the command post clarified the situation on the front, my men and I came to understand that personally we had based ourselves in a dangerous area. We were alone in a field and were without means of defending ourselves. Thus, that night we all took turns standing guard in an effort to give ourselves warning should the Syrians continue in their advance. Sadly, that evening we suffered a loss, not totally unconnected with the war, but not associated with any battle. A young artillery officer, who was exhausted from the more than forty hours he had been awake and fighting, fell asleep behind a half-track that he believed would not be used until the morning. Unfortunately, the half-track had to be moved and the driver, in the darkness, did not notice the young man sleeping on the ground behind him. This young officer of great potential was crushed to death. Any death is sad, but a death by accident, while a war is raging, is sadder in its irony.

Toward dawn we had a little scare as we received reports that the Syrians had landed commandos by helicopter approximately three quarters of a mile from our headquarters. Our reports stated that our Air Force Mirages had destroyed all the helicopters, many before their commandos disembarked, but that some Syrians had successfully landed. We dispatched a patrol to comb the area, and they found and eliminated the Syrians who had managed to land.

That night, a tank company from the Seventh Brigade, commanded by Meir Zamir, a brilliant commander and genuine hero, engaged in one of the most heroic and amazing battles in the history of warfare. Zamir's company had been assigned to assist Dan Laner in the southern sector, as he was facing a Syrian onslaught on his left wing. In a night battle of tremendous importance to the war, Zamir's company of eight tanks held back and ultimately destroyed the advancing Syrian Tank Brigade 43, which had one hundred tanks. This feat was achieved without the benefit of night-sighting systems and without losing one Israeli tank. Had Zamir failed to stem the tide of the Syrian assault the battle of the next day, Monday, would have been dramatically more difficult and dangerous.

As we had expected, heavy Syrian pressure developed north of Quneitra at dawn on Monday, the third day of the war. The strategic outposts along the front line were attacked and harassed, but stood their ground in heroic battles of defiance, preventing the Syrians from capturing even one position in the whole sector. We ordered the evacuation of two positions; the remainder of the outposts were isolated in the enemy's rear. The Syrians attacked them furiously and each time our forces succeeded in repelling the assault. The men of the Golani Brigade and the paratroopers fought with immense bravery, destroying Syrian tanks with their personal weapons and fighting with skill and boldness. One strategic outpost succeeded in destroying six Syrian tanks that had entered their compound; others succeeded in turning back Syrian tanks before they penetrated the base. In all instances, the soldiers acted with tremendous courage, and I am only sorry that I cannot name each and every act of bravery. These young men literally secured the existence of the State of Israel and their actions are engraved in the memory of our whole nation.

The positions in the northern sector, from the foothills of Mount Hermon to the Little Hermon, were not under particularly heavy pressure, although a large Syrian commando force had successfully penetrated the Little Hermon itself and Buq'ata, the Druze village. The Syrians also blocked the Hermon-Mas'ada-Naffach road. Sadly, a patrol from the seventh brigade suffered many losses in a battle with these Syrian forces in the western foothills of the Little Hermon.

The presence of the Syrian commando forces in Buq'ata did not concern me as much as the very heavy Syrian pressure that had begun to develop in the "Valley of Tears." The sector through this valley was under constant heavy artillery fire and attacks by Syrian rockets and planes. The shooting did not stop for even a moment. On Monday, toward noon, our positions reported that the Syrians were rushing a huge force of tanks, APCs, jeeps, trucks, and artillery to the front. They crossed the protective fence, the border markings, and were approaching the first anti-tank trench and minefields in the "Valley of Tears." The Seventh Brigade, spread out along the width of the sector, from the Little Hermon southward to Quneitra, held the Syrians in a valiant battle. Our men in Position 107, which was now situated behind enemy lines, fought daringly and, for lack of a better anti-tank weapon, destroyed Syrian tanks with their bazookas.

The Syrian tanks were advancing and placing our forces under enormous pressure. They succeeded on crossing over our mines, and overcame our anti-tank ditches by building bridges over them. The Seventh Brigade was under constant, heavy shelling, and fought desperately, temporarily stopping the Syrian attack. However, the heavy Syrian pressure was resumed when fresh forces from their rear arrived, and slowly the Syrians managed to advance their tanks closer to the brigade's positions. Ultimately, some Syrian tanks passed the brigade's position and others found the way to the foot of the Little Hermon, effectively outflanking the main body of the Seventh Brigade. The brigade's difficulties were magnified by the fact that our ammunition trucks could not reach their positions, due to the heavy Syrian artillery shelling. The tanks could only be re-stocked with ammunition if they traveled to the rear of the battle front, which was very close to my command post.

During the night the Syrians continued their pressure. The darkness brought with it many potentially dangerous situations. Syrian tanks were passing our forces at times at a distance of only several yards. Luckily, the Syrians did not notice us, and we had the opportunity to cause their advance some damage. The commander of Battalion 77, Avigdor Kahalani, for example, hit a Syrian tank that was passing only one yard in front of him. In certain instances, the tank battles were like hand-to-hand combat, with barrels of tank cannons actually rubbing against each other. On Tuesday morning the battle scene revealed the peculiar battle of the night before, as Syrian tanks, some hit and some undamaged, stood in the rear of the Seventh Brigade, facing west along the Merom Golan-Elrom road.

Our forces continued to arrive to the front all that night, as men arriving from abroad came directly from the airplane to the battlefield, and wounded who had been treated in hospitals rejoined their units as soon as they were physically able. The process of repairing tanks also continued with an urgency, and every tank that was repaired was immediately sent back into combat.

By Tuesday morning, the fourth day of the war, the situation was critical. Although, in the southern sector the Syrians had already been pushed back to their border, in most part due to the efforts of the division commanded by Musa Peled, the situation was very grave in the northern sector. The Syrian assault had been dramatically intensified during the night, and the Seventh Brigade had received no reinforcements. Their forces were dwindling, their ammunition supply had been depleted, and we still could not reach them with additional supplies because of the heavy Syrian shelling.

In this situation we presented a gap for the Syrians to break through every time one of our tanks turned around to get more ammunition. Furthermore, the tank crews had been fighting since the beginning of the war, without a moment's rest, and under constant pressure. Under these conditions, I feared for our troops and the positions they were defending. I knew these men were skilled soldiers who were motivated by a deep sense of responsibility for the fate of their country, and I trusted that they would mobilize every drop of their strength and will in their battle. But, the Syrians were close, having advanced even further during the night. I wondered how long my brave young men could hold out.

The men of my command staff were asking themselves the same question and after hours of restraining themselves began to openly plead with me to have the Seventh Brigade pull back. They were not talking about a withdrawal, for they knew that we would all fight to our death rather than open up the whole north of Israel to Syrian domination. They simply wanted me to order the brigade to pull back a few kilometers, so that they would be under less Syrian pressure. I strongly considered their advice, and I knew it was not without merit. However, I also knew that any ground we gave the Syrians was ground we would not be forcing them to take. I knew it was excruciatingly difficult for the fighting soldiers, but I also felt that the Syrians, who were not as motivated as we, would soon break.

When things were most critical, that is, when the chance for holding the advance of the Syrian armor had been lost, my good angel appeared again, this time in the guise of Yossi Ben-Hanan. When I heard Yossi's voice over the radio, I was not sure my exhaustion hadn't affected my hearing. I knew Yossi, an excellent officer, had gone on a tour of the Himalayas just after leaving the army, and did not know he had managed to return to Israel. It seems, when the war broke out, Yossi, a battalion commander on the Golan Heights, transferred from plane to plane, and country to country, until he was able to arrive in Israel. Naturally, he came straight from the airport to the front. And here my angel had brought him to me, just when I needed him most. Yossi had about twenty tanks under his command and was asking me where I would like to position his forces. I told him to advance to the oil pipeline and await further instructions. His presence gave me new hope.

After speaking with Ben-Hanan, I immediately called Yanush Bengal, the commander of the Seventh Brigade, and informed him that "the son of Mr. Morning Exercise has arrived." This reference to Yossi was in connection with his father, who for years had been the broadcaster of a morning exercise program on Israel radio. Yanush instantly realized who I was speaking about and shared my feeling of relief. Yanush informed me that Ben-Hanan's forces were most needed on the road leading up to our Position 107, which was isolated behind Syrian lines.

Yossi did as I instructed and succeeded in linking up with Position 107. In the few minutes that followed, the Syrian attack was broken. Finding themselves behind enemy lines, Ben-Hanan's unit began firing on Syrian tanks, armored personel carriers, and half-tracks, scoring direct hits, shooting at them from behind their own lines, the Syrians found themselves to be surrounded by tanks. In addition to the tactical advantages this provided us with, it also damaged the Syrians psychologically. They did not know that the Seventh Brigade was on the verge of collapse, or that the brigade's ammunition supply was down to about three or four shells per tank. All they knew was that they had not succeeded in breaking through, and that they were now being hit from the rear as well. I breathed my first easy breath when I heard the radio operator from Position 107 report that the Syrian tanks were turning around and beginning to withdraw. At that moment I understood that the awful Syrian attack, which had lasted longer than twenty-four continuous hours, had been stopped.

Toward noon the shooting died down. The Syrian flight was a heartwarming sight, as they abandoned their tanks, many of them in sound, battle-ready condition, loaded with ammunition. With the sector relatively quiet, we decided on Tuesday night to afford ourselves the luxury of a few hours sleep, an indulgence we had not granted ourselves since the Syrian bombardment began. The next day, Wednesday, the fifth day of the war, all of the Golan Heights was in our hands. We started urgent preparations to organize our forces, restock ammunition, and refuel the tanks. We decided we would counter-attack and break through to the Syrian side of the Golan Heights. I received a paratroop brigade and we did a thorough search of the sector. After determining that the sector was empty and that the Syrians had all fled, I sent a now famous telegram to the Chief of Staff informing him that "the Golan Heights are in our hands." I could say no more, although I knew he understood that the magnificent heroism of our troops was hidden behind the words.

Now that the Israeli Army had retaken control of the Golan Heights and left the Syrians beaten and defeated as they fled for their lives, the Commander of the Northern Command, General Hofi, crossed the Jordan River, and for the first time, joined us. While we were fighting for the very control of the Golan, and perhaps for the fate of Israel, he stayed in the headquarters of the Command. Thus, I was not surprised when I heard from Musa Peled that when the war broke out he found Hakka Hofi lying on a field cot, broken and mumbling "everything is lost...everything is lost." I understand the tremendous responsibilities that were on his shoulders at that very moment, but because of that great responsibility, I feel that he should have done all he could to remain strong and lead our war effort. I tremble at the thought of the consequences had other members of the General Staff suffered similar panic attacks, similar feelings of defeat. With such an attitude, the fate of the war would have been decided in advance. From the moment the war began, I too felt that the situation was desperate. I did not, even for a brief moment, pretend to myself that things were anything other than critical. I understood what hung in the balance and was frustrated, angry, and even nervous. However, I not only believed we would overcome our difficulties and triumph, I knew we would. I saw the strength of our soldiers, their motivation, their spirit. I saw their will to win and drew my own strength from it. I had sworn I would not leave the Golan alive and I knew that as I pledged my life in the defense of our nation, so did the thousands of other men who were fighting beside me. I overcame my fear when I realized our pledge was a very formidable power indeed, a power the Syrians could not possibly defeat.

We deployed our forces for an offensive against the Syrian sector of the Golan Heights. The Seventh Brigade, which had initially suffered losses at the hands of the Syrians, were anxious to continue the fight. The brigade mobilized their forces and produced more than one hundred tanks fully manned and ready for battle. I was also given command of the Golani infantry brigade and a select commando unit.

On Wednesday night, as I was allowing myself the luxury of some rest, a senior officer who had once been the commander of the special commando unit came to my room and requested that I not include his former unit in the front of our offensive into Syria. He argued that the young men serving in the unit were among the best of Israel and that they should not be placed in dangerous situations when it was not absolutely necessary. His words angered me quite a bit. I told him all of our youth were the best we had to offer, and none of them should be placed in danger when it is not absolutely necessary. We were at war. To me, that made it absolutely necessary. He left my room feeling ashamed and I believe he regretted his words because he told what had happened to the present commander of the unit, Yonatan Netanyahu. The next morning

Netanyahu, who died rescuing hijacked passengers in the Entebbe rescue in 1976, came to me and apologized for the words of the former commander. He informed me that his men were ready to do whatever was necessary to achieve the breakthrough into Syria. The commando unit did participate in the offensive and fought bravely, justifying the prestige bestowed upon it.

The next day, Thursday, the sixth day of the war, the Chief of Staff, Commander of the Northern Command and several other senior officers visited the Golan Heights. They had come to review and approve my plan for breaking through into Syria, but also took the opportunity to tour the area. It was the first visit by the Chief of Staff since the war started, and I must confess that I was angry that he had not come while the balance of forces favored the Syrians. His presence then would have served to motivate our forces and shown his recognition of the bravery that was being displayed so often.

Once we secured the Chief of Staff's approval for our plan, we set the time for our assault for noon that same day, Thursday. I was pleased that my plans were approved, and also pleased that a bandage I was wearing on my left hand, due to an injury I received in my carpentry shop, was finally able to come off. The brigade doctor had given his approval and, despite the fact that the bandage had been useful for wiping off pencil marks on maps, I was glad I wouldn't have to continue explaining to everyone that I had not been injured in the hand during the war.

As the Chief of Staff and the Commander of the Northern Command walked to their helicopter to leave the Golan Heights, I heard Hakka mention my name to Dado. As I moved closer to hear what they were saying, I heard Hakka recommend that I be given the rank of General for the defense I had organized and commanded on the Golan. Dado responded that it was not the easiest thing to do, and I thought to myself that Dado was too hesitant, that I would not receive it.

After the senior officers left, we set up our command center at Tel Ben-Tal, in a location that allowed us the ability to respond to events in the field. At exactly noon, with the help of artillery and aerial attacks by our planes, we began the breakthrough into Syria's northern sector of the Golan, in the direction of Mizra'at, Beit-Jinn, and Tel-Shams.

The breakthrough was executed exactly as planned. We broke through without losses, and by the evening of the same day we were already in Mizra'at and Beit-Jinn and in control of the road from Mizra'at, Beit-Jinn, Herfa, Khalas, and Tel-Shams. The overall plan called for Dan Laner's division to initiate an assault on the Syrian central sector in the direction of Quneitra and Khan-Arnebeh at two o'clock that afternoon. This assault ran into difficulties as the troops passed over minefields and suffered heavy losses. In spite of this, we all took note at where we stood six days after the Syrians had attacked us. We were in Syria, and the only way we were leaving was if our government told us to.

20

Hatred for Dayan

Not until Friday, the seventh day of the war, did the Minister of Defense, Moshe Dayan, come to visit the Golan Heights. As I had felt with regard to the Chief of Staff and the general Command, I was angry that the Minister of Defense had not found the time to visit us while the situation on the ground was against us. As it turned out, we did not need his support or advice, but there were moments when the circumstances looked as though we did. Instead, on the seventh day of the war, with our troops already in the Syrian sector of the Golan, Dayan arrives, listens to the story of our battles, instructs us to shell Damascus with our artillery and leaves. I found it interesting to see the anger with which he was received by the officers and soldiers, with some acting toward him with open hostility. Some men even expressed a bitter hatred, and I was sure that he felt the tension. How could he not understand the meaning behind clearly spoken words of resentment? His order to shell Damascus only served to increase disaffection because it was seen as an effort on his part to vindicate himself and lift himself out of the embarrassing situation he found himself in.

The attack on Israel on Yom Kippur by the Arab forces was not a surprise, or should not have been. There was intelligence data that clearly indicated that the attack was imminent. Yet Dayan did not correctly interpret the data, and failed to properly evaluate the situation. He underestimated the enemy's strength and was overtaken by an inflated sense of self-confidence. He did not believe the Arabs would attack, despite all the evidence that suggested the contrary. Thus, on the day of the attack our reserve units were not at the front, supplies were not at the front, and the borders were not properly fortified. The soldiers who were guarding the borders were few in number, without proper weapons and totally unprepared for the Arab onslaught. The number of casualties we suffered, particularly during the first few days of the war, was the sad indicator of how greatly unprepared we were. Minister Dayan was responsible for the decision not to mobilize more men and not to move supplies to the fronts. The resentment of our men, who had fought the difficult battles and watched their friends die, was an expression of their anger for the errors Dayan had made. What was even more frustrating was Dayan's refusal to admit that he had made mistakes. In fact, he never did admit that he had erred.

Personally, I had always questioned the legend of Moshe Dayan. During the days of the Palmach, Dayan's unit often engaged in daring raids, but this was not uncommon for many units. By the 1950s, Dayan had become a close associate of Prime Minister David Ben-Gurion, and used this relationship to climb the ranks to power. His legend of courage was artificial to my mind. Even during the Six-Day War, when he was also Minister of Defense, he only visited areas after the fighting was already over. He was not a leader who threw himself into the thick of the battle or strove to set a personal example of bravery for his men. He had his legend to lean on, and I must admit, it served him well.

The legend served him well, that is, until his true nature came to light in the Yom Kippur War. As he stood before our troops, his arrogance and attitude of superiority were obvious. The troops were angry, and his supposed deeds of bravery in the past were not shielding him from the anger. What he failed to understand was that each soldier sitting before him was not impressed with his reputation for bravery, because each of them had displayed at least as much bravery in their recent battles with the Syrians. We literally had thousands of heroes sitting before him. I personally despised the man, and I knew he felt the same way toward me.

I had been told that Dayan's hostility toward me was rooted in an old rivalry between our families, although I do not know of any such rivalry. However over the years I could not help but notice his aggressive behavior toward me. Actually he was aggressive toward everyone, treating brave soldiers as if he were a feudal lord, but he was particularly belligerent toward me. During the period of reprisal raids along the Jordan River, he treated me with contempt and tyranny, often attempting to ridicule me in front of my troops. Even after the very successful raid on Beirut Airport he overemphasized the fact that we had not destroyed the airfield and reprimanded me for this oversight, despite the fact that the Chief of Staff Bar-Lev explained to him that destroying the airfield was not part of our instructions. Perhaps the most openly aggressive he had ever been toward me was during the episode of the terrorists' landing of their hijacked Sabena airliner at Lod Airport. As Chief Paratrooper Officer my presence at the scene was requested by the Deputy Chief of Staff, General Tal. I participated in consultations and contributed to the formulation of a plan of action. When Dayan saw me there his face immediately turned sour. When he suggested that we remove the hydraulic oil from the plane, I countered that the terrorists had threatened the life of the passengers when they demanded more fuel, and would most likely do the same to receive more hydraulic oil. Dayan was furious that I would contradict him, he, who could do everything, knew everything, and understood everything. He lashed out at me, screaming, "What are you doing here? Who asked you to be here? Who asked you to speak? Who asked you what you think?" Everybody in the room was frozen with shock. I too did not know what to say, but recognized that he attacked me so viciously because he realized I had made him look foolish. This was not my intention, however. My intention was to engage in an intelligent and thoughtful planning process that would result in the freeing of the hostages on board the airliner. After Dayan's assault, I understood that my presence would not be helpful, and I left the room. That evening as many of us lay on the ground beside the airliner, a member of the Belgian crew came down from the pilot's cabin through an opening in the forward landing gear mounting to check the airplane. After his inspection, he returned to

the plane's cabin, not having noticed we were there. The actions of
the crew member sparked my imagination and, after surveying the
possibilities, I reported to the commanders at the scene that I
believed there was a possibility of having our troops enter the plane.
My answer to Dayan's foolish and childish behavior toward me was
seen in the satisfaction I received when the commanders accepted
my suggestion. Our troops entered the plane, killed the hijackers
and freed the hostages.

As he stood on the Golan Heights that Friday morning and
issued his orders to bombard Damascus, I did not take him very
seriously. The task would have taken a great deal of preparation, as
the big guns and artillery machines needed for such a task were not
presently available. We would have to transport the equipment from
the central Northern Command post and set them up under my
authority. I had other priorities and other things to worry about.

Only the night before, the tank force commanded by Yossi
Ben-Hanan had entered the Syrian zone at Tel-Shams. The Syrian
force defending the highway to Damascus confronted Ben-Hanan's
tanks with heavy anti-tank fire from the slopes of Tel-Shams, placing
his forces in a dangerous position. Throughout the night,
Netanyahu's special unit worked to rescue the tanks and their crews,
evacuating the wounded, of which Ben-Hanan was one. On Saturday night, the eighth day of the war, the paratrooper brigade
captured Tel-Shams. The victory was due to a deep, forceful flanking movement from the southwest to the south, where the Syrians
were least prepared for an assault. When I presented this plan to the
brigade commander he objected to this movement and requested
permission to implement a plan of his own. I denied his request, and
luckily my stubbornness proved to be the right decision.

On Friday night, we received information that fresh Iraqi forces
were streaming to the front and some among our General Staff
expressed concern. I did not share this concern because I felt the
Iraqis were entering a losing war effort and that the tide had turned
in our favor. As it turned out, the Iraqis, an armored brigade and a
mechanized brigade, had wandered into a chaotic situation, straying

from place to place with no maps or Syrian guides. They were shot at from all directions and never knew exactly who was shooting at them. Often the Syrians and the Iraqis engaged in battles with each other, each convinced they were fighting the Israelis. The only fear I shared was the reports that the Iraqis would attack in Dan Laner's sector, on my right flank. To neutralize this threat, I ordered one of the battalion commanders from the Seventh Brigade to take tanks and capture Khan Arniyeh, which would serve as a defensive position. In addition, I told him to do what was necessary to assure that the Iraqis did not take the major intersection in the area. Later that night I received his report that the axis was empty and that the Iraqis were not on their way to Quneitra.

Although I felt relieved at the news that the Iraqis were not advancing, I understood and respected the concerns of the others. I am a believer in caution, particularly during wartime. Actions should not be taken on assumptions, and a good commander is never indifferent to any change, no matter how small he may perceive it to be. The definition of war requires the taking of risks, but each risk should be measured and calculated. Thus, as I listened to the radio, I heard a conversation between Dan Laner and the central Northern Command in which Laner expressed concern and that he was considering withdrawing his forces. I interrupted the conversation and informed Laner that there was no serious threat of an Iraqi assault, and that most of what he was hearing from the Iraqis were empty gestures designed to impress and appease the Syrians.

The use of empty gestures and colorful rhetoric was not unusual in the Arab world. Although it was alien to us, as we placed a special emphasis on accuracy, we found that Arab commanders often lessened the extent of their failures, or at times presented failures as successes, when reporting to their headquarters. This was the case in the battle for Tel-Shams. The Syrians had seriously fortified the area because it was clear that Tel-Shams was crucial to the IDF's advance to Damascus. As the battle raged, and it was clear to all that the Syrians had absolutely no chance of defending Tel-Shams, the Syrian commander informed his commanders that his forces were standing fast and pushing our troops back. His efforts were praised by headquarters, and we enjoyed a good laugh when we heard his commanders call him a "hero among heroes."

After our forces completed the capture of Tel-Shams the Syrians rained extraordinary amounts of artillery on the area, targeting not only Tel-Shams, but also Khalas, where my command post was located. The bombardment was the heaviest we had seen since the first days of the war.

We moved our command post westward and waited until the Syrian fire eased up. Once there was relative quiet, we moved our big guns forward and opened fire on Damascus, raining shells on the Al-Mazeh neighborhood and Damascus Airport. I believe this artillery attack left a deep impression on the Syrians and they began to understand their vulnerability. Our ground forces then widened their attack toward Tel Mas'hara, Tel Maar, Tel Karin, and Tel Fatma, a chain of hills in the Syrian Golan. These hills completed the turf that was targeted and captured by the IDF during the Yom Kippur War.

The next day, the divisions commanded by Laner and Peled pushed back the Iraqi forces and caused them heavy losses. Meanwhile, my forces fought a battle with Saudi units and inflicted heavy losses on them as well. We recovered some Western weaponry from this battle and for the first time I realized the international nature of the forces that we were fighting against.

Throughout the night we dug in and fortified our position at Tel-Shams. The Syrian artillery attack, frightful in the number of shells they were firing, maintained heavy pressure, but did not prevent us from completing our task. At one point their shells came extremely close to the Armored Personnel Carrier that was serving as my command post. Luckily, we managed to leave the APC before a shell pierced its armor. Shells were exploded literally inches away from us as we squeezed ourselves between rocks for protection.

The Syrians tried to retake Tel-Shams with an infantry assault. One evening we spotted a large Syrian force of infantry and heavy artillery five kilometers to our east and immediately initiated artillery fire. The Syrians responded by shelling our position with phosphorus shells, which covered our camp with thick, black smoke. I calculated that the Syrians were going to land troops by helicopter to the rear of our position and attack under the protection of the smoke screen and while our attention was focused on the Syrian infantry forces to our east. I ordered the Nahal company of the Seventh Brigade, which was located south of our position, to redeploy to our rear and take up defensive positions against a Syrian attack. Our movements had their desired deterrent effects and the Syrians did not attack.

The battle to retake Mount Hermon was initiated before the cease-fire. Although our effort was a success, we suffered many losses, among them my friend and neighbor from Tel Adashim, Shmaryahu Vinik, who was commander of the Golani reconnaissance unit. Shmaryahu was a good man and a good commander and he was well liked by his neighbors and soldiers.

Although there can be no doubt as to the Israeli victory in the war, it did not end the way our previous wars had. Our victory did not totally decimate our enemy and the Syrians were able to engage in a shooting war of attrition that continued for months after the cessation of wide scale hostilities. As we had done against the Egyptians during their war of attrition against us in the late 1960s, we took many initiatives to undermine Syrian security and exact a heavy price for the war they were raging against us. We executed raids behind Syrian lines, attacked their anti-aircraft positions, and laid ambushes and mines in their rear. We also inflicted damage through artillery and tank shelling, targeting their installations and positions. We gradually established an environment in which the Syrians preferred to keep away from us rather than engage us in conflict. My division was given the responsibility for the whole attrition effort in the Syrian zone and I located my forward command post in Tel-Da'ur, close to the line of action.

This was a difficult period, as the Syrian shelling caused losses and the cold winter made it even more difficult to maintain the border. During this time a most unprecedented event occurred when the Minister of Defense, Moshe Dayan, visited our base. Dayan was an archeology buff and had been told that we had discovered, in a small village at the foot of Tel al-Mal, a stone doorpost with Hebrew writing on it. Dayan did not come to visit our troops, but rather to see the archeological find. While he was at our camp, my troops, mostly reservists, hurled insults at him in a way I had never seen before or since. Never have soldiers addressed a Minister of Defense with such defiance and lack of respect. But Dayan ignored the chorus of insults and criticisms, not so much as offering a reaction or word of defense. He simply got up and left.

The Syrian willingness to soften their stance and agree to a full cease-fire, thus ending the war of attrition, was considerably influenced by our aggressive initiatives and continued military pressure. We had taken the momentum away from them and had placed them in a position in which they could do little except shell us from afar and await our next assault. We threw them off balance by maintaining the element of surprise. They never knew when or where our next strike would be.

Yet, the Syrian President, Hafiz Al-Assad, was still stubbornly insisting on emerging a victor from the war in which he had been defeated, and making absurd demands as his price for agreeing to a cease-fire. The American Secretary of State, Dr. Henry Kissinger, was shuttling back and forth between Damascus and our tired government in Jerusalem. In addition, our government was concerned with the political ramifications of their actions prior to the war and were therefore interested in reaching an agreement and bringing our soldiers home as soon as possible.

Under these circumstances, Minister Dayan and Chief of Staff Elazar came to my forward command post at Tel Da'ur and briefed some senior officers about the negotiations with the Syrians. It was clear from his words that the government was considering actions that would appease the Syrians, in the hope that they would agree to a cease-fire. I knew Dayan was not talking only about a withdrawal from the Syrian side of the Golan, but was also considering a partial withdrawal from areas we had controlled prior to the war. It seemed crazy to me that we would reward the Syrians for starting and losing a war against us. I was angered by this approach and spoke out. I asked why we, the victors, should try to appease those who had started a war with us and had subsequently been defeated. According to my logic, it should be us making demands on the Syrians and threatening them with continuing hostilities, if they did not comply. Dayan got angry, as he would have no matter what I said. He responded that unless we were forthcoming with concessions on the Golan Heights, the Syrians would not agree to a cease-fire. I was appalled and confused at the lack of will and political courage being displayed by our leaders. I continued to voice my opinion and questioned our weakness. Why were we accepting their refusal to agree to a cease-fire and viewing it as a position we were obligated to change? It did not appear to me that the Syrians, with their forces in disarray after a substantial military defeat, were in any position to refuse anything we demanded. Since when, I asked, does the defeated dictate the terms of a cease-fire to the victor? Dayan did not have answers to the fundamental issues I was presenting. As he always did when a situation got too difficult or embarrassing, he simply turned and left the room.

It was frustrating for us, who had risked our lives to prevent the Syrians from achieving their goals, to watch them get what they wanted, despite the defeat we handed them. Yet, we came to realize that our government did not have the political strength to resist the pressures being placed upon them by the Americans, Arabs, Soviets, and other nations. None of these international players could tolerate the thought of a Jewish victory. Whatever we won on the field we would have to forgo at the negotiation table. For example, it was clear that our forces were going to withdraw from Quneitra. One of the explanations given for our returning Quneitra was that the Syrians vowed to rebuild the town and repopulate it with civilians. Our leaders argued that once civilians were there, the Syrians would be less likely to use Quneitra as a springboard for war, because such an action would lead to the suffering of the civilians residing there. I do not believe that our leaders truly believed their own argument, but this was the case they made before a post-war Israeli public. In any case, to this day, the Syrians have not rebuilt or repopulated Quneitra, and I doubt they ever intended to.

By the time the cease-fire had been completely negotiated David "Dado" Elazar was no longer Chief of Staff and was replaced by Mordechai "Motta" Gur. Dado had been forced to resign after the Agranat Commission, which looked into the reasons Israel was unprepared for the Yom Kippur War, placed a great deal of the blame on his shoulders. Oddly enough, and most likely as part of a political whitewash, Dayan escaped all blame. With our new Chief of Staff in place I did all I could to impress upon Motta my position that we should not return any of the land we had captured to the Syrians at this time. I did not know his position, or whether he was able to express it. I did not know whether the political establishment would listen to what he had to say. I only knew that I had to do all within my power to prevent us from making a grave mistake. I understood my words had not been heeded when we received the order to evacuate Positions 114 and 116, as well as Quneitra.

The winter of 1973 was very harsh on the Golan. The area under our control was covered with deep snow and movement was difficult. The temperature remained consistently below freezing and at times was close to zero degrees Fahrenheit. Despite the cold and the difficulties maneuvering heavy equipment, we were well equipped for the cold and had "bear cub" waterproof heavy winter coats to keep us warm.

Yet, Israel is a nation of Jewish mothers and they will not sit by quietly while their sons are on the Golan Heights freezing. A big commotion was under way in Israel that declared that not every soldier had received a "bear cub" and that even if they had, the coats did not keep us warm and dry. The campaign was so intense that one evening as I was driving back to base after having spent the day in the forward positions in the Herfa region, which was still under occasional Syrian bombardment, I met a Member of the Knesset on an isolated Golan road. This Member of the Knesset, Yossi Sarid, with whom I have since had a series of combative political encounters, announced that he had come to the Golan to check that every soldier had a "bear cub" coat. I explained to the young politician that there was no basis to the concern being expressed in Israel and that I too was very concerned for the well being and comfort of my soldiers. I informed him that he would not be permitted to review the forces under my command and cordially asked him to leave the area. I understood, and even in some ways appreciated, what the young man was trying to do. However, there is great merit in the idea that the military does not interfere with the political sector, and there is equal wisdom to the notion that the politicians should not tell the military how to best achieve their tasks. Their place is to tell us what objectives we are to achieve; our task is finding the way to achieve them. The IDF has a tradition of concern for its men. Of course every man had a "bear cub" coat.

Immediately following the war, once the magnitude of our losses became apparent, the whole nation of Israel was swept with a deep sense of anguish and bereavement. In this atmosphere, naturally, I had little thoughts about my own career and personal future. I had been good friends with Chief of Staff Dado Elazar, and perhaps I could have exerted pressure on him to promote me, but I was too busy with my chores on the Golan and with my own feelings of sorrow and frustration. Consequently, when Dado summoned me to his office in Tel Aviv on October 29, I did not have any clue as to the purpose of our meeting. As I entered his office, Dado showered me with praise for the manner with which I had conducted the war on the Golan and promoted me to the rank of major-general. I was pleased with the promotion, but taken aback when he informed me that he was still unsure of the position I would be receiving. I took the opportunity to once again request the position of Commander of the Northern Command, but Dado informed me that this position was most probably going to be assigned to Herzl Shafir, who as Adjutant-General was a member of the General Staff. I boldly asked Dado the reasons why Shafir was being chosen over me and was shocked when he responded that Shafir had done excellent work on the computer system during the war. I knew this was not the criterion for choosing the Commander of the Northern Command, and pushed Dado for an explanation. He would only admit that there were additional reasons for my being overlooked.

I dropped the matter and was prepared to leave when I noticed Dado was waiting to say something else. I stood waiting and was surprised to hear the Chief of Staff begin to pour his heart out to me. He told me he had done everything he possibly could to fight the war, but that it appeared others were trying to blame him for the sins of omission and commission that occurred directly before and during the war. "I have a feeling big troubles are in store for me," he said sadly. I listened with embarrassment, as comforting a person who is hurting inside has never been a talent of mine. My embarrassment grew greater when Dado began to cry. I did not understand my own feelings. I had not accumulated much experience in consolation, and in addition Dado was on one hand an old friend, and on the other the man who was preventing my advancement in the IDF. I was feeling both anger and pity. Yet, this grown man, the Commander of the whole IDF was standing before me and weeping. I understood his dilemma and in some ways I felt his pain. I left him after a short time and returned to the Golan a major-general. The date was seventeen years to the day since the Mitla Pass jump of the Sinai campaign.

After Dado was forced to resign, Hakka Hofi was appointed acting Chief of Staff and Motta Gur was appointed Chief of the Northern Command, a post he had held in the past. It was clear that both appointments were temporary and that one of them was going to be appointed Chief of Staff. One day Motta informed me that both he and Hakka had agreed that whichever of them got appointed Chief of Staff, he would appoint me Commander of the Northern Command. I was pleased when Motta was appointed and kept his word. I had finally been appointed to the post I had long coveted.

I had another emotional meeting with Dado, as he came to the Golan to take leave of the soldiers, as is done by every commander as he leaves his post. Motta Gur had already been appointed Chief of Staff and Dado had already been found wanting by the Agranat

Commission. Yet, Dado had had a long and glorious career with the IDF and I knew that he deserved a proper parting ceremony. We drove to the peak of Mount Hermon in an APC and as we arrived we were greeted by a Syrian 240 mm mortar shell which fell only a yard away from us. Luckily, there was still deep snow on the ground, which swallowed up the shell. Still, we were close enough to feel the heat emitted from the bomb. We entered a big cave that was sheltering the unit stationed on the Mount. Once inside, Dado was very restless and sat quietly. The soldiers in the cave sat facing us, also silent. Finally, I broke the silence and told the troops that Dado had come to take leave of them and that they were invited to ask questions and make statements, if they wished to. When the cave remained still in an eerie silence, Dado requested that we leave. I took him to a luncheon that had been prepared in his honor at El-Hama. Dado sat without speaking, and when I presented him with a gift on behalf of all the soldiers in the north, he could do no more than mumble his thanks. I was saddened by the response he had received from the soldiers and knew that he had been deeply hurt.

On June 5, 1974, at 10:30 in the morning the separation of forces agreement was signed between Israel and Syria. As per the agreement we evacuated Quneitra and the two hills dominating it. In Tel Shams I showed a great measure of self-restraint as I spoke to reporters. I said, "We are a victorious army, but we are handing territories over to the Syrians in exchange for the agreement that has been signed."

As I spoke, a storm was brewing in my heart. I had great difficulty controlling myself and wanted to say that it was wrong of us to hand over territory to Syria, in essence to reward them, despite their defeat. The Israeli fighting men were being punished in spite of their victory. This was a war for survival and the boys had fought with self-sacrifice and courage as in no previous war. The political echelon had disappointed the soldiers, indeed betrayed them. The politicians had acted callously and did not understand the emotions involved for those of us who had fought the war and watched the best of our men die before our eyes. Our politicians had shown that they lacked the strength to deal with the opposing side. The Syrians had displayed greater political will. Syria had been defeated in war, and yet its politicians had won at the negotiating table. I resented this very much and was sure many of my fellow soldiers shared my views. I was particularly angry in light of the fact that the Agranat Commission had laid all the blame on the army and had minimized the blame of the political echelon. I felt vindicated only when the public showed that it too rejected the notion that the government bore no responsibility. Before the 1974 elections the leaders of the Labor party, Golda Meir and Moshe Dayan, were forced to resign, and in 1977, particularly in response to the cover-up of the Agranat Commission, the Labor Party was voted out of office for the first time since the creation of the State.

The whole idea that the government would dare try to pass the blame onto the army was an insult to the average Israeli's intelligence. It was well known that the army acts only on the orders of the Minister of Defense. Our problem was not a lack of ability, it was a lack of preparedness. The cause of this was solely the notion in Moshe Dayan's head that the Syrians and Egyptians were too weak and would not dare attack us. Only three weeks before the war began I had participated in a deliberation at which I suggested that each settlement in the Golan Heights be armed with an artillery cannon that could be hidden and used against any enemy force that entered the area. Not only was my suggestion rejected by the Minister of Defense, he also ordered that the cannons that already were positioned in the settlement be removed. In his blind confidence that there would not be another war, Dayan simple could not see the purpose of positioning cannons in settlements. Thus, Dayan, the symbol of Israeli military strength, was in no small way responsible for the biggest blunder in our history. Yet, he used his image and his political clout to transfer all the blame onto Dado. His claims of innocence should have been held in complete contempt, as it is clear that a Minister of Defense cannot be involved in army affairs and escape at least partial blame for army mistakes. But Dayan never accepted blame, at any time or for any reason.

If for nothing more, Dayan held a great deal of the responsibility for our failure to deliver a pre-emptive strike. Such a strike should have been directed at least against the Syrians, particularly when it became clear that they were going to start a war. An aerial strike could have hindered their opening moves and would have signalled to them that we were aware of their intentions and ready to resist their advance. Instead, our boys were left unprepared and unknowing. After the war, Prime Minister Golda Meir explained, with the enthusiastic support of Dayan and other Cabinet members, that a pre-emptive strike was ruled against for political reasons, so that Israel could not be blamed for starting the war, which they feared would result in the country being isolated internationally. In my mind there is no greater foolishness. The very existence of our nation was hanging in the balance. Our army was not mobilized and its communications system was shut down for the holiday of Yom Kippur, which meant that we could not initiate a call up and mobilize the reserves quickly. Under these circumstances, the political ramifications of a pre-emptive strike should have been the last and least important consideration. I believe that any leader who takes into consideration what other nations will say about Israel at a time when we are faced with armies poised to attack our borders and threatening our existence is not qualified or capable of leading this State.

The war had a great many lessons to be learned, the first of which was that Israel must never be caught unprepared for war and that it must deal with its affairs in accordance with the deployments of the Arab armies and not our estimations of their intentions. In addition, the ground forces must be able to absorb the initial blows of an attack, which would then allow the Air Force the time to destroy enemy anti-aircraft batteries. During the war, the Air Force's potential was greatly hindered by its need to repeatedly come to the aid of ground forces, and the lack of freedom it had in the skies, due to a saturation of Syrian anti-aircraft missiles. Thus, the effectiveness of the Air Force, and by extension the whole war effort, is enhanced when the Air Force has the freedom to deal with enemy missile sites at the outset of the war. Once the missiles are knocked out, the Air Force would enjoy freedom over enemy skies and can assist the ground forces by harassing enemy troops and damaging supply lines.

As Commander of the Northern Command I sought to institutionalize the lessons I had learned. As a member of the General Staff I also argued for certain changes in all sectors, and for a re-evaluation of the ideology that had led us away from civilian territorial defense in borderline villages. I also attacked the army's policy of exclusive reliance on armour and artillery. In my own sector I built up civilian borderline settlements, setting up fortifications, distributing weapons, conducting training exercises and developing an awareness of territorial defense. My efforts spanned from Rosh HaNikra in the west to Ti'at Zvi in the east and throughout the Golan Heights. We also restored the remains of the defensive infrastructure on the Golan that had been damaged during the war.

I found the General Staff and Chief of Staff in agreement with my claim that it was necessary to reinforce the status of the infantry in the army and upgrade its training, facilities, and equipment. I called for a reorganization of the infantry and a considerable increase, not only of armour corps, but also of the paratroopers, other infantry units and artillery. It was clear to the General Staff that the infantry had proven its worth during the war, as every infantry unit on the Golan held its ground and prevented a Syrian advance. Foot soldiers proved they were essential and preferable even in night attacks and in actions against fortified objectives and missile zones. The ability of the Egyptian infantrymen, armed with personal anti-tank weapons, to cause severe damage to our forces in Sinai during the Yom Kippur War was yet another indication of the potential of the infantry. To this day I believe there is no replacement for the infantryman, despite the modern refinement and variety of electronic weapons.

21

Connections with the Christians

I arrived at my headquarters in the Northern Command with a wide variety of tasks that required my immediate attention. In addition to replacing equipment that had been damaged in the war, and bolstering my infantry brigades, I also decided to set up new tank divisions and infantry units. In addition, the terrorists were now using Lebanon as their base for infiltrations into Israel, and I put great emphasis on frustrating their efforts.

My approach to the war with the terrorists was consistent with the methods we had used in the past. I immediately set up a civilian territorial defense apparatus, armed and trained the residents of the border settlements, and installed a security fence along the border. In addition, I instructed my officers to prepare a series of offensive strikes that would sabotage the terrorists by disrupting their organization and damaging their infrastructure.

In many ways the challenge posed by the terrorists was similar to the threat we faced in the late 1960s, in that the terrorists attempted to infiltrate our borders by land and sea, and targeted our civilian population. In one very important way, however, the struggle against the terrorists from Lebanon was different, and therefore, more difficult. In the Jordan Valley we did not have any settlements directly on the Israel-Jordan border. When a terrorist group infiltrated Israel the distance between our border and our settlements gave us valuable time to hunt down and neutralize the terrorists. However, in the case of Lebanon, we have a vast network of settlements directly on the border. Thus, it was necessary for the army to detect each infiltration immediately, and capture or kill the terrorists before they had time to advance to their civilian target.

The task before us required a great deal of energy and ingenuity. Our forces engaged in numerous pursuits, one lasting as long as four days. In this particular hunt, a gang of terrorists had succeeded in infiltrating deep into Northern Israel's Hanita Region. After four days of chasing them, having captured one and wounded another, we concluded that the group would most likely try to re-enter Lebanon. After careful analysis of the border, where they had entered Israel and where they were presently located, we determined the spot where they would most likely attempt their border crossing. We laid mines and set ambushes at this site, and sure enough, that evening the gang attempted to cross over, and were killed in the minefield. Not all our efforts ended in success however, and the terrorists killed some of our civilians in Kiryat Shmona, Kfar Yovel, and Kibbutz Rosh HaNikra.

In a terrorist attack on Kibbutz Shamir we encountered a phenomenon that we had not seen until then, but have seen in practically every terrorist attack since, namely, terrorists who have explosives attached to their bodies so they can commit suicide. In many cases the terrorists did not detonate the explosives, but there have been numerous instances, like the one at Kibbutz Shamir, where they did. In this particular attack, the terrorists murdered a number of civilians as they worked in the kibbutz beehives. Our security forces tracked them to the Kibbutz and surrounded the area, but before we could take any action, the terrorists blew themselves up.

Perhaps one of the most barbaric attacks occurred in the northern border town of Ma'alot, where a group of children touring the north were taken hostage by a group of Palestinians. We had a plan that called for penetration of the school building in which the children were being held, but unfortunately in its execution the commander of one of the units miscalculated and entered the building one story higher than was necessary. This error, always a possibility in any operation, gave the terrorists an additional minute or two to recover from their surprise, and they opened fire on the children. The terrorists slaughtered twenty-two of our youngsters in total disregard of their age and innocence.

Another brutal attack occurred in Nahariya, when terrorists killed a mother and her two children. The terrorists had entered their building, and the victims were trying to escape out their window when they were spotted and killed. I will never forget the gruesome, heartbreaking sight of that woman, hanging dead from the sheet she had tied around her, the limp body of her young son hanging from a sheet next to her, and her dead infant son, pacifier still in his mouth, still wrapped in her arms, secured by yet another sheet.

During this period we were also confronted, albeit on a lesser scale, with terrorist penetrations from Jordan as well. Our towns of Beit Shean, Ashdot Ya'akov, Ramat HaGolan and Ramat Magshimim were all attacked, the last one resulting in the death of two yeshiva students.

We paid a heavy price in our struggle, but our system of defense was getting stronger with each terrorist attempt. We learned a different lesson from each of their successes and eventually our border with Lebanon became almost completely sealed.

Meanwhile, in Lebanon itself, a civil war raged that was in many ways rooted in that nation's political and historical past. This war reduced the authority and capabilities of the central government and Lebanese Army, and this situation was exploited by the Palestine Liberation Organization, which built for itself a virtually autonomous entity in Southern Lebanon. This posed a threat to the security and interests of Israel.

Our first Prime Minister, and great Zionist leader, David Ben-Gurion, had stipulated in his political doctrine that Israel's isolation in the Middle East and the hostilities of its neighbors, demanded that Israel seek alliances with other minority groups in the region. This was, for example, one of the motivational factors in the assistance we provided to the Kurds in Iraq. Additional ties were established with the Shah's regime in Iran and the Emperor's regime in Ethiopia. The notion of forming ties with the Christians of Lebanon, and particularly the idea of assisting a Christian officer in controlling parts of southern Lebanon, were first entertained in the 1950s. In his memoir, Moshe Sharrett, who served as both Prime Minister and Foreign Minister in the 1950s, recalled discussions in the Israeli government concerning relations with Lebanon's Christians. Yet, it was not until the mid-1970s and the Lebanese civil war that these relations became an absolute necessity.

One direct result of the Lebanese War was that the PLO, which was involved in the infighting in Lebanon, no longer had the resources to try to infiltrate our vastly improved border security. Thus, the Palestinians initiated a new strategy of firing rockets randomly into Israel from Lebanese territory. This new development required that we increase our assaults on Palestinian targets inside Lebanon, a factor that also brought us into conflict with remnant elements from the Lebanese Army, which had virtually disintegrated.

Our first contact with Lebanon's Christian community began with a note attached to our security fence, near our northern town of Metulla. The note read, "I am a Lebanese soldier. I will come to this point tomorrow night. I would like to meet someone from your army." The note was brought to my attention, and I instructed a small unit to wait in the orchards near the spot in the fence where the note was found, and to bring the Lebanese soldier to me in Metulla. That evening a frightened, pale, mature Lebanese soldier, dressed in uniform, was brought before me. He gave his rank as Master-Sergeant and explained that he was a Christian from the town of Kfar Kley'a. He proudly told me that prior to our War of Independence members of his village were involved in a scheme that helped smuggle Jewish children out of Syria and into Israel. Today, he said, his village was in dire need of assistance. He told us that the Lebanese Army had all but fallen apart, and that there was now no force to protect the Christians from the will and brutal force of the Moslems and PLO terrorists. He had come to us to ask for help, for weapons so that his village could defend itself from its enemies. Without making any promises, I asked him to return to his village and gather a list of all Lebanese soldiers who resided in Kfar Kley'a and a detailed listing of the weapons they would require to defend themselves. He was to bring the information the next day. After the man left, I contacted the Chief of Staff and informed him of the details of our meeting. He authorized me to continue contacts with the Lebanese soldier, but made no commitment that he would approve any aid.

When the man arrived the next evening with the lists I had requested, he informed me that he had failed to mention the lack of food and medical supplies that was causing his village leaders great concern as well. I surprised the man by informing him that I and a group of my officers would join him in his journey back to his village, so that we could judge the situation at first hand. Although the man was uncomfortable with my decision, complaining that his neighbors would not have time to roast lambs and greet us properly, he understood the purpose of our trip.

We crossed the border at midnight and arrived at the village to find the leading notables gathered in one home. We sat for many hours as they detailed the dangers they faced from the Moslems and PLO and the supplies they needed most urgently. I believed their situation was grave and was sufficiently impressed to recognize that they were determined in their will to fight for their homes.

I returned to Israel and placed a recommendation before the Chief of Staff that we supply Kfar Kley'a with weapons and basic foods. I received permission to provide English rifles, ammunition, and hand grenades, as well as flour, oil, and sugar.

After we delivered the supplies, the first occasion we had lent assistance to Lebanese Christians, the rumor of our good will spread rapidly across Southern Lebanon. We even received requests for assistance from the village of Aitaroun, a Moslem village.

Our ties with Kfar Kley'a became broader and were characterized by closer relations. However, the village was isolated and did not have links with neighboring towns. In this sense it was not suitable to lead an effort we had decided to initiate, which called for us to assist a series of villages that were closely situated, and that would result in a strip of villages that had close relations to Israel. When leaders of the Christian village R'meish met with me in Nahariya, I realized that their village was ideally located, and requested that they inform the leaders of their neighboring villages that Israel was willing and interested in assisting them, if they were committed to a policy that stood up to the terrorists and denied them power in southern Lebanon. The leaders of R'meish did as I requested and in a short time Israel had relations with a variety of south Lebanese villages. Thus, what began as a private initiative on the part of some individuals from Kfar Kley'a developed into the beginning stages of a network of relationships between Israel and Lebanon's Christians.

After a short period our troops were visiting these villages almost daily in a show of moral support, to learn their needs and to offer military advice in their war with the PLO. Another Israeli initiative was the opening of a medical facility at the "Good Fence," along the border, near Metulla. In an effort to provide some desperately needed medical aid, and in a gesture of friendship, the Lebanese, both Christian and Moslem, were invited to seek medical treatment at the clinic.

As the war in Lebanon raged, the word of our assistance in the south began to reach the Christians fighting in northern Lebanon. Many of the Christian forces in the north were from the Phalangist party, and I had a very close relationship with two young, energetic brothers, both officers in the Lebanese army, whom I had met in Kfar Kley'a. During our meeting I had assisted them in devising plans for an assault against a terrorist stronghold in southern Lebanon. Under their command, the Christians succeeded in capturing Marj Ayoun from the PLO, which marked a turning point in the balance of power in the area. The battle was evidence that the Christian cooperation with Israel had transformed them into a force to be contended with in the south.

After the assault on Marj Ayoun, I received a visit from a

Phalangist army officer, Major Shidyak, and a Christian civilian, George Farrah, who brought his Jerusalem-born wife, Esterkeh Arazi, with him to our meeting. Farrah made a particularly good impression on me. I found him to be intelligent, honest, sincere, loyal, and above all, a Lebanese patriot. He was later killed leading an assault on a terrorist base in Kfar Yaroun.

The escalation of our role in the Lebanese conflict began in 1976 when a Christian emissary from northern Lebanon came to Israel. He arrived at Haifa Bay by boat in the middle of the night. In addition to meeting with me, he also met with our Minister of Defense, Shimon Peres. The meetings resulted in our continued assistance to the Christians in the south, and the establishment of a base in the Galilee for the training of Lebanese Christian soldiers. This base flew the Lebanese flag, and upon the completion of the first course, hosted a graduation ceremony during which both the Israeli and the Lebanese national anthems were played.

Christian leaders began visiting Israel often. These meetings, by Phalange leader Bashir Gemayel, Dany and Dori Chamoun, and others were kept a secret for fear that any open statement of active Israeli cooperation would lead to a major Moslem and PLO offensive. Still, it was not until the visit by Major Sa'ad Haddad, the one who had the greatest impact on our policy in Lebanon, that Israel was genuinely hopeful about protecting southern Lebanon. I personally had a great deal of respect for Major Haddad, and it only increased as we got to know each other better. He was a candid man, who opened our first meeting with the words, "President Franjieh has sent me to save the south and has instructed me to cooperate closely with Israel." Haddad was a man we were able to rely on. He was true to his word and above politics. He was motivated only by his hatred for the foreign forces that were threatening Lebanon's sovereignty, and his deep love for and commitment to his country. In the end, the cooperation between Israel and his forces grew to be closer than either of us would have ever dared to predict during our initial meetings.

As the terrorist efforts were targeted more toward the Christian population, which was being subjected to artillery shelling and Katyusha rocket attacks, the Christian confidence in Israel began to increase. We had shown the Christians that we were very cautious with the promises we made but quite meticulous in carrying out our word. In my meetings with Christian leaders I often repeated our stand that Israel will not promise what it cannot or does not wish to provide. I reminded them that Israel would not fight for them, but assist them by giving them the means to fight for themselves. I often reminded them that Israel was not interested in any Lebanese territory, nor would it force on the Christians a policy that was in Israeli interests but against their own. Simply put, Israel was interested in fighting the terrorists, as were the Christians. This common goal was Israel's motivating factor in supplying assistance.

Our policy was the same with the Phalange in the north, although they were the recipients of some heavy armor and tanks, so that they could withstand constant Moslem assaults. The war they were involved in was often cruel and bloody, and in the Christian areas of Jounieh and Beirut unusually heavy and severe. When the Christians lost the town of Damur, the Moslem forces perpetrated a terrible massacre of Christians. Later, when the Moslems lost the town of Tel az-Za'atar, the Christians perpetrated an equally brutal slaughter. Yet, the Christian and Moslem worlds were silent and turned a blind eye to the sufferings of their brethren in Lebanon.

A central issue between the Israelis and the Christian Lebanese was Israel's refusal to promise to assist the Christians actively if the Syrians should ever attack them. This issue came to the fore in a meeting I had with Bashir Gemayel at the end of 1976. We met on an Israeli missile boat in the Jounieh Bay, five miles off the Lebanese coast. Bashir arrived at our boat on one of our rubber rafts, having been brought out to sea on a Lebanese fishing vessel. He boarded the boat wearing a mask so that no one, neither those on the fishing boat nor my soldiers, would recognize him.

During our meeting Gemayel again detailed the aid that was needed from Israel and commented that his forces were extremely worried about a Syrian offensive. He even went so far as to insinuate that part of the Syrian wrath that the Christians would have to bear was a direct result of their cooperation with the Israelis. I re-stated our position that we would assist the Christian forces by providing them with the means to defend themselves, and that anything further than that, such as direct military support, could not be promised at this point. Furthermore, I reminded him that the Christian cooperation with Israel was not due to noble Christian efforts to help Israel, but rather because Israel was providing them with the only chance they had of withstanding the Moslem offensive.

Despite the frankness of our dialogues, or perhaps because of them, I enjoyed a friendly relationship with Gemayel. He and I were similar in our simplicity. He was a brave man, who was prepared for self-sacrifice, and I knew him as an intelligent, sophisticated thinker who had an excellent understanding of his Moslem and PLO rivals. Furthermore, Bashir had a true vision of an Israeli-Lebanese Christian alliance, one that would remain beyond the present conflict and continue as a friendship between two nations. His views were based on his belief that a Christian Lebanon would never be accepted in the Moslem Arab world, and that therefore Israel, in a similar predicament, was their natural ally.

For these reasons I liked and trusted Gemayel more than other Lebanese Christian leaders, such as Dany Chamoun. Although Chamoun spoke in exalted phrases to emphasize his patriotism, I always doubted his sincerity and willingness to sacrifice. In addition, he was very sensitive to the status of the Christians in the Arab world and, despite his hatred of the Moslems for the war they had brought to Lebanon, never completely cut his commercial links with the Arab world. Chamoun also had close relations with Jordan's King Hussein, and believed his future, and that of Lebanon, was with the Arab world.

A great source of frustration for me, which remained with me during the time I served as Chief of Staff, was the lack of unity within the Christian community of Lebanon. Although they shared the same identity and fate, they rarely coordinated their efforts to free Lebanon, and almost never came to each other's aid. During my talks with the leaders of the north, I often suggested to them that they send forces to the south and begin their war there. I argued that the south, with its close proximity to Israel, was in a position to receive greater aid, allowing for initial successes before the war got moved to the north. Yet, despite my words, the Christians of the south were left to fight alone. Although there were elements of apathy, the failure to help the south was also due to the fact that the leaders of the north were short-sighted and bogged down with their own affairs. The north, with its French roots and European sophistication, was alienated from the needs of the south, which was seen as inhabited by poor, uneducated peasants. In addition, the leaders of the north had a limit to the strength they could mobilize, although I and many others greatly overestimated their potency. The fact was that it was a militia force composed of men who worked and studied during the day and carried arms at night. They suffered from a high turnover rate and a lack of organization. However, much of this could have been overcome if there had been an interest in getting involved with the war in the south.

In contrast to the leaders of the north, Major Haddad, the leader of the Christian forces in the south, was a bold, stubborn man who believed in taking chances. His forces worked closely with Israel, and we provided him with supplies and advisory support. Haddad was wounded when his forces were repelled from the Moslem town of Tel Kneyssa, which they had captured earlier the same day. The village of Tel Knayssa was in Lebanese territory only a few miles from the Israeli kibbutz, Misgav Am. We evacuated Haddad to one of our hospitals, and later that night sent troops into Tel Knayssa to blow up a tank we had given to Haddad, so that it would not fall into the hands of the terrorists.

Haddad's strong, determined personality was often a source of conflict and difficulties between us. Although he was a loyal friend of Israel, he refused to be subject to the wishes and needs of Israel. In spite of the fact that his men were armed and trained by the Israeli army, he also refused to be considered under the command of Israel's senior officers. Consequently, there were numerous occasions when

Haddad fired artillery at the terrorists' bases despite Israel's interest in a temporary cease-fire, or attacked bases against the expressed wishes of the Israeli General Staff.

In the framework of our relations with various groups in southern Lebanon, and after great internal debates, we responded positively to a request for aid we had received from Asiyya, a Christian village north of the Litani River. Upon delivery of the ammunition, weapons and equipment, we again reminded the village leaders that their cooperation with us would attract the wrath of the PLO and that if they were attacked, we would not be in a position to come to their aid. A short while later the village was overcome by a large Palestinian force. Despite our statements that we would not assist, we did lend artillery fire, but it proved to be of no avail. Some of the town's residents succeeded in fleeing to Kfar Kley'a and Marj Ayoun, but many others were massacred with the typical brutality that had become so commonplace in Lebanon. When word of the massacre reached me I was very bothered and felt that we had failed in our pledge to assist these people. I knew that we had warned them that we would not come to their aid and that the responsibility was their own. I knew that under the circumstances we had done all we could, but I questioned the validity of the limitations and prohibitions we had placed on ourselves.

In late June of 1976 an Air France airliner with Israeli and Jewish passengers was hijacked by German and Palestinian terrorists and taken to Entebbe airport in Uganda. On July 3rd, while I was in my home entertaining guests from Tiberias, a message from the Chief of staff arrived informing me to pick up the commander of the Armored Corps, Musa Peled, who lived in nearby Nahalal, and fly to Tel Aviv at once. As we were being driven from the Sde Dov base where I landed, our driver, a female officer, asked me if "the operation was a go." I did not answer her, partly because if it was a "go" it would be top secret information, but mostly because I had no idea what she was talking about. I later learned that our driver was the ex-wife of Dan Shomron, the Commander of the Entebbe Raid. She obviously knew things I did not. When we arrived at the

offices of the Chief of Staff we were informed that the planes were
in the air and we were awaiting Cabinet approval. When we received
the word that the government had approved the mission we waited
with anxious anticipation. We were overjoyed when we received
word that the rescue was a success, and that both troops and
passengers were on their way home to Israel. We had not received
word that Yoni Netanyahu was killed, and so we had no reason to
repress our jubilation. I returned home to Tel Adashim and shared
the good news with my wife and son, who was already at that time
a combat pilot. I did not sleep much that night, as I was energized
and excited by the scope of the operation and the incredible skill it
had taken to execute it successfully.

The 1977 elections in Israel brought about a political revolution,
endeding twenty-nine years of rule by the Labor Party. The Likud
party was now leading the government and Prime Minister
Menachem Begin appointed Ezer Weizman to the post of Minister
of Defense. I had always had friendly relations with Weizman and
was pleased at his appointment. My relationship with the Labor
government that had just been defeated had also been quite smooth.
I had no areas of friction with the Labor Minister of Defense Shimon
Peres, and had enjoyed the trust of the Prime Minister, Yitzchak
Rabin. Rabin, who had also risen through the ranks of the IDF, had
been Commander of the Northern Command and also Chief of
Staff (during the Six-Day War). When he was elected Prime Minister I initially had apprehensions because during his tenure as
Commander of the Northern Command, when Arik Sharon was a
battalion commander and I was a company commander, Rabin
showed a reserved coolness toward the paratroopers. He even went
so far as to forbid the paratroopers to operate in the Huleh Valley,
which bordered Syria. Naturally, I was concerned that his feelings
toward the infantry remained, but it seems that his attitude then was
only a reflection of his apprehensions about Sharon. As it was, my
relations with the Rabin-Peres government were cordial. I anticipated that my relations with Begin and Weizman would be the
same. In fact, I hoped that Weizman would be more in line with my

notions of the type of assistance we should be providing the Christians in Lebanon than Peres had been. The Chief of Staff, Motta Gur, was not in favor of an active Israeli approach, and he often joined forces with Peres to oppose the more active approach favored by Rabin and myself.

During the period of our government's transition, the General Staff were called to the Chief of Staff's offices in the center of Tel Aviv. These offices, although removed from the front, are the nerve center of the IDF during any war. It is from these offices that decisions are made as to the direction and scope of a war. As such, it is understandable that security is tight and the offices are considered to be extremely safe. Yet, during our meeting we heard glass shatter and one of our colleagues, Aryeh Biro, remarked that he felt something fall on his back. At closer examination we noticed that the pane of the window behind him had been splintered and a bullet from a Russian-made Kalashnikov rifle was lying on his clothing. After further investigation, we discovered that terrorists had seized the Savoy Hotel in Tel Aviv. In addition to the innocent people they brutally killed, the terrorists had inadvertently shot a bullet into our offices. They had almost killed a general engaged in a discussion with the entire General Staff.

As tensions between the PLO and the Christian forces commanded by Haddad became more intense, I began to doubt Haddad's ability to withstand the pressure. He had attempted to broaden his area of control into the Marj Ayoun Valley, but was repulsed by intense PLO shelling. I pressured the political echelon to grant the Christians more active aid by introducing tanks and artillery support. In light of my request, Begin and Weizman visited the north to size up the situation personally. While in the area, Begin met with Haddad and Shidyak, while Weizman and Gur visited strategic locations. At a meeting at the home of the head of the Metulla Regional Council, Begin told Haddad and Shidyak that Israel would still commit itself only to helping the Lebanese Christians help themselves. "Do not expect us to come fight your battles," Begin plainly told them.

Later that night a senior Christian representative telephoned the
Prime Minister at home and described the desperate situation of the
Christians in Jounieh, which was under the pressure of a Syrian
artillery bombardment. He implored Begin to expand the Israeli
commitment to protect the Christians against a full Syrian assault.
The Prime Minister, always a cautious man, responded that Israel
would utilize its Air Force if the Syrians employed aircraft against
the Christians.

This additional commitment was very much against the wishes
of the Chief of Staff, Motta Gur. The conflict brought to light a
problem that had never occurred before in the history of Israel.
Until 1977 the Labor Party, or Mapai, had always ruled Israel, and
the Chief of Staff was always a military officer who identified
strongly with their policies. Suddenly, Motta Gur, a Labor Party
sympathizer, found himself with a year to serve until his term of
office expired, and under the authority of a government with concepts that were alien to his own. Gur, rather than accept the legal
authority of the government, used his position to voice opposition,
which in turn caused a great deal of controversy for the IDF. For
example, he gave press interviews near the time Egyptian President
Sadat visited Israel that criticized the government. Many senior
officers felt Gur was wrong for voicing opinions on issues that were
in no way connected to issues of security and defense, but in many
ways Gur was at war with Defense Minister Weizman and his
Deputy, Mordechai "Motkeh" Zipori, both of whom he did not like.
For his part, Zipori did not like Gur very much either, as Gur had
forced his retirement from the IDF.

After Gur's interview to the press Weizman had decided to
dismiss him and called him back from a secret mission he was
engaged in overseas. When I entered Gur's office he was still in
civilian clothes and on the telephone, nervously seeking advice from
various friends. Weizman had called Gur and told him to report to
his office later that afternoon, and as I entered Weizman's office, I
heard Begin overrule Weizman's intentions, saying "There will be
no dismissal of the Chief of Staff in the State of Israel, if for no other

reason, then as a sign of honor to the position."

Although Gur was to remain Chief of Staff, the great deal of infighting and internal controversy that he had instigated and the opposition of Weizman precluded his chances of having his term as Chief of Staff extended. With this in mind, most senior officers were beginning to speculate who would be chosen to replace him. Naturally, the next Chief of Staff, to be presented for government approval by Minister of Defense Weizman, would have to be a professional soldier who would serve the government and security interests of the State of Israel without entering into political debates that were totally unconnected to security issues.

Shortly after Weizman was appointed Minister of Defense, he summoned me to his office and informed me that he intended to appoint me head of the General Staff Branch. I recalled that I had once asked Minister of Defense Peres if the position of head of the General Staff Branch was a necessary prerequisite to the post of Chief of Staff, to which he had answered that it was not. Still, I was encouraged by the appointment. Weizman officially appointed me head of the General Branch Staff three years and three months after I had been appointed Commander of the Northern Command.

I am not sure that my appointment was to the liking of Gur, although our relationship had been good and he did not attempt to block it. I was aware, however, that General Yekutiel "Kuti" Adam and Herzl Shafir were both quite upset. Kuti had just completed his tour as head of the General Staff Branch and had been send abroad to study, always a sign that compensation was felt necessary. Shafir was serving as Commander of the Southern Command and had previously served as head of the General Staff Branch. Both men were candidates for the position of Chief of Staff and they knew that my appointment placed me as a candidate as well. When Weizman made clear his intentions to appoint me Chief of Staff, Shafir protested, and Gur advised him against the selection, despite the fact that he had told me that he would recommend my appointment.

With Sadat's visit to Israel, an era of official and semi-official visits by Israelis to Egypt and Egyptians to Israel began. On one of his visits to Egypt, Weizman took Herzl Shafir with him, which raised my suspicions and insecurities. Weizman and I have always had an open, familiar, honest relationship and I knew I would have to bring up my feelings with him. We had always shared our thoughts and, in spite of the fact that we at times argued, rather heatedly, I believe we both valued the honesty. Our relationship was such that, although both of us were strong-willed men who at times lost our tempers, we had a clear, tested method for easing tensions. Whenever one of us felt a temper flare-up emerging, we would simply offer the other a small glass of wine or liquor, and the tension would ease. When I approached Weizman about his selection of Shafir, he reassured me that I had little to worry about. When I pushed him for an explanation, he informed me that I would understand "as time goes on." When I requested an immediate understanding, he responded, firmly, yet simply, that the time for me to understand had not yet arrived. Later, in February 1978, as I was in the Negev reviewing a military exercise with Gur and others, we received word that Weizman wished to see us in his office after the completion of the exercises. When we entered his office, without preliminaries Weizman announced, "I called you here to inform you that Raful will be replacing Motta as Chief of Staff." Still later, Weizman told me that he had taken Shafir to Egypt with him because he had already decided on my appointment.

While Gur was still Chief of Staff and I was head of the General Staff Branch, the IDF entered southern Lebanon up to the Litani River in a large scale retaliatory raid. In February 1978 I received a call at home from Motta informing me that a terrorist attack had occurred on the main coastal road. He asked that I go to the scene as soon as possible, and advised me to drive through Wadi Milk and south along the coastal road. As I passed Kibbutz Ma'agan Michi'el, north of the town of Hedera, I met policemen and soldiers from our border guard unit. There was a rubber boat and other equipment often used by terrorists on the side of the road. The men spoke to me of a "bloody bus," but I did not understand the full meaning of their words. I continued south, and as I neared the Country Club, outside of Tel Aviv, I saw a bus in flames and chaos all around. I continued to Sde Dov, where Motta had set up a command post. We were unsure whether the terrorists had died in the bus explosion, or whether they had managed to escape. We clamped a curfew on the entire region and our forces were engaged in a massive search.

Our command post was heavy with a depressive mood. We were all trying to come to terms with what had gone wrong, with identifying which part of our system had failed. Our coast was not protected, and this allowed the terrorists to land on a rubber boat. Our inner defenses also did not function, as the terrorists hijacked a bus and made the driver travel toward Tel Aviv.

The following day the government decided to retaliate with a massive assault on southern Lebanon, so as to destroy the PLO infrastructure there and drive home to the Palestinians that Israel has the power and will to punish them severely for their terrorist attacks. The army presented the government with a plan for Operation Litani which would have the IDF clear a five-mile strip, from the Israeli border moving north into Lebanon, of all PLO and hostile Palestinian forces. The date of the strike was set for March.

Our troops entered Lebanon under dark clouds and rain. There was practically no resistance, with the exception of a unit of terrorists that fought meekly at Bint Jebail. By dawn we had advanced more than the five miles we had intended, and had Palestinian units surrendering to us on all sides.

Once we reached the edge of the Litani River, I proposed that we expand the nature of our mission and capture the city of Tyre, where the PLO had its headquarters, and destroy the Kasmiya Bridge. Situated, as we were on the Litani, we controlled the entrances to Tyre and could have easily launched an assault on the city. The Chief of Staff was vigorously opposed to the idea, citing the possibility of high casualties to the IDF and the Lebanese civilian population. The Commander of the Northern Command, Yanush Bengal, also hesitated. Under these circumstances, Minister of Defense Weizman declined to authorize the assault, preferring not to override the objections of the Chief of Staff, without the confidence of the Commander of the Northern Command.

I thought the decision was a tremendous error, and to this day believe that our failure to capture Tyre and destroy the PLO infrastructure greatly contributed to our need to re-enter Lebanon four years later when we initiated the Peace for Galilee War. If we had captured Tyre, United Nations UNIFIL observer troops would have been stationed in the city, which would have prevented the PLO from operating there. Only a short while after the Litani operation the PLO began shelling Nahariya from a cannon they had set up in the cemetery of Rashidiya, near Tyre. If UNIFIL troops had been stationed in the whole area south of the Litani River these attacks would have been impossible. There are those who argue that the PLO was bombing Kiryat Shmona from the north side of the Litani during the same period they were bombing Nahariya, and although this is true, it is also true that the PLO did not shoot Katyushas from the UNIFIL zone. The more territory we would have captured in the Litani operation the more territory we would have turned over to UNIFIL, which in turn would have left the PLO with less area to operate in that was in striking distance of Israel. Our failure to capture Tyre meant that they could reach our borders in the west from Tyre, and in the east, from points north of the Litani. Had they not had complete access to our whole borderline, perhaps we would have been able to find a less extensive means of neutralizing the threat, as opposed to the massive assault we decided upon in June 1982.

Furthermore, our failure to remove the PLO from Tyre resulted in the UNIFIL troops developing relations with the terrorists. We had placed great hope in the UNIFIL troops because their soldiers were from nations like Norway and Holland, which were very friendly to Israel. However, these troops were soon inundated with PLO propaganda, and being in constant contact with PLO forces in Tyre, they soon became convinced that Israel was, as the Palestinians had claimed, the villain of the conflict. If we had removed the PLO from Tyre there would have been no need for the UNIFIL forces to have liaison offices with the terrorists. We further compounded our error when we allowed the UNIFIL troops to be situated in areas that infringed on the freedom of movement of Major Haddad's troops.

When I assumed the role of Chief of Staff on April 16, 1978, our army was still stationed in Lebanon, but the UNIFIL forces were beginning to deploy and it was to late too reverse the decisions that had been taken. The maps detailing UNIFIL deployment and the areas the forces of Major Haddad would control was signed by an American officer and presented to me. I would bring this map with me each time I met with General Siilasvuo, commander of the UNIFIL forces.

22

Easing Pinto's Punishment

Only a few short weeks after I began my tenure as Chief of Staff, I was confronted by some fundamental issues about the nature of the IDF. Although the Litani operation had not lasted long, it appeared that some of our soldiers had found the time to deviate from standing orders and commit acts of looting, and, some believed, murder. For me, the crime of looting was easy to define, for it constituted the taking of goods that do not belong to you. During wartime, it is often easy for soldiers to see "opportunities" to "acquire" goods and merchandise from stores and frightened civilians. In my mind this is nothing short of robbery and looting has always been strictly forbidden by the IDF. In fact, Israel has always been proud of the fact that its soldiers have always behaved cordially and fairly to civilians, and despite the noise some were making, the truth was that there were very few cases of looting during Operation Litani. Those who were caught, however, were tried and punished.

The charges of murder were more difficult to me to define. The IDF has always had a standard of "tohar haneshek," purity of arms, that attempts to regulate under what circumstances a soldier is legitimately entitled to use lethal force. These standards, like the regulations against looting, have always been upheld by the over-whelming majority of our soldiers. Yet, what exactly is the concept of purity of arms in a combat situation? Is not a war fought with the single goal of killing one's enemies? Although clearly defined in reference to civilians, is not the concept completely blurred with regard to enemy forces?

I do not wish to minimize the importance of morality in combat. It is important not only because it is, in principle, correct, but also because strategically it focuses one's soldiers on the objectives of the war. Thus, with these questions in mind, one of my first acts as Chief of Staff was to reduce the sentences of three IDF officers who had been tried and sentenced to prison for charges stemming from the deaths of Palestinian fighters killed during the Litani operation. My actions were controversial and the controversy was further fueled by the international press, which had attached great symbolic meaning to my decisions. Naturally, this was nonsense, but I had learned that the press was only interested in drama, and most importantly, drama that could be twisted to make Israel look bad.

My decision was based on a variety of factors. My personal confusion with regard to the concept of purity of arms was certainly one factor. If these officers had been convicted of killing civilians, I would not have intervened. But this was not the case. They were convicted of killing Palestinian terrorists in situations when, in the view of the court, the terrorists did not have to be killed. Yet, was this not the purpose of our operation? Didn't the Prime Minister announce that the IDF was going to "cut off the arm" of the terrorists? Didn't the Minister of Defense announce that we were going to "destroy" the terrorists? The Litani operation was launched after the Coastal Road bus massacre. The terrorists had gone too far, and the time had come for us to remind them of the powers that be. These were the orders that were presented to the IDF. It was an operation of vengeance. If soldiers killed terrorists when it was not absolutely necessary, then let them be punished, but let us have the punishment reflect the atmosphere and environment in which the "crimes" were committed.

The first of the three cases that came to my attention was that of Lieutenant Pinto, who had been charged with murder, although the bodies of those he allegedly murdered were never found. The court sentenced him to twelve years in prison, which was reduced by the

Appeals Court to eight years. I reduced the sentence further, to three years. I examined Pinto's file carefully. The judge who tried the case had determined his guilt primarily on the basis of the testimony of one man, Yoav Hirsh, who initially brought Pinto's act to the attention of the authorities. Hirsch had followed Pinto as company commander, but had never been able to attain the same status and respect that the soldiers had afforded Pinto. There were definite elements of jealousy, which I believed could have been motivating Hirsch. Moreover, Hirsh had been sentenced to two years incarceration for looting during the Litani Operation. Although his sentence was suspended by the Commander of the Central Command, Moshe Levy, who later followed me as Chief of Staff, I questioned his sincerity and purpose. Furthermore, I saw looting as a far more serious crime, because it cannot be said that the soldier simply got caught up in his mission. Hirsch took something that was not his, and used his authority and power, bestowed upon him by the IDF, as the means for his thievery. Thus, I concluded that eight years was too severe, and knowing he should be punished, sought a sentence that I felt better reflected the misdeeds and intentions of Pinto. There were those in Israel who were outraged at my decision and I understood their concern, but they did not have access to all the information I did, and they were not aware of the exact circumstances of the deaths in question. However, some were so bitter that they even went so far as to claim I reduced Pinto's sentence because he was engaged to be married to the daughter of an IDF general, Danny Mat. Although Mat had testified as a character witness on Pinto's behalf, his rank in the IDF had no influence on my decision. My sense of justice and professionalism, as well as those of Mat, would never have allowed it. Still, it was not beyond many in Israel to question my integrity and fight to have an IDF officer rot in prison, so as to avenge the deaths of some Palestinian terrorists.

The second case that came to my attention was that of a battalion commander in the Engineering Corps named Sadeh who was accused of instructing his men to kill a terrorist gang they had caught during the war. Sadeh was given a light sentence because of the circumstances surrounding his actions, and I felt his sentence warranted an additional reduction and lowered his sentence to one year. Sadeh had not acted out of malice or ill intent. He did not instruct his forces to kill the terrorists out of a desire to be evil or brutal. He understood his orders to be the destruction of the terrorists and ordered his men to complete their mission. My decision was further influenced by the difficult personal problems of the Sadeh family, which would have been further exacerbated had he spent a long time in prison. The issue with Sadeh, as it was with Pinto, was whether he had acted with intent to violate the rules of the IDF and the spirit of the orders presented to him. Our concept of purity of arms includes the notion that we do not kill men once they have been captured. Thus, these men were guilty. My task was to place the offense in its proper context and make sure the punishments were fair, to the spirit and morals of the IDF as well as to the men being punished.

Although the Pinto and Sadeh cases received a great deal of press, a similar case, involving a Kibbutznik who was a battalion commander from the Nahal infantry brigade was totally ignored by the press. I had assigned a military prosecutor to the case after receiving a letter from a soldier that informed me that the commander had issued an order over the radio for his troops to kill a group of terrorists they had captured while on patrol during the Litani operation. The author of the letter was involved in the incident, and citing the press reports surrounding the Pinto and Sadeh cases, wrote that his conscience was bothering him and he was questioning whether he had committed a crime.

I summoned the battalion commander to my office, and he did not deny my allegations, but informed me that the circumstances of the incident were such that he felt his men would be in danger if the terrorists were not eliminated. This is always a difficult decision for a commander and one which is not given the benefit of guidelines by the concept of purity of arms. I found the commander to be very sincere and honest, and was surprised when he informed me that he had raised his actions with the Kibbutz educational institution, which had deliberated his case and found him to be innocent.

Naturally, I could not be satisfied with the ruling of the educational institution, although I was impressed that the young officer had sought their ruling. The military prosecutor had decided to place the officer, and the soldiers who had done the actual shooting, on trial. Yet the officer was a man of integrity and honesty in the truest sense. Before the trial began, and numerous times during the course of the trial, he reported to me and expressed concern for his soldiers. He knew that his lawyers had an excellent case that would most likely result in his acquittal, yet, he was concerned that his men, who had carried out an order according to his instructions, would serve time in prison while he was left to go free. In the end, he was acquitted, as his lawyers were able to raise questions as to the identity of the individual who spoke through the radio and actually issued the order. The soldiers who carried out the order were found guilty and were sentenced to terms of imprisonment of one and a half to two years. I suspended their sentences. Interestingly, not a word from the media and no public outcry. I wondered what had made the Sadeh case, and particularly the Pinto case, so deserving of media and public attention. They certainly did not have any dynamics that were missing from this case. I believe that the difference was rooted in social prejudices that were, and in many ways still are, prevalent in Israeli society. The Kibbutznik officer, coming from a Kibbutz, was seen as being educated and moral. Although he was accused of the same crime, it was assumed by the press that he had legitimate reasons for issuing his orders. Sadeh was not given the benefit of the doubt, and Pinto's case was blown totally out of proportion by the presence of the international press.

In an even more controversial ruling I reduced the sentence of a man named Lederman who had been sentenced to twenty years for murdering an Arab in revenge for the death of a soldier at a hitchhiking rest stop in Jerusalem. Lederman was a member of the Civil Guard, a volunteer civilian nighttime patrol, which is made up of men above the age of fifty-five. He had been deeply affected by the murder of a soldier and sought to personally avenge the act by taking the life of an Arab. The Appeals Court reduced his sentence to ten years and I intervened and further reduced it to three years. Lederman was an older man, who had acted, as he saw it, according to the principle of revenge, as espoused in the Torah, "an eye for an eye, a tooth for a tooth." He had broken the law, and had violated some of our sacred principles, but he was a mature man with a family to support. I felt three years would be enough time for him to understand his crime and repay his debt to society.

It must be understood that in all these cases my wish was not to get involved in the politics of the issues brought to the fore by the actions of the defendants. In almost each case the left wing of the Israeli political spectrum chose to make a public outcry over the defendant's actions, while the right wing sought justifications. My task was to judge the events with an eye toward the intent of the defendant, and then to arrive at a punishment that was fair.

I do not intend to appoint myself judge of my own term of service as Chief of Staff. A man is by nature inclined to exaggerate his accomplishments and underestimate his failures. I only sought to do what I saw as correct and never denied coming to the post with a certain world outlook, which I tried to impress upon the army. I approached each failure with my understanding that big failures are not born out of nothing, but rather, begin with small failures, with presumably thoughtless breaches of discipline and irresponsibility.

I was a simple man of great discipline and the army I commanded was to be the same. I was concerned with discipline, with waste, with pride, and with motivation. Thus, among my first actions I ordered that all soldiers, including officers, were required to wear the beret at all times, except when indoors. This may appear a strange issue to place emphasis on, but I viewed the beret, the symbol of each unit, as a symbol of pride in that unit, and felt it should be worn by the soldiers with the proper amount of pride. I felt my order would restore the pride, and by extension some motivation, and since it was a direct order from the Chief of Staff, it would serve to increase the level of discipline as well. The need to wear berets at all times had been lifted by my predecessor, Motta Gur, for reasons I do not understand.

I was also very interested in cleanliness and appearance, because I feel they reflect a soldier's pride in himself and his unit. I issued orders that required bases to be maintained and kept clean, and for soldiers to be required to shave and to shine their boots daily.

I also believe that an army, particularly a citizens army like Israel's, must serve as an example for the people. Thus, if there is a need for people to cut down on waste and careless spending, so too must the army. I knew we were a country without great resources that was required to maintain a large, strong army. We had the task of training and equipping that army. Our foes were formidable, and forced many wars upon us, as they continued to refuse to come to terms with our existence. We therefore had no choice but to assign huge sums to the army, and in fact have the largest military budget, per capita, of any country in the world. This does not mean that our oil-rich enemies do not spend more than we do, and do not have more weapons than we do, it only means that they are nations wealthy enough to spend the money without having their citizenry pay for it. Israel does not have this luxury. Our budget comes from our taxes and the assistance we receive from Western nations that have an interest in our security and the military assistance we provide. Waste for us would be foolish, yet I discovered that it was rampant. I found food was often thrown away, and ammunition cartridges were often lost or disposed of. I issued orders designed to cut down on waste and remind the soldiers that they were literally paying for everything they threw away that could have been used. I strove to set a personal example, and even went so far as to order a soldier aboard a missile boat to remove a whole loaf of bread, that had not been opened, from the trash, and to make french toast with it. That evening I made a point of joining the crew for their french toast dinner. Our system needed to economize and our army had to behave like a poor man's army. I repeated this theme constantly, wherever I went. I even ordered that all empty cartridges from rifles and light and heavy machine guns be retrieved. The metal for producing bullets is imported from abroad and a bullet goes through a process of sixty machine steps until it is ready for use. The cartridges lie scattered on the ground after shooting. Picking them up is an activity of major importance in educating in the benefits of frugality. I was strict about having the order carried out, even though I knew it was the subject of discontent and jest.

I understood that it is hard to change people's habits and hoped that I would help encourage a gradual shift in the way we used our resources. I believe that my campaign was at least in part successful, and that people's awareness of what they were wasting increased. They learned to conserve and that there is no such thing as owner-less property. Each individual has a responsibility to do his or her own part.

I believe the principles of cleanliness, pride in oneself and one's environment, personal responsibility and conservation were lessons that the army helped incorporate into the consciousness of all Israelis. In this sense the army was once again a pioneer in Israeli society.

23

LIBI —
Renewed Pride

A great believer in education, I understand that the army presents a unique opportunity to further enhance a soldier's education. Children in Israel should be educated about the Land of Israel as small children in kindergarten and they should learn to know the country over the years by walking through its valley and plains, hiking its mountains and wadis. Only through personal experiences can a child be bonded to the land, learn to love the flowers and trees, the sea and the desert. In this manner, the IDF had the means to enrich the soldiers and allow each one to aquire a deep personal feeling for the land and the nation he or she was serving.

Yet there was another educational challenge before us. Like most nations, Israel's society is economically stratified, and like most nations, those who find themselves at the bottom do not receive the attention and governmental services they need to help lift them up the social ladder. In Israel, this problem has been intensified by the fact that most poor families are of Arab or eastern origin, while the upper and middle classes are predominantly of European background. One of the major services that are not delivered to the poorer communities is education. Often the failure of education must be shared by the schools and the community, but assessing blame does little to change the fact that poor children are not given the educational tools they need to lift themselves out of poverty. Thus, I found that a whole sector of our youth was behind most others of their age, not only in history and science, but also with regard to the basic skills of reading and writing. These youth did not study or work, and were literally left to fend for themselves. They had slipped through the educational framework, and when it came time for them to enlist in the IDF they were most often deemed unfit for military service due to their illiteracy. Thus, what was happening was that the military, like the governmental and civilian institutions, was abandoning them to their fate.

I could not come to terms with this and upon assuming the position of Chief of Staff began to set up a system, within the framework of the IDF, that would allow these young people the chance to join the army, and learn the skills they needed. I followed up on its formation daily, and was not beyond using my authority to remove senior officers who were against my plans and attempting to sabotage my efforts. I understood that these officers felt that it was not the task of the army to educate our youth and that the program would require resources that were better spent elsewhere. I argued that the IDF had an obligation to society, as well as to the children, to do all we could, particularly if the civilian sector had failed. I wanted to give these young people a new start and a chance to feel pride in themselves. It was in the long term interests of the IDF, as these individuals, once educated, would perform on a higher level as soldiers.

As could be expected, most of the opposition I faced came from within the civilian sector. Many felt that the task of education was not the responsibility of the army, and others, mostly those responsible for education, were angered because I was, in effect, exposing their failure. I admitted that traditionally the army has not been involved in education, but argued that, in principle, we were not a nation that did not give every one of its young a chance. I also argued that Israel was in no position to waste its most valuable resource, its youth, and in this respect, the army had every right to do what it felt necessary to improve the standard of its soldiers. If this included education, then it was our obligation and right to educate.

The IDF was mobilized to the task of providing these young people with education and culture in a positive environment. I was very sensitive to the fact that they had known poverty all their lives and strove to guarantee that all their personal needs were met. They were to receive, and they were to serve. My hope was that the combination would give them the basis they would need to leave the army as confident, proud, decent young men and women.

I assigned some of our best instructors to the project, and ordered them to do all they could to help these people. There are no short cuts in education and there are no immediate results. The problems were great and the solutions we developed were not simple. We needed patience and perseverance. We began by taking these young people and giving them back their sense of pride and self-worth. We found that this had an extraordinarily positive effect, not only on the youth, but on their families and the people closest to them. When they first arrived in the army many were rebellious, alienated, withdrawn, and unkempt, yet we had each one returning home clean, well-dressed, proud of himself and his uniform, and carrying his personal rifle. For those adults who had known him as a troubled child, the sight was encouraging and hopeful. For the neighborhood children who remembered him as wild and unruly, he became a model to emulate.

Our army basic educational system graduated young men who went on to become quality soldiers. If the gauge of success is quantitative, nearly fifty percent of those completing their studies went on to serve in excellent combat units and were incorporated into these units as fighting men equal to their peers in all respects. This proved that these young people had potential, and that we had been losing the benefits of their services because of an alienating society, and a lack of will to change things. We showed that these young people needed only the opportunity and proper conditions to develop, and that once given the chance, they were enthusiastic in their desire to repay society.

One particularly successful story involves nine young men who served in the Engineering Corps. Although the Chief Engineering Officer was against my request to train these nine young men in the operation of heavy mechanical equipment, I compelled him to admit them to a course, which they finished with high grades. Upon their completion of the course they served in the IDF's bases in the Negev Desert, where they excelled. Their success gave me a great sense of personal satisfaction, for I knew these boys had no real homes to speak of and that the IDF had become their home. They gave their duties one hundred percent of their energies, and the IDF repaid their efforts with praise and respect. These nine young men remained in the army after the completion of their conscripted duty, and were trained as instructors. They spent much of their time traveling through the country finding young men similar to themselves, recruiting them and training them to operate heavy equipment. Interestingly, a disproportionate number of the heavy equipment operators in the IDF were graduates of our program, and many of them went on to this profession in civilian life, which was another "side-benefit" of our programs.

One of our biggest problems was our lack of funds. Our school buildings were really converted warehouses, and although the program's initial successes won many supporters to my position, we were unable to find governmental sources of funding. In fact, each new budget session would include attempts to cut the Defense budget, because it was assumed that money could be saved by discontinuing the army's basic education program. I fought the efforts to cut our budget with all my energy and argued that the army educational project was a national and moral concern of the first priority. I maintained that the army budget needed an additional one billion shekels for education and that I, in an effort to set a personal example, was donating one day's pay per month to the education fund.

Many people laughed at my gesture and ridiculed my attempts to have all IDF officers follow my example. My efforts succeeded, which was reflective of the character and quality of the IDF officer, and I moved my campaign to the public and private sectors where I demanded that those earning middle and upper level salaries donate as well. The officer's donations had laid the foundation of the LIBI Fund, and soon other donations began to flow in. To this day, the LIBI Fund for Israel's Defense, used for education and other needs of our soldiers, is a vibrant charity that has collected many billion of shekels for its worthy projects.

We converted an old rest home in Givat Olga, north of Tel Aviv, into a special school where young men were taught to read and write. The school was a great success and I invited the Prime Minister, President and other Cabinet Ministers to visit the school. While there they saw how effective our program was, and President Yitzchak Navon had tears in his eyes as he watched a young man writing the Hebrew alphabet on the blackboard. It was the first time this boy had ever written the word "Abba," father, in Hebrew.

The word of our successes began to spread and many people started to take note of our programs. We received more building space and professional educators, psychologists, social workers and others began volunteering their time and talents. Great interest was shown in the methods we had developed to teach these young adults the fundamentals of reading, since we obviously could not employ the methods they would have been exposed to in kindergarten. Special programs were also developed to help our students learn to live together and get along with one another.

The first time I instructed the officers of the various army corps to go to the basic education schools and choose soldiers for their units, they could not hide their dissatisfaction. They did not believe in the ability of our students. Yet, as time went on, these students proved themselves to be excellent, highly motivated soldiers and became sought after, even for combat units. They served in every branch of the IDF, in every unit, both combat and support, service and technical. When a soldier turned out to be a disappointment, when he failed to function properly and was not capable of serving in a unit framework, we did not reject the individual. He was not released or given an exemption from service, but rather sent back to school for another month or two, during which time the specific difficulties he had displayed were addressed.

Our students brought great pride to their families as well, and we took the opportunity of meeting their parents to demonstrate our respect. At commencement ceremonies, as the parents watched with pride, their children stood dressed in the Israeli Army uniform, polished, adorned with badges. After the ceremony I would often greet the parents personally, a sign of respect they took notice of. At one particular party I joined the tears of joy with my own tears as the parents, in appreciation, passed around a donation cup. These people were poor, yet they wished to contribute to the work of LIBI.

We worked with the Ministry of Labor in helping find our graduates jobs. We helped the street gangs division of the Police. We even made a deal with the Ministry of Justice on behalf of our students that called for the clearing of all police records if the young men successfully completed their military service. This agreement became a motivating factor for them, but also served to give them a fresh start in life when they left the army's structured way of life.

After my tenure as Chief of Staff and my retirement from the army, I was pleased to see that the LIBI fund and the programs I had initiated remained as an essential part of the IDF. The LIBI Fund has been integrated into Israel's everyday life and every young child has heard about it. To this day, although I am no longer in a position of authority over the army, I never miss an opportunity to solicit money for the LIBI Fund, and often agree to public speaking engagements in exchange for a LIBI contribution.

In addition, again in an effort to be a man of deeds, my family has adopted a poor family from Afula, and we have made our house in Tel Adashim open to them at all times. We have spent many hours assisting the children in their studies and enjoying recreational activities with the family.

During 1978-79, terrorist activity along our northern border continued, especially through artillery and Katyusha fire. We combatted the terrorists by utilizing our air force, navy, and ground forces. We attacked their bases and arms depots, harassed their forces and disrupted their momentum. During this time, the Lebanese civil war was still raging, and the PLO was very actively involved in the Moslem effort to dominate Lebanon's Christian population. The additional power that this gave the Palestinians, and their use of that power to violate Israeli sovereignty and endanger Israeli lives by engaging in terrorist infiltrations and Katyusha attacks, was increasingly becoming a great concern to the leaders of the Israeli government and the IDF.

Part Five:
CHIEF OF STAFF OF THE ISRAEL DEFENSE FORCES

24

Good Advice for the Americans

A short while after I assumed the position of Chief of Staff I received an official invitation to visit the United States, and agreed to a tour at the end of 1979. As the first Israeli Chief of Staff to be visiting the United States in an official capacity, I was showered with gestures of respect and affection. The members of my entourage were received graciously throughout the country and I was even awarded the Legion of Merit medal in an impressive ceremony on the lawn of the Pentagon. We even had an airplane placed at our disposal.

Although I felt honored by the kind and respectful gestures, I understood that the Americans were bestowing honor not on me as an individual, but rather on me as the symbol of Israel and the Israel Defense Forces. In this sense, I was very proud and accepted the American gestures with pleasure.

While on my tour, I had many interesting and enjoyable meetings with American soldiers I had gone through the Marines School with in 1961. Many of these men were still in active service and were senior officers. We shared many laughs as we recalled the days when we were junior officers in our respective armies.

Although I had not traveled to the United States in the capacity of military advisor to the American Army, my opinions were often sought, as my trip corresponded with the seizure of the American Embassy staff in Teheran, Iran. The Americans were understandably frustrated by the blatant Iranian violation of international law, and were searching for ways to free their hostages. When asked for advice or a suggested course of action, I almost always chose to remind my American friends that they were the leaders of a great army, and that they would find a solution without my assistance. The only advice I was willing to offer was a caution in the use of armed force. This advice, particularly in that it was coming from me, sounded strange. I was the general from Israel, and hadn't Israel used armed force to free its hostages in Entebbe, Uganda? I reminded my friends that the Entebbe rescue, as heroic as it was, was carried out with the benefit of the element of surprise, and at an airport on the outskirts of the city. The American hostages, on the other hand, were located in the center of Iran's capital city, and the Iranian revolutionary guards were prepared for, in fact were anticipating, an American assault. Thus, I explained, my advice was not to use force to free the hostages.

Another consideration that occurred to me but that I had declined to mention to my American colleagues was the difference in combat experience of the Israeli and American forces. Our soldiers who executed the Entebbe raid had been on many other strikes across enemy borders, and many had fought in at least one war. The American troops, although highly trained, did not have the level of actual combat experience I believed necessary to better the chances of a successful mission.

As we know, the Americans did not heed my advice, as I did not expect them to. While I was still in the United States, it seemed to me that they had already begun planning a military operation to free the hostages. It is the obligation of the military to offer the political leaders an option. I did not have much confidence in the possibilities, but I was disappointed when the rescue attempt was aborted after a series of serious and unfortunate errors. A short time later, many of the officers who had participated in the rescue effort visited Israel and shared with us the causes of its failure. Unfortunately, there were no great differences between my estimations prior to the attempt and their analysis following it. I did not believe that it was a wise mission to attempt, and would have recommended against it if Israeli hostages were being held in similar circumstances.

During this period I visited Egypt twice. I was not impressed and left believing there is no cure for the ills in Egypt. Cairo will never be a clean city; there will never be a sewage system; and the telephones there will never work properly. The great powers of the east and west could join together and they would never succeed in making Egypt into a modern state. The artificial impression they make on their important guests when they free the roads of all traffic jams does not actually alleviate the hell that returns once the guest has passed. My encounter with Egypt was typified by the leaking faucets in my luxury hotel room, the wallpaper peeling from the walls, the filth, the rotten fruit that I found on my table, and the apathy and indifference I saw in the average Egyptian citizen. I saw no chance of Egypt ever solving its true problems and couldn't help but wonder how an army born out of such a crumbling country succeeded in surprising us on Yom Kippur, 1973.

I knew that the Egyptian success was in part due to our own errors. We helped them by incorrectly interpreting their actions. Our arrogance had dulled our senses. Yet, it occurred to me that perhaps Egypt was a crumbling nation not in spite of its success in surprising us, but as a result. The Egyptians were willing to sacrifice everything in order to win even a temporary victory over the Jews. They were willing to forgo important services such as education and health, and necessary infrastructure like highways and a telephone system. They were even willing to do without food. Such a policy of mass sacrifice would not be acceptable in Israel, or any other Western nation. Yet in Egypt, as an Egyptian official once commented, "Egypt was set back twenty-four years in all areas of life while preparing and paying for the Suez Canal crossing of 1973." The same official also commented that another Egyptian attack on Israel could result in a total collapse of the Egyptian economic and governmental structures.

My second visit to Egypt was in 1981, after President Sadat had been assassinated. I was accompanied by the Commander of the Air Force and the Commander of the Southern Command and we were treated to a tour of factories manufacturing and assembling military hardware. I did not have great respect for what I saw, as it was many years behind our own technology, but we were courteous to our hosts, as they were to us. We laid wreaths on President Sadat's grave and participated in other official functions. I had to leave Egypt earlier than I had planned because of tensions on the Golan Heights; however I had seen enough to make me realize that our peace with the Egyptians was a fragile child.

When I first heard that Sadat had been shot I did not see it as being necessarily bad for Israel. In some sense, any disarray among the Arab leadership works in Israel's favor. Anything that sows confusion and undermines authority in the Arab world ultimately weakens the Arabs. The Arab leaders do not differ from one another in their displeasure at the existence of a Jewish State. They differ only on the tactical measures that they feel should be applied against Israel in order to achieve their goals.

Sadat, and later Mubarak, would not do anything to hurt Israel before we completed our evacuation of all of the Sinai. It was only after the evacuation that Mubarak made efforts to return Egypt to the Arab fold and restore its position of leadership in the Arab world. That this would require a freezing of relations with Israel was not of importance. That the peace treaty would have to be relegated to a position of minimal importance with no real manifestations or expression was also irrelevant. These were not prices too high to be paid. Unfortunately, I must say that I cannot state with absolute confidence that a future Egyptian leader would not resume armed conflict against Israel, if Arab solidarity, or Egypt's position in the Arab world warranted it.

When I learned that Israel had agreed to evacuate all the Jewish settlements in the Sinai I knew, as Chief of Staff, that my duty would be to execute the government's wishes. My unconditional readiness to fulfill every government order notwithstanding, I requested a meeting with the Prime Minister, Menachem Begin. I believe that the Prime Minister sensed my deep emotional involvement, although I tried to present things logically, without emotion. I respectfully told Begin, "Mr. Prime Minister, despite the often tragic history of the Jewish people, never have we evacuated Jewish settlements on our own initiative. It has never happened! We have never evacuated Jewish settlements under the pressure of a difficult war. Are we authorized to evacuate Jewish settlements under the pressure of peace?"

The Prime Minister addressed me in a fatherly manner and explained that the evacuation of the Jewish settlements tore at his heart too. Yet, he saw no choice. It was true that the Jewish people had never voluntarily evacuated a settlement, but, the Prime Minister said, it was also true that they had never signed a peace treaty with an Arab State. Thus, there were two historical firsts, peace and evacuation. He hoped that they struck a certain balance.

Begin thanked me for expressing my views and I thanked him for listening. I was impressed with his readiness to listen and the attentive manner with which he followed my words. He appreciated my openness and my willingness to speak my mind without consideration for who might or might not be pleased with what I felt I had to say. I had long ago vowed to myself that such considerations would not guide my words, nor my actions.

25

Between Ezer
and Myself

Ezer Weizman and I differ in many ways, the least of which is my tendency to be outspoken and voice my opinion without consideration of its popularity. Ezer is a charming, likable man, yet Ezer the soldier, the fighter dedicated to the Land of Israel, bears little resemblance to Ezer the politician, the diplomat eager to placate everyone. Ezer lost his commitment to the Land of Israel and Judea and Samaria when he sought favor in the eyes of the Americans, Egyptians, and Western Europeans. In Israel he seeks the approval of all, hoping to cross over the conflict-laden spectrum of views. He searches for praise and recognition, wishful that all will acknowledge his virtues. In reality, this need caused Ezer to lose one of his most redeeming qualities, his ability to formulate a position and loyally fight for what he believed.

It is not easy to criticize Ezer Weizman. In contrast to Arik Sharon, who is calculating and cold, Ezer is an emotional man, who, although at times subject to extreme mood swings, is nonetheless very human. We always found ways to reduce tensions between us and bridge our differences of opinion. He used to tell me that the disagreements we had were born out of the fact that we were raised in contrasting environments. The nephew of Chaim Weizman, the great Zionist leader and Israel's first President, Ezer was brought up a son of the aristocracy. While my roots in poverty did little to advance my career, Ezer was offered major appointments, in part, because of his background and upbringing. While I do not wish to imply that he was not qualified for the positions he was offered, or that he did not fulfill his duties with great talent, there were times when he acknowledged what he saw to have been a natural, primary advantage he had over me. While he was perceived as an educated man of the world, I was often seen as provincial and narrow-minded. Our relationship had its periods of tension, and moments of agreement. At times Ezer did not share his political troubles with me, and other times he wanted to, but did not always find me willing to get involved beyond the point necessary for me to fulfill my duties as Chief of Staff.

We had our most intense disagreements about the Land of Israel. Although we shared basic views at the beginning of his term as Minister of Defense, during the course of his term Ezer underwent a transformation of opinion. I remained loyal to my vision of the Land of Israel, while Ezer began to speak in terms of concessions and compromises. He would argue that my opinions were the thoughts of a soldier and farmer, a man of the soil, while he was obligated to think as a politician, like a man who has seen the world.

In many cases it was possible to change Ezer's mind. Although he was confident in his decisions, he was not too proud to listen. He was a pragmatist, and there was always the chance that if your arguments were good he would follow your advice. He did not believe in stubbornly sticking to a decision or that his prestige as Minister of Defense precluded challenges to his positions.

There were many times that I would question Ezer's approach to our conflict with the Arabs in Judea and Samaria. Ezer would often remind me that there were no quick, easy solutions to the conflict and that "we will have to live with these Arabs." This approach always seemed to me one-sided and unfair in that it places the responsibility for co-existence solely on Israel. Is it any less true that the Arabs "will have to live with us"? If we are obligated to act with deliberation, moderation, and caution so as not to offend or alienate the Arabs, should they too not show consideration for our sensitivities and sense of honor? If we are expected to understand their aspirations, why are they not required to understand our commitment to remain a free, independent Jewish nation?

The fact that Weizman was very emotional made it difficult to accurately predict his reactions and decisions. He would often swing from moderation to the authorization of stern action. Most often, stern action was taken after an event that reminded Ezer of the senseless violence perpetrated by the terrorists. After five yeshiva students were murdered in Hebron, I entered Ezer's office with a recommendation to deport the pro-PLO mayors from Judea and Samaria. I was prepared to argue my case, and was even ready for a long evening of heated disagreement. Yet, to my surprise, there was little need for debate, and Ezer accepted the recommendation that same evening.

A major conflict in our relationship evolved over an attempt by Jewish settlers to establish the town of Elon Moreh three miles east of Nablus. Although Ezer had once been a great supporter of Jewish settlements, as Minister of Defense he came to oppose it. Despite my efforts to have Weizman meet with the settlers to discuss a compromise, Weizman simply stated that they were to leave the site, or the Israel Defense Forces would remove them.

The settler's defiance of the Minister of Defense elevated their efforts to an issue of concern for the whole government, and the Cabinet held a session on the stand-off at Elon Moreh. While I was convinced that the settlement was important from a security perspective, Ezer felt differently, and shared his views with the Cabinet. When the Cabinet asked me to present my views in writing, I did so, in effect contradicting Ezer's appraisal. I wrote that in my view Elon Moreh was situated on a security sensitive site and was therefore an important location to have a settlement in for security purposes. Although this was not the first time that a Minister of Defense and Chief of Staff had disagreed, Ezer was angry and felt that I had overstepped my authority by contradicting him before the whole Cabinet. I tried to calm Ezer by reminding him that I had told the Cabinet nothing new and that the Elon Moreh site was designated a strategic security location as early as 1973. Yet, Weizman felt that I had betrayed the relationship between

the Minister of Defense and Chief of Staff. Under ordinary circumstances, if a disagreement between the two is not solved by one
person successfully convincing the other of the validity and logic of
his argument, then the Chief of Staff must subordinate his position
to that of the Minister of Defense. Yet, under these circumstances,
this arrangement was unacceptable to me. Weizman was not my
"commander," but rather the representative of the government
relegated the responsibilities to liaison with the army and carry out
government policy. The government, the full Cabinet, were my
"commanders" and they had requested my professional opinion.
Under the circumstances, I was obligated to contradict Weizman's
analysis of the strategic value of the settlement site.

There were many additional differences of opinion between us,
including our retaliation policy against the terrorists operating in
Lebanon. Our problem was a lack of consistency, aggravated by the
fact that Ezer changed his policy after every terrorist attack or
Katyushas barrage. In addition, although I argued for the strict
enforcement of the law in Judea and Samaria, Ezer was flexible and
at times willing to overlook the law and act on the basis of other
considerations. I do not believe that Ezer fully understood the Arabs
and think that he was like many Israelis in that he thought he could
appease the Arabs by making concessions. I used to argue with him
that the Arabs misinterpret concessions as a sign of weakness and
fatigue. Israeli concessions only serve to re-enforce their view that
their struggle will be successful and that more concessions will be
forthcoming if they continue to deny Israel its right to exist.

Yet, despite the disagreements and ideological debates we, Ezer
Weizman and I, were not adversaries, but friends involved in controversy. We often found ourselves close to each other, as we
traveled together and spent much time together. In most situations
we were able to find a common line that would allow us to unify our
differing opinions. In all situations, despite the ideological differences, we were always able to cooperate with one another and work
well together.

There were times when Ezer would share with me stories of the events that led up to the signing of the Camp David Accords. Although I cannot state as fact that Ezer joined forces with Moshe Dayan to convince Prime Minister Begin to make additional concessions to Egypt, I do know that Weizman's statement, calling for a "national peace government because this government does not want peace," served as a vehicle for additional pressures on Begin and the government. I do not believe that Weizman was wise in making such a statement, particularly in light of his position as a senior minister in the government he was criticizing. Yet Ezer was seduced into moderation by the hopes for peace and the gestures of respect bestowed upon him by the United States' President, Jimmy Carter. Ezer proudly told me how Carter once visited him at his cabin at Camp David unannounced, and that the two sat on the porch drinking whiskey and eating chocolate. Such recognition was difficult for Ezer to ignore.

Although many people know Ezer as the good natured, friendly person he often is, he is also a man of great rage and quick temper. Many times I watched as Ezer burst into fits of anger, screaming and pounding his fists on his desk. The worst incident I ever witnessed was when Ezer had not been informed of a Cabinet meeting which was being held on a non-military issue Ezer was quite concerned with. His anger was taken out on Brigadier General Ephraim Poran, who was the military secretary of the Prime Minister. As I entered Ezer's office, he was screaming as I had never seen a man scream. In truth Ezer's anger was caused by his realization that he had not been notified because many senior members of the Cabinet had lost confidence in him and were pushing him out of the circle of decision makers. I suspect that this was in part the reason he decided to resign as Minister of Defense and from the Cabinet. He did not consult with me prior to his resignation, but I understood beforehand that he was considering resigning. He would often complain to me that he was unhappy with the other Cabinet members and frustrated with the constant political maneuvering. I had tried to comfort him and encourage him to continue to serve because I was fond of him and we worked well together. But it was to no avail.

I believe that Ezer thought his resignation would result in the fall of the entire government. Paradoxically, what his resignation caused was the rise of Arik Sharon, as it provided an opportunity for Sharon to pursue the position of Minister of Defense. After Ezer's resignation Prime Minister Begin assumed the responsibilities of the Minister of Defense. This decision was acceptable to me, and I saw nothing odd in it as Prime Ministers Ben-Gurion and Levi Eshkol had also served as Ministers of Defense during their tenure. I respected Begin a great deal and did not expect difficulties in communicating with him. Yet, what I did not foresee was that Begin, as Prime Minister, would be too busy to be readily available for consultations and discussions with me whenever I felt it was necessary. I could not simply enter his office or call him up on the telephone at all times as I had done with Weizman.

Thus, a void was created that was eagerly filled by the Deputy Minister of Defense, Mordecai "Mottkeh" Tzipori, who had long felt that his advancement in the army had been blocked because of his more hawkish views. Tzipori was waiting for the opportunity to exert his authority, and the Begin decision to assume the post of Minister of Defense, presented Mottkeh with his big chance. Whereas Begin did not have the knowledge of the inner workings of the army, nor the time to learn, Tzipori knew the system and his status rose as he became the connecting link between Begin and the army.

There were moments of great tension between Tzipori and myself, mostly over his support for budget cuts in military spending, Menachem Begin was unable to resume Weizman's campaign to avoid military spending cuts because as Prime Minister as well, he felt he had an overall commitment to the entire economy. The cause should therefore have been taken up by Tzipori, but instead he stood with those calling for spending cuts. I was left to fight the political battle alone, and the result was a significant cut in the funds made available to the army.

The struggle between Tzipori and myself only intensified when he voiced extremely strong opposition to the proposal to destroy the Iraqi nuclear reactor.

26

Destroying the
Iraqi Reactor

The decision to attack the Iraqi nuclear reactor in June 1981 was reached only after prolonged, often heated, debate. Joining Tzipori in his opposition were many senior officials in the defense establishment and many Cabinet Ministers. They argued that bombing a nuclear installation near an Arab capital would not be understood by the world and that the action would serve to alienate Israel's few friends. Furthermore, they contended that the development of nuclear weapons by the Arab world could not be completely halted and that Israel would simply have to learn to deal politically with an Arab nuclear capacity. We could accomplish this, they claimed, by maintaining a deterrence posture which would call for all sides to refrain from the use of nuclear weapons, because such use would result in mutual destruction. In addition to these arguments, at least one Cabinet member questioned the legitimacy of the action by declaring that Israel cannot simply blow up an installation in a foreign country, even one officially at war with us, if the country in question has not committed an act of war.

In my view the attack on the reactor was a rescue mission and an unavoidable action. We had to do all we could to prevent or delay the Iraqi nuclear capacity. I joined many Cabinet Ministers in sharing the Prime Minister's opinion that the Arab leaders were too irrational, too unpredictable, and too ruthless for Israel to depend on a policy of deterrence and mutually assured destruction to counter an Arab nuclear threat. We argued that Israel was not able to model its approach after the United States' strategy vis-à-vis the Soviet Union because whereas the U.S. has the ability to withstand an initial attack and respond, Israel would be totally devastated by an Arab nuclear attack. Moreover, we pointed out that an Iraqi nuclear weapon would raise the possibility of political extortion. What would be Israel's response, we asked those in opposition to the plan, if a nuclear-armed Iraq announced that it would bomb Israel if we did not withdraw from Jerusalem within forty-eight hours? The instability of the Iraqi regime, and its leader have taught us that anything is possible.

In addition to the political and logistical issues, some Cabinet members felt that rather than attack the Iraqi nuclear site, Israel should destroy anti-aircraft missiles Syria had moved into Southeastern Lebanon in violation of an unofficial agreement we had with them. We had long advised the Syrians that we would not be able to tolerate any Syrian maneuver that would hinder our freedom of movement in Lebanese skies. The crisis that developed over the Syrian deployment included numerous Israeli warnings and threats of action and an effort at mediation by the Americans that ended in total failure. The question before us was whether the political fallout of the Iraqi attack would preclude any action on our part against the Syrian missiles. If this was the case, which action was more important, more immediate? The Prime Minister argued that the Iraqi reactor presented an existential danger for Israel, while the missiles, although a threat to Israel's ability to carry out its missions in Lebanon, did not. Conversely, he stressed the possibility that an attack on the Syrian missiles might draw political fire that would prevent Israel from launching the Iraqi assault.

Politically, the Cabinet argued that the new United States President, Ronald Reagan, should not be greeted with such an action, and that the French, who were assisting the Iraqis and had French workers at the site, might react with great anger. Yet, Begin felt that on issues of Israel's very existence we could not base our decisions to act solely on the needs and reactions of other world leaders. The destruction of the Iraqi nuclear reactor would serve American and

Western interests as well, and if they did not understand that immediately after the attack, they would come to understand it in the future.

As Chief of Staff, my concerns were more centered on the operational issues of the mission. There were a great many dangers, as the mission was complex and a far distance away from Israel. In addition, the timing of our attack was extremely important and there was a need to act quickly because the circle of officials who were aware of our plans had grown to over three hundred and we feared a leak that would serve as a warning to the Iraqis. Such a warning could mean that the Iraqis would prepare for our attack and we would suffer casualties, or worse, that we would be forced to cancel or postpone the mission. Yet, postponement was not really an option because our experts had advised us that the reactor would soon be "hot", that is, that it would be ready to begin to irradiate uranium, and "milk" plutonium that the process produces. Once the Iraqis began this process we would no longer be able to attack, because any destruction of the facility would cause the deaths of tens of thousands, and perhaps even hundreds of thousands, of Iraqi citizens, as the reactor would release radioactive radiation. Thus, we worked under a feeling of urgency and developed a plan that we felt would succeed, should the government approve the action.

After difficult deliberations, I concluded that the reactor should only be destroyed by means of an aerial attack. We performed various exercises with the planes that we had, Phantoms and Skyhawks, and gathered information on the Iraqi air defenses and radar systems.

Before our plan could be implemented, our Air Force received F-16 fighter jets, which dramatically improved the level of our assault capacity. I instructed the Air Force to review the attack plan and make the necessary adjustments so as to suit our new planes. When the plan was revised we ran a mock assault on a fabricated installation at a distance similar to the mission's target. I participated in this "dry run" and was extremely confident that the plan would work. I immediately reported my opinion to Prime Minister and

Minister of Defense Begin and recommended that the mission be approved as soon as possible. Once Deputy Prime Minister Yigael Yadin lent his support to the strike, a Cabinet majority was secured and we received the authorization for the strike.

Before the pilots left on the mission I went to their base in the south and shared a few words with them. I knew that each of them understood the importance of the mission, and that they also understood what their fate would be should there be some kind of breakdown and they got shot down or had to abandon their plane. At times such as this, before an important dangerous mission, there is little room for personal feelings. The pilots were quiet, confident of their ability, yet understandably anxious.

Personally, being at the base was an extremely difficult and emotional experience because my son, Yoram, had died on the very same airfield in a training accident only a month earlier. To everyone's surprise, and in a complete departure from my usual behavior, I publicly betrayed my true emotions, and asked to see my son's room. After standing in his room a few moments, I went and spoke to his squadron commander, and then returned to my command post. During the time our planes were away I sat quietly, reflecting on my son, and the brave pilots who were in the process of completing a daring attack. When all our planes returned safely, I called the Prime Minister and informed him that the Iraqi nuclear reactor had been successfully destroyed. There was a great sigh of relief throughout the government and military.

The attack was implemented exactly according to the plan. We had equipped the F-16's with video machines that recorded the mission from the view of the pilot. The evening after the attack we viewed the films and confirmed the pilots' contentions that the reactor had been totally destroyed. A few months later, during a trip to the United States, I shared these videos with my American counterpart and other top American military leaders. They were excited to review the F-16 under combat conditions, and expressed their admiration for the complexity and success of our mission.

Israel's involvement in Lebanon on behalf of the Christian

population there increased during Begin's tenure as Minister of Defense. In addition to the clear need for Israeli involvement from a strategic perspective, Begin also felt strongly, as a humanitarian, that Israel had to do all it could to prevent a complete massacre of Lebanon's Christians. It was clear to Begin that the combined forces of the Lebanese Moslems, the PLO, and the Syrians were destroying Christian villages, and he was unable to understand the silence of the Christian Western countries. Their lack of intervention clearly influenced Begin's decision to upgrade Israeli aid.

As the situation worsened for the Christians, requests for our assistance increased. Begin met some Christian leaders in his home in Jerusalem and listened attentively to the plight of the Christians in Jounieh. Although he was plainly disturbed by what he had heard, Begin reminded the visitors that they would have to fight the Syrians with their own forces, and that Israel would assist them only if the Syrians introduced their Air Force into the conflict. It was Begin's view that use of the Syrian Air Force would present the Christians with a threat they had no means of countering, and would also pose a security threat for Israel.

During the time that we were increasing our role in Lebanon, we were also continuing our attacks on the terrorist bases situated in Southern Lebanon. With so much activity, I was not in favor of any structural changes in the IDF and rejected a plan to restructure that was being promoted by Israel "Talik" Tal. Tal was in charge of the Merkava tank project and had an excellent reputation. His plan was given further strength with the support of Tzipori. However, I felt that the plan would only result in unnecessary upheavals without bringing any real benefits. Once my views were articulated, Tal withdrew his proposal.

The summer of 1981 was also a period of great tension between Israel and PLO forces in Lebanon. After numerous PLO Katyusha attacks on our northern cities, we responded with a concentrated campaign of strikes and bombing raids. In addition, the Syrians had moved anti-aircraft missiles into the Beka'a Valley, crossing a "red line" Israel had set as a condition for the presence of Syrian troops in Lebanon. The Americans were concerned that the new tensions could develop into a war with the Syrians and sent their emissary, Philip Habib, to mediate a cease-fire and secure the removal of the missiles. He was only partially successful. The PLO agreed to cease attacking Israel, a promise they were soon to break, but the Syrians refused to remove the missiles.

At the time of all this activity the Israeli voters went to the polls and re-elected the Likud government of Menachem Begin. Sensing the opportunity, Arik Sharon began to pressure Begin to appoint him Minister of Defense. Prior to his fulfilling Sharon's request, Begin asked my opinion of the appointment. Although I naturally had my thoughts on the subject, I informed the Prime Minister that it was inappropriate for a Chief of Staff to voice an opinion on who should be selected as Minister of Defense. I would do my best to work with whomever was chosen.

27

Begin as
Minister of Defense

Many are those who have tried to claim that Begin's relationship
with me while he served as both Prime Minister and Defense
Minister was similar to Levi Eshkol's relationship to his Chief of
Staff, Yitzchak Rabin. Eshkol, serving as both Prime Minister and
Defense Minister, did not have a military background and placed
great trust in Rabin's advice, and some would say allowed Rabin to
in effect run the ministry. While Begin also lacked a military
background and listened carefully to my opinions, he understood
concepts quickly and was a strong leader. The argument that I ran
the ministry is not intended as a compliment to me, but rather as an
insult to Begin, and is simply untrue. In fact, until my experiences
with Begin, I had thought that the Minister of Defense should be a
man who had held a senior position in the army. Begin's ability to
consider the options and arrive at well thought out, strategically
sound decisions proved to me that this was not necessary.

One of the characteristics that most impressed me about Begin
was his strength and willingness to take whatever action was necessary to preserve the interests of Israel. He was not a leader intimidated by the thought of what "others," which in Israel usually
is translated as "the Gentiles," would think. His decisions were
determined only by the national interest.

Yet, there were times when Begin and I disagreed profoundly.
The most serious disagreement concerned the cease-fire Israel
signed with the terrorists after we had spent most of the summer of

1981 answering PLO artillery assaults with air raids. Unlike Weizman, Begin did not believe that the IDF had to wait for the terrorists to commit an atrocity before we acted against them. I had long advocated a policy of hitting the terrorists whenever and wherever our intelligence data indicated it was possible, and Begin permitted us to pursue this policy. Thus, we were engaged in an extremely active campaign against the terrorists in Lebanon, using air, land, and sea forces. It was also evident that our strategy was effective, as we often succeeded in causing damage that disrupted the terrorists' operations, and therefore prevented an assault on Israel. There was even an occasion when we were advised that a group of terrorists was stationed in a building near the sea and that they were planning to launch a sea attack against our coastal town of Nahariyya. We sent our Air Force to destroy the building, killing the terrorists and preventing the attack. I always felt that this was preferable to a policy that required we wait for the attack, suffer the losses, and only then send the planes to destroy the building.

During the height of this small war of attrition, we had destroyed the whole terrorist infrastructure in Lebanon. It was clear that they were on the verge of collapse, which would greatly serve Israel's interests. Sensing the severity of their situation, the terrorists appealed to the Saudis for assistance, who in turn, asked the Americans to pressure us to stop our campaign. With Begin under intense American pressure, I appealed to him to remain firm. We had destroyed the terrorists' bases and bunkers, their headquarters in Beirut, their training camps throughout Lebanon, and the openings to their weapons storage areas, usually located in mountainside caves. We had them on the verge of collapse, and it would have been a terrible mistake to agree to a cease-fire, so that they would have the time to reorganize and re-supply.

Yet Begin and the Cabinet agreed to the cease-fire, apparently under tremendous American pressure and in an effort to limit the damage some of our attacks in Lebanon, particularly the Beirut air raid, had done to our image in the West. This was indeed even more tragic in that it made necessary the Lebanon War, which was to be launched a year later.

For in truth, if the Cabinet had permitted us to continue with our efforts, the PLO would have collapsed, and history would look entirely different. A year later, after the Soviets, the Eastern bloc and the Arab States helped restore the terrorists to their original strength, it became clear to the government that the situation in the north was intolerable. The seeds of the war were sown the moment we allowed the world to once again rescue the Arabs at the moment they were on the verge of total defeat. The real shame is that the average Israeli was too busy enjoying the economic prosperity to realize just how close war really was.

28

Between Sharon and Myself

Shortly after the Likud's re-election in June, 1981, Prime Minister Begin appointed Ariel "Arik" Sharon to the position of Minister of Defense. Begin had been hesitant in making the appointment and had often asked me if I thought Sharon should be given the post. In such situations, I always declined comment because as Chief of Staff my opinions on such matters are irrelevant. It is the task of the Prime Minister to decide on the Cabinet Ministers and it was my task to serve the Cabinet. My only concern at the time was that Sharon had publicly stated that he supported cuts in the defense budget and I was adamantly opposed to all cuts. Luckily, his position changed after he was appointed Minister of Defense.

The first time I met Sharon was in 1952 at the border town of Berta'a, an Arab town that had been the site of many encounters with the Jordanians. At the time I was serving as the operations officer of the Ninth Brigade and he was the intelligence officer for the Northern Command. On this particular occasion the Commander of the Northern Command, General Assaf Simhoni, had joined our forces as we responded to a Jordanian sniper attack. Arik and I acknowledged one another, but did not exchange many words.

A year later the unit that Sharon had been associated with, Commando Unit 101, was merged with the paratroopers and Sharon was named battalion commander. At the time I was a commander of a reserve paratroop company and was not against Sharon's appointment. Other officers, however, left the paratroopers as an expression of their dissatisfaction with the manner in which the top men of Unit 101 were placed in command. In August 1955 I was to grow closer to Arik when I was asked to return to full service to replace a company commander in the regular army who was killed as he traveled over a mine near the Gaza Strip.

Sharon generally treated the officers under his command poorly. He was a strict authoritarian who continually reinforced his superiority and authority. He often scolded and chided his officers, shouting and screaming whenever he felt it necessary. Yet my relationship with Sharon was different. Whereas all the other officers below him were young and relatively inexperienced, Sharon and I were roughly the same age, and we had both experienced a great deal during the War of Independence. Sharon knew the only difference between us was that he had continued to serve in the army, while I had chosen to return to my farm and to serve only as a reserve officer. When I returned to the standing army my rank was lower than Sharon's, but he knew this was a merely a reflection of the difference in time we had served. He recognized my experience and abilities and quite often entrusted my company with important missions and central functions.

As a result of our activities, my company, Company E, acquired a prestigious reputation and many soldiers were requesting to serve under me. After I was wounded in the Sea of Galilee operation, a wound that required time to heal, I decided to leave the company. After I left the hospital I was appointed deputy commander of Battalion 890, under the command of Aharon Davidi. At this time Arik was named commander of the paratroop brigade.

Six months before the Sinai Campaign War in 1956 a plan was developed to land troops at Sharm el Sheikh in order to open the Straits of Tiran that had been blockaded by the Egyptians. Although the plan was not executed due to political considerations, Sharon was deeply insulted when Haim Bar Lev was assigned commander of the attacking force instead of Sharon. As a result, Sharon left the paratroopers and served for a time in the Armored Corps. A long period of time passed before we were to work together again.

During the Six-Day War, Arik served as a division commander and I served as a brigade commander. After the war Chief of Staff Rabin appointed Sharon head of the training department and Arik assigned me to review and develop a report on the lessons to be learned from the war. When I completed my assignment I mentioned to Sharon that I was interested in receiving the post of commander of the Jordan Valley. Sharon brought my request before the Chief of Staff and I received the appointment. Still later, while I was Chief Paratroop and Infantry Officer, I worked closely with Sharon, who was Commander of the Southern Command.

During this time the War of Attrition was being waged on the banks of the Suez Canal and Arik and I joined forces to encourage IDF raids and strikes at Egyptian targets on the western side of the canal. The Chief of Staff, Haim Bar Lev, was adamantly opposed to our proposals, but we combined forces and continued to pressure him. Finally, confident that Dayan would agree with his position, Bar Lev brought the matter before the Minister of Defense. To our surprise Dayan agreed with us and we were granted permission to launch a strike against the Egyptians.

Our first raid across the canal was code named "Victoria" and took place just north of Qantara. The raid was successful and achieved the desired effect of quieting the Egyptian guns. The Victoria raid also marked a period of cooperation between my forces and Sharon's and during this time we got along very well, enjoying a relationship of mutual respect and understanding.

Once our relationship graduated to the level of Minister of Defense and Chief of Staff I was a bit apprehensive that Sharon would at times act to restrict my authority or take positions on basic matters that were different from mine. I decided that were this to happen I would resign my position, but do so in a quiet manner that would not be interpreted as a political statement.

Yet the idea that Sharon would serve as Minister of Defense scared many people, as they thought he would use the position to expand his power base and take charge of policy. Prime Minister Begin was obviously one of those apprehensive and quite often admonished Sharon before the other members of the cabinet for actions he had taken without the Prime Minister's express consent. At one particularly heated meeting during the Lebanon War Begin yelled at Sharon, "You are not in charge here, I am, and don't you forget it!"

Indeed one of Sharon's first acts as Minister of Defense was aimed at infringing on the authority of the IDF General Staff. In an effort to gain independence from us in military and security related matters Sharon set up a "National Security Unit" within the Ministry of Defense, which served him as a sort of junior general staff. No other Minister of Defense had ever needed such a unit and its real value was aptly revealed when Moshe Arens, who followed Sharon as Minister of Defense, disbanded the unit almost immediately upon taking office.

The National Security Unit was the source of much tension between the IDF and the Ministry of Defense. Their mandate was in absolute competition with the aims of many IDF personnel and a great deal of resentment was felt toward the National Security Unit. Matters that had previously been concluded quickly and efficiently were now difficult and time consuming. My role as Chief of Staff, and my relationship to the Minister of Defense were also hindered, as the National Security Unit became a barrier between myself and Sharon. Furthermore, because the National Security Unit was new, it felt a tremendous need to make its presence felt and influence events. This also served to complicate matters and added to the tension.

Sharon assumed his post during a relatively quiet period, but there was great potential for tension. The American sponsored cease-fire was in effect between us and the terrorist forces in Lebanon and the American mediator, Philip Habib, was still actively involved in trying to resolve the crisis that arose when Syria moved anti-aircraft missiles into Lebanon. Sharon also inherited the plans for a variety of large and small scale assaults to be carried out by the IDF in Lebanon if the need were to arise. We were aware that the terrorists were using the cease-fire as an opportunity to re-organize,

dig in and acquire new weapons and that they would break the
cease-fire after they had completed their build-up. We also knew
that the terrorists, with the possible assistance of the Syrians, were
planning to attack and destroy Christian bases in northern Lebanon.
Furthermore, along with Habib's failure to get the Syrian SAM-6
missiles removed, we were concerned with Syrian movements that
clearly indicated a military build-up inside of Lebanon.

In addition to the flow of reports indicating a build-up in the
respective and combined strengths of the Syrians and the terrorists,
it became clear that the terrorists had no intentions of actually
keeping the cease-fire. They announced that their interpretation of
the agreement did not prohibit them from attacking Israel, rather,
it required that they launch their attacks from somewhere other than
Lebanese soil. Thus, attacks were launched against us from Jordanian territory and Katyusha rockets shot from Jordan fell near
Ma'oz Haim and the Sea of Galilee. Our government chose not to
react to this blatant violation only because no Israelis were killed or
injured.

Although these issues were pressing, Sharon's biggest and most
difficult task was assuring that Israel withdraw from the Sinai, as was
stipulated in the Camp David Accords with Egypt. This was a very
sensitive issue, particularly because the Jewish settlements in the
Yamit area were being evacuated.

Personally, I too was deeply saddened by the need to evacuate
the settlements and even tried to convince Prime Minister Begin to
not complete the evacuation. Yet, Begin understood that this
evacuation was of supreme importance to the Americans, who
viewed it as a matter of principle and hoped it would serve as a
precedent for the evacuation of other Jewish settlements. Indeed,
Begin and many other Cabinet ministers, many senior IDF officers
and many Israeli civilians were heartbroken at the thought of leaving
the area. Yet, of all those who ached at the thought, I was the one
who had to issue the orders that the evacuation be carried out. It
was, without a doubt, one of the most difficult things I have ever
done. The difficulty was compounded by the fact that many Jewish

settlers and their supporters had refused to leave and the possibility of violence, Jew against Jew, was quite real. I and other officials visited Yamit and appealed for calm, and in the end the resistance was symbolic and mostly peaceful.

During my tenure as Chief of Staff I served under four Ministers of Defense, Ezer Weizman, Menachem Begin, Ariel Sharon, and Moshe Arens. Of these, Begin and Arens had not been senior officers in the IDF, while Sharon and Weizman had both aspired to the position of Chief of Staff, but were not appointed. Although it can not be proven, there is reason to believe that both of these men were not chosen to lead the IDF, at least in part, because of their political world views.

Although I know this is a politically sensitive issue, and that my words are controversial, I must admit that I strongly support the concept that a Chief of Staff must have the same basic world view as the government he is serving. Although this means a politicalization of the process under which the Chief of Staff is chosen, this process has been politicized unofficially anyway, and this because it is only natural. One need only look at the tenure of Motti Gur, who was the first Chief of Staff to serve during a period when the government switched parties. Committed to his Labor Party world view, Gur often made public statements that were in opposition to the policies and goals of the Likud government. I did not support Gur's comments and I do not believe he or any other Chief of Staff should publicly oppose the government he is serving, but this problem would not arise if the two were in agreement at least on the fundamentals. However, in all cases it is the duty of the Chief of Staff to obey the instructions of the government and this obligation is absolute. It is one of the key tests of democracy.

Today it is more difficult to consider the world view of the candidates for Chief of Staff because the government is more volatile, with the Labor and Likud parties often swapping power. Under these circumstances, only men who have risen through the ranks of the IDF without strongly expressing their world views are viable candidates.

I was appointed by a Likud government and shared their basic approaches to the Land of Israel, Jewish settlement, and the war against terrorism. Although we had disagreements, many of my problems with Weizman and Sharon were not connected to policy issues, but rather their efforts, at times, to live out their unfulfilled dreams of being Chief of Staff by infringing on my authority. While both of them denied trying to be "super Chiefs of Staff," both men knew the army very well and tried to have a say on certain issues that have always been at the discretion of the Chief of Staff. Naturally I resisted these efforts and informed both men that I would not tolerate intervention on any issue that is the exclusive domain of the Chief of Staff. Perhaps this was one of the reasons Sharon tried to circumvent my authority by setting up his National Security Unit. The Minister of Defense is the individual who serves as the government's representative and he has the authority to instruct the army to engage or refrain from operational activity. The Minister of Defense determines the timing, objective and magnitude of all operations. Yet, it is the Chief of Staff who decides on the manner of execution, which units participate, and the tactics to be employed. Similarly, promotion of officers, structure of units, and the daily activities of the IDF are also under the authority of the Chief of Staff.

Of the four Ministers I served under, I was most friendly with Ezer Weizman. Although we had our disagreements, we always sought to solve them through dialogue. Ezer frustrated me the most in his approach to Judea and Samaria, where he sought compromises with the Arab residents. He believed that a soft Israeli hand would lead to Arab moderation, while I knew that the Arabs respect law and order and interpret a soft approach as a sign of weakness. Rather than encourage moderation, I argued, the compromises will serve as proof to the Arabs that their hardline stand is reaping benefits. Ezer was not a methodical man who thought out his positions with great care; he was an impulsive man and often took the advice of the last individual he had spoken to. Still, I very much enjoyed his company and developed feelings of great affection for him.

My relationship with Menachem Begin was completely different. While Ezer and I had a great many things in common, Begin and I did not share a common background. Yet, I had a great deal of respect for him and appreciated the attentive manner with which he listened when I presented an analysis or request. Begin had a great deal of respect for soldiers and often asked my opinions on issues unrelated to security, such as the economy. I often told him that I felt our Cabinet ministers needed to set an example for the general public and cut back on their standard of living. Although Begin himself lived very moderately, he was unable to enforce his standard on his colleagues.

As I have mentioned, I was a bit apprehensive when Begin appointed Sharon Minister of Defense, yet despite his efforts at times to overshadow my authority, I believe our relationship was one of mutual respect. Sharon and I had similar views on Judea and Samaria, Jewish settlement, and how to fight the terrorists. We also shared similar experiences in the army and were able to look at a situation and isolate, consider, and solve complex problems.

Before Sharon assumed his post, the army had developed a variety of plans to enter Lebanon on both a large and small scale. Sharon and I shared the view that if the IDF were to enter Lebanon the objective would be the terrorists and not the Syrians, unless they chose to enter the conflict or block our actions against the terrorists. Sharon also shared my concern for the Christians and personally went to Lebanon to meet with Bashir Gemayel and other Christian leaders. During these meetings Sharon never mentioned our plan to enter Lebanon and tried to avoid raising the Christians' hopes. In fact only after the first day of the Peace for Galilee War did I call Bashir Gemayel to my headquarters to explain to him the aims of our campaign. I informed him that we were going to reach the Beirut-Damascus highway and if possible we would link up with Christian forces in the area. However, the main reason I had called him to my office was to warn him that the Christians were not to take our actions as a sign that they were entitled to begin military initiatives of their own. We did not want them to begin to pursue their interests under the umbrella of our forces, nor did we want their actions to interfere with our progress. Gemayel understood my concerns and departed from my office hopeful that our presence would ease the plight of his people. At this stage of the war he was still very interested in cooperating with and supporting Israel. Unfortunately, later he would change his policy, seriously hindering the success of our actions and securing the Syrian occupation of Lebanon.

Part Six:
THE PEACE FOR GALILEE WAR

29
The Inevitable War

Many things have happened in Lebanon since the Israel Defense Forces first entered in June 1982. Despite these developments, and despite the fact that it must be said without hesitation or denial that the results of the war were, in the last analysis, entirely different from Israel's intentions and objectives, I remain firm in my belief that the war in Lebanon was, from Israel's perspective, absolutely inevitable. It is clear that this war would have been initiated by the Arabs at a later time had we not taken the opportunity to fight the war on our terms and while the advantages were on our side. Their intentions of war were clear from the quantity of weapons being stockpiled by the terrorists, the infrastructure they were building, and the actions they were taking, such as training maneuvers, that were designed to increase their strength. When considering these developments and the terrorists' history of initiating hostilities against us, most often aimed at our civilian population, we had every reason to believe that war was on the horizon. The cease-fire that had been in effect from June 1981 had been appropriately exploited by the terrorists and they had managed not only to restore themselves to what they had been prior to June 1981, but to enhance their power. Their proclaimed goal of destroying Israel and replacing it with a Palestinian State was not abandoned, despite attempts by their leaders to change the means of the struggle to gain international support and place pressure on Israel.

Moreover, we were concerned with the improved status of the PLO in the Arab nations. History has taught us that a strong PLO has managed to pressure and taunt the Arab states into military action against Israel. We understood the danger of the PLO's increased strength and realized that we had to act to diminish it. Also, many other nations had come to view a Palestinian state as a vehicle for peace and as a prerequisite to a resolution to our conflict with the Arabs. Conversely, our history and our experiences with our neighbors has taught us that the fight for a Palestinian State in Judea and Samaria is merely a modality being employed by the Arabs as a means of forcing an Israeli withdrawal. Once we withdraw, needless to say, their claims on the rest of Israel will be voiced and the war will be renewed. The world is used to seeing the Jewish people homeless and persecuted, and it is difficult for many to come to terms with a Jewish State strong and willing to fight for its survival. Yet, we know that no resolution can be achieved until the Arabs show us, through deeds and not words, that they have come to terms with our existence as an independent Jewish State in the Middle East. The only way they will ever come to terms with our presence is if they conclude that they have no military option against us and that they cannot destroy us.

We knew that the terrorists did not have the ability to destroy Israel, but the obligations of the government and the IDF were not limited to the prevention of an attack that would lead to the conquering of Israel. We were also obligated to insure the safety of our population, and the terrorist threat to our northern towns and villages demanded government action. This threat included artillery barrages, raids on transportation, terrorist incursions, and even the temporary capture of civilian outposts. Such a campaign would lead to increased tensions between Israel and the other Arab states that could easily escalate to war. Thus, in determining whether to embark on the Peace for Galilee War, we had to consider the possibility that if we did not strike a death blow to the PLO now, we might be forced to fight a full-fledged war against the combined forces of the terrorist and Arab states, most definitely Syria, and perhaps even Jordan and Iraq, in the not so distant future. Such a war would be dramatically more difficult and cause many more casualties than the war against the terrorists alone would. Therefore, we concluded that the initiation of the war was in our long term-interests. These considerations, and the need to protect our northern settlements led to our determination to enter Lebanon.

The argument by many Israelis who opposed the war that the terrorists would have needed twenty years to inflict on Israel the number of dead and wounded we suffered during the war is not a fair approach to judging the wisdom of our decision. First, with the modern weapons the terrorists were stockpiling, the potential for large scale damage and destruction was very real. Furthermore, if this war in fact prevented another large-scale military conflict with the Arab states, then the number of dead and wounded we suffered was far less than that which we would have suffered in a larger conflict. I do not wish to minimize our losses, and my heart genuinely aches for each soldier who died or was wounded, but war by definition brings casualties, and we cannot judge the wisdom of a war solely on this consideration. Our interests and the security of our nation demanded that we act by sending in our forces to destroy our enemies. We did so with a heavy heart, concerned and saddened by the cost we would have to bear, yet with confidence that it was the best option available.

Furthermore, all members of a nation are obligated to share the burden of national security, and it could not be expected of the residents of Kiryat Shmona, Hanita, Metulla and the other border towns to suffer the effects of a strong PLO by themselves. These residents had spent the summer of 1981 in bomb shelters and had been forced to bear almost daily barrages. Obviously we could not expect them to return to such an unbearable situation.

It should be made clear that Lebanon was not the target of our campaign. In truth, there was a Lebanon only in name, as the civil war, which had erupted in 1976, had all but destroyed any semblance of a unified nation. There was no central government in Lebanon that was capable of protecting its sovereignty or enforcing its laws. The nation was under Syrian occupation in the north and east, and under Palestinian terrorist control in the south.

During the war, immediately after it, and to this day, the war in Lebanon has aroused great opposition in Israel. The war was called a war of choice and criticized as not having been necessary. In addition, because of the opposition, and the debate it caused, the war was also condemned for harming unity. Both of these criticisms were politically motivated, and if examined, are revealed to be foolish and inconsistent.

The argument that the war caused a collapse of national unity is so unfair as to border on the absurd. After all, the same forces who were condemning the war for this reason were the very people causing the lack of unity. Never in Israel's history had citizens campaigned against a war while the war was in progress. The disunity that this caused was the responsibility of those who felt the need to voice their opposition while our boys were still fighting. This opposition had very little to do with the war, or the reasons for the war, but was politically motivated. The leaders of the anti-war movement were the ones responsible for the disunity, and their efforts to place the blame on the political leadership was just a manifestation of their anti-Likud campaign. These same forces condemned the war because it was a war of choice, yet they gave little consideration to the fact that of all Israel's wars, only the War of Independence and the Yom Kippur War were not initiated by Israel. The Sinai War in 1956 and the Six-Day War of 1967 both officially began when Israel attacked and could therefore be interpreted as wars of choice. However, both were preceded by acts of war and military build-ups in Arab states that made it clear to Israel's leaders that war was imminent. Israel is a small nation with an army that is mostly made up of reserve soldiers. We do not have the ability to absorb a concentrated first blow and therefore have adopted as a central component to our defense strategy the notion of pre-emptive strikes. The war in Lebanon was consistent with this strategy. The only difference was that the war was initiated under the leadership of a Likud government and many liberal forces in society chose to oppose it. In reality the Lebanon War was in many ways no different from our other wars. In 1956 we could have avoided attacking Egypt and waited until Nasser completed training his forces on the advanced Soviet weaponry and attacked us. In 1967 we could have refrained from striking the first blow and allowed Nasser to evict United Nations forces from the Sinai and waited for him to attack us. Similarly, in 1982 we could have waited until the terrorists, with Syrian assistance, completed their build-up and resumed their campaign of harassment and destruction. In each instance the definition of the war as a war of choice is absurd when considering the evidence that war was pending and by striking the first blow we assured ourselves an advantage and saved countless lives. The tragedy of 1973 was that we did not strike first, and as a result we lost more than 3,000 men, many more than we would have if we had preempted the Syrian and Egyptian attacks. As the Chief of Staff my obligation was to consider these variables and act as I saw necessary to preserve the national security and minimize casualties.

The truth is that if we had not fought the terrorists and Syrians in June 1982, we would have been forced to fight them at a later date and under conditions that most likely would not have been to our advantage. In fact, the war should have been fought a year earlier, but was postponed after we destroyed the Iraqi nuclear reactor because the government wanted to wait for the political storm to subside.

During the period that the cease-fire was in effect, the terrorists violated the spirit and letter of the agreement on numerous occasions. Each time such an incident occurred the army would present the government with a plan for a retaliatory raid, and each time the government refused to respond because no deaths had been caused by the violation. Yet during this time the government became increasingly aware of the need for a large-scale assault against the terrorists, so as to neutralize any future threat they would pose. The army never demanded of the government that we be permitted to enter Lebanon, and they arrived at the conclusion that there was a need on their own. The only question was one of timing, and naturally this decision was made by the government. Our task was to present the government with a variety of operational plans they could consider.

When the terrorists tried to assassinate Israel's ambassador to England, Shlomo Argov, the government decided that a response was necessary. Contrary to the claims of some academics, the Argov assassination attempt was not used as an excuse to begin the war. In fact, our response was not designed to serve as the opening blow. We bombed the terrorist bases because the government felt that it was time to explain to the PLO that their interpretation of the cease-fire agreement (that the terrorists were not allowed to strike at Israel from Lebanon but could do so from other fronts and in other countries) was unacceptable and all such acts were to be considered violations of the agreement. What brought the war on was the severe response to our raid, during which the terrorists bombarded northern Israel with great intensity. This bombardment made it clear to our leaders that the terrorists had indeed enhanced their fighting capacity and that there was a pressing need to destroy them before they caused great damage. Thus, on Saturday evening, June 5, 1982, I was joined by some of my senior officers in the Prime Minister's home in Jerusalem as we presented the government with the plan to enter Lebanon. The government authorized the plan, and it should be pointed out that the plan, as presented that evening, included the capture of a segment of the Beirut-Damascus Highway. The battle for this area later became a controversial issue in Israel, as some Cabinet members tried to claim that it represented an expansion of the plans they had authorized. However, the maps we presented that evening clearly had this area marked with arrows, and our intentions were clearly expressed.

It is true that we never presented the cabinet with plans to conquer Beirut. This is not because we were attempting to hide our intentions, but rather because such plans genuinely did not exist. We even explained to the Christians that we would not consider an assault on Beirut and that it was not part of the campaign's objectives. This changed only when the circumstances on the ground changed and it became clear that the only way we would achieve the goal of expelling the PLO was through the capture of Beirut.

The Cabinet was primarily concerned with three issues: the possibility of a confrontation with Syria, the timeframe for the operation, and naturally, a projection of losses for IDF soldiers. We informed them that while our plans did not call for a confrontation with the Syrians, we could not promise that the Syrians would not try to intervene on behalf of the PLO. We advised the Cabinet that any attempt by the Syrians to assist the terrorists or hinder our efforts would be responded to appropriately. The amount of time necessary to complete the operation was estimated at five to six days, but once again we advised the Cabinet that the operation could take longer if the Syrians intervened. Finally, with regard to the number of wounded, I responded that I was unable to give such an estimate as this is impossible to even attempt to calculate. Although this question always came up in deliberations with the cabinet on any IDF operation, I never answered it, as I felt it was an unfair and difficult question. Casualties on a battlefield result from too many unforeseeable elements to be able to predict accurately.

The claims that the fighting ability of the army was hindered by a lack of clarity in the objectives and delays in the Cabinet's approval of certain maneuvers is patently false. The army fought the war well and did not fail in the attainment of the goals in accordance with the timeframe anticipated. The government was placed under tremendous American pressure to agree to a cease-fire after five days of fighting and had they not succumbed to the pressure, we would have reached the Beirut-Damascus Highway on day six, just as I had advised the cabinet prior to the war.

Other accusations concerning the war included the lies that the army had promised not to advance beyond a certain number of kilometers, that the cabinet was either willfully misled or did not understand the pre-war deliberations, and that Sharon, and possibly I, willfully provoked the Syrians into the war, as they too were secretly the targets of the war. The bitterness and politically motivated viciousness that provoked these lies should anger me, but rather than anger, I feel sorrow. At no time did the army present the Cabinet with a maximum number of kilometers we would enter Lebanon. We advised the Cabinet that a minimum of forty kilometers would be necessary so as to push the terrorists' artillery out of range of Israel's border, but we never indicated that once that was accomplished we would cease our advance. It was clear that the goal of the war was to destroy the terrorists, not merely push them back temporarily. Furthermore, although the cabinet session on the war plans was tense, the ministers had every opportunity to question the plan and received answers to each of their questions. To assume that they were misled is to call them naive. To assume that they did not understand is to call them stupid. They were neither. They questioned, they got answers, and they understood. Finally, neither Sharon nor I had any pre-conceived plan to intentionally draw the Syrians into the conflict. Fighting the Syrians did little to enhance the attainment of our objective of destroying the PLO and required a diversion of resources from the PLO to the Syrians. We did all we could to avoid a conflict with the Syrians. Yet, this too is an example of the inflammatory falsehoods that the forces of disunity spread during the war.

The confrontation with the Syrians started on the first day of the war, as the Syrians attempted to protect the terrorists by flying above their positions. Our Air Force, still under threat from the Syrian missile batteries, confronted the planes and downed them. We did not view this Syrian provocation as a cause to expand the war and refrained from attacking them on the ground. During the second

day of fighting the Syrians directed artillery barrages at our positions, yet we again refrained from broadening the scope of the
conflict. We considered the possibility that these limited Syrian
gestures might be an attempt on their part to fulfill their pan-Arab
duties and avoid accusations later that they stood idly by while we
destroyed the PLO.

However, on the third day of the war our considerations were
proven wrong as it became evident that the Syrians were determined
to confront our forces and prevent our reaching the Beirut-Damascus Highway. As our forces moved northward on the mountain ridge
with the aim of reaching the highway, we received information that
a Syrian tank force was advancing toward the town of Jezzine, which
was strategically located at the axis of our advance. Our force
continued up from the Beka'a Valley, past Lake Qar'oun and settled
on the approach to Jezzine. Meanwhile, I called Minister of Defense
Sharon, appraised him of the situation and requested permission to
order an Air Force strike against the Syrian force. Sharon agreed
with me that the prospect of a Syrian force in Jezzine was not in our
interests, and authorized the air raids. While our planes attacked the
Syrian convoys, some of our armored forces were dispatched to
Jezzine to confront any Syrian tanks that might succeed in getting
away from our planes. In the end Syrian T-62 tanks did reach
Jezzine, but were destroyed by our tanks in the first armored battle
of the war between Israeli and Syrian forces.

That evening the General Staff and the Minister of Defense met
to consider the implications of the Syrian actions. We realized that
we had to consider the Syrian decision to intervene in all future
actions, and that this in turn meant that we would have to destroy
the missile sites they set up in the Beka'a, as they severely restricted
the movement of our planes. Although Sharon wanted the missiles
attacked immediately, I advised caution and reminded everyone
present that the destruction of the missile sites was a very dangerous
and precise operation.

The Minister of Defense returned to Jerusalem and received
authorization to attack the missiles on Wednesday, the third day of

the war, at two o'clock. The Air Force prepared itself for Operation Drugstore and performed its mission with dazzling precision. Not one of our planes received so much as a scratch and all the Syrian missile sites were completely destroyed. Once we achieved this, the Syrians began to work for a cease-fire. As has happened in all our other wars with the Arabs, as soon as we begin to achieve the upper hand, the Arabs call for a cease-fire and the Americans in effect impose one upon us. Thus, we are never really able to deal the Arabs the final blow, the defeat that might in fact convince them that war with us is not in their interests. The cease-fire was set for Friday, and we spent the rest of our time mopping up pockets of terrorists and securing control over the whole coastal strip.

At the time the cease-fire took effect, the Israeli Army was very close to the Beirut-Damascus highway in two separate locations: in Dar-al-Baydr on the ridge facing the Beka'a, and in the eastern suburbs of Beirut. With these positions in mind we made it clear to the Syrians through the media that we would maintain the cease-fire as long as they did, but that we would not feel restricted to responding to their violations under terms they dictated. In other words, in a departure from the past, we were telling the Syrians that we would not be drawn into a war of attrition with them and that if they broke the cease-fire we would choose the time, place, and magnitude of our response. In fact, if they fired at us, we would reserve the right to view the cease-fire as null and void and proceed to capture the positions on the highway we were so close to. We would choose our response based on our interests and our strategic judgments.

Despite all our public warnings, the Syrians violated the cease-fire and we, true to our word, responded by taking a portion of the Beirut-Damascus Highway. The violation was actually perpetrated by terrorists and not Syrian soldiers, but this was irrelevant as the Syrians were responsible for maintaining the peace on their side of the line. Were we not to hold them to this obligation they could easily have begun to employ the terrorists as their proxy and strike out at us with relative impunity. The violation occurred on the Mansouriyya-Bhamdoun-Aley-Dar-al-Baydr axis, which leads to the Beirut-Damascus Highway. The cease-fire line was Wadi Sakha and the attack occurred as an Armored Personnel Carrier of ours was attacked by a missile while on patrol. After the attack, I received permission from Sharon to take a segment of the highway and our forces advanced along the axis until we arrived at the highway. This action later proved decisive, as our presence on the highway convinced both the terrorists in Beirut and the Syrians of the severity of their situation and convinced them to capitulate to some of our demands.

In East Beirut, we linked up with the Christians and West Beirut was surrounded from every direction. This fact, together with the massive bombardments of chosen terrorist targets in West Beirut, finally caused the surrender of the Syrians and brought about the terrorists' evacuation of the city.

30

"Don't Hit Civilians"

Although the world press and certain groups in Israel that were against the war condemned Israel for the siege of Beirut and the air raids we conducted as a means of keeping the pressure on the Palestinians, I must state without any doubt that their accusations that we were bombing civilian targets were totally false and without any basis in fact. Simply stated, no nation at war, in the history of the world, ever took more care to avoid civilian casualties than Israel did during the war in Lebanon. There were many times that we had accurate information with regard to the location of the terrorist leaders, but did not bomb the site because the terrorists had intentionally placed themselves among civilians. Our bombing raids were exact, surgical strikes that delivered their payloads on the precise target, most often without causing any damage to any of the surrounding structures. We took these precautions to save civilian lives and always acted in accordance with our concept of purity in arms. We did so even though we knew that if the circumstances had been reversed the Arabs would have been bombing us indiscriminately. Yet despite our efforts, there were those in Israel, and outside, who maintained that Israel was intentionally targeting civilians. The fact that they had no proof to support these slanderous claims did not stop them from pronouncing them, nor did it prevent many from believing them. Yet, I know that I issued orders that clearly required the strict adherence to our concept of purity in arms, and I know that my soldiers and pilots would have held to this concept, even if I had not ordered them to do so.

The ability of our pilots to score exact hits on targets was astounding. Using aerial photographs and intelligence reports to identify terrorist facilities, we would also determine the identity of surrounding buildings. Almost always, these buildings were hospitals, schools and other such civilian facilities. The terrorists intentionally located themselves around such institutions because they knew that we would do all we could to avoid harming civilians. In an effort to review operational procedure for myself, I accompanied a bombing raid and served as a navigator on a Phantom jet. I was truly amazed to watch with great pride as the pilots used the intelligence data and state of the art equipment on the plane to score direct hits. None of the buildings on either side of the target were damaged, and the target was completely destroyed.

In addition to the lie that we were intentionally targeting civilians, there were many other lies that were eagerly accepted and reported by the international press. One of these lies had to do with the number of casualties, as the terrorists often inflated the number of injured in a particular area to beyond the actual number of residents. Another fabrication was that Sharon and I had plans to enter West Beirut even before the murder of Bashir Gemayel. The IDF entered Beirut only because we feared that the death of Gemayel would lead to a collapse of the already fragile social order. Were chaos to break out, we would in effect lose all we had gained up to that point. Under these conditions, we determined it was necessary and in our interests to enter West Beirut. While Gemayel was alive we had no reason to even consider entering Beirut. The Christians were in control of the area, and we had already been disappointed with their performance, as they had not kept their promises or lived up to our expectations. We felt no reason to assist them any more than we already had. Furthermore, when Gemayel was elected President he had voiced his commitment to removing the buildings the terrorists had built, so we had no interest in entering West Beirut.

In my last conversation with President Gemayel, he vowed that Lebanon was going to sign a formal peace treaty with Israel. He remarked that the Lebanese people had suffered greatly at the hands of the Arabs and had to look for alliances outside of the Arab world. In this regard, he stated, our two states were natural allies, Israel and Christian Lebanon. Gemayel continued to compare my country and his, declaring that both states shared a common enemy, were surrounded, and leaned toward the west. Thus, when he was murdered, many of Israel's interests were placed in great jeopardy.

The murder of Gemayel came after the terrorists had already agreed to evacuate West Beirut, and had in fact officially left the country. However, we knew that they had not honored many important clauses of the evacuation agreement. The chaos that promised to follow Gemayel's death would provide the terrorists with an opportunity to re-establish themselves in the area. Many terrorists had managed to stay in the country by posing as civilians, and, in defiance of the agreement, the terrorists had hidden weapons throughout the city. Although we were aware of these violations, we did not intend to act against them because they did not pose any great danger. We saw the violations as a Christian problem and an issue the Lebanese army would have to deal with. Again, however, once Gemayel was assassinated, we recognized that this new development posed a threat to our objectives.

On September 17, 1982, the night of the assassination of Gemayel, the Prime Minister and Minister of Defense, after consulting with me, decided not to leave a power vacuum in Beirut and ordered the IDF to enter the city. The Cabinet gave its consent at seven o'clock that evening. The operation to take and control the city was one of the most comprehensive operations ever performed by the IDF. Within twenty-four hours our troops were in control of the city, at a cost of eight men dead. Once in the city we discovered huge caches of weapons hidden by the terrorists in warehouses and residential buildings. Many of the arms depots were positioned on the lower floors of residential buildings so as to discourage our attacks. The terrorists knew that we would not risk harming the civilians in the building in order to destroy their weapons supply.

The role of the Christians during the war has been another point of controversy. Many believe that the Christians did not join the fighting, but rather waited on the sidelines until Israel had handed them a victory. Although in many ways this is true, it is so due to decisions on our part not to include the Christians in our plans. We were not confident of their fighting ability and hesitated to share our plans with them for fear that they had been infiltrated by Syrian or PLO informants. Also, we feared that any prior knowledge of our plans might lead to their taking dangerous actions against their enemies, as they knew we would soon enter the country and rescue them, if need be.

During the war there were various forms of cooperation with the Christians, as was required by the development of events on the ground. In coordination with us, the Christians secured locations that had been taken by the IDF, cared for the population and set up control barriers. They performed these tasks well, and their familiarity with the conditions in Lebanon, and with the population, proved helpful to us.

However, at various stages of the war the Christians did not fulfill our expectations. There were many times we felt they could do more to advance their own interests and share the burden of the war, and despite the fact that we urged them to act, they refrained from taking concrete action. Many of our soldiers became bitter over this, as it seemed to them that the Christians were interested in benefiting from the labors of Jewish blood, without making the same sacrifices.

Yet another point of debate was the number of casualties we suffered. Often those who felt that our casualty count was too high were basing their analysis on their prejudice that the war was not a worthy endeavor. Others had the more legitimate point that some soldiers died as a result of error and a lack of coordinated leadership. This is to a certain extent true, but it is true of every war that was ever fought. Planes sometimes bomb their own forces, infantrymen fire on their other infantry units; and artillery barrages are fought between forces of the same side. These errors are cataclysmic, and all is done in attempts to prevent them, but, under the pressure of war, mistakes will be made. These deaths and all casualties of war are an unfortunate and sad occurrence. I have stood by the graves of our fallen many time and watched as the mothers, wives, sisters, and daughters mourn their loved ones. My heart aches with pain that is overbearing. And yet, I know that these young men's lives were bravely given in the pursuit of security, and that if we wish to remain free, we must never shy away from paying this awesome and tragic price.

Another issue that must be addressed is the internal debate within Israel concerning the validity and wisdom of the war. I do not agree with some politicians who claimed that the internal debate led to the deaths of more IDF soldiers, but I am convinced that it did add to the determination of the terrorists to withstand our pressure. The terrorist forces in Lebanon gained strength from the debate in Israel and also believed that we were being weakened by it. Thus, they adopted a more militant, defiant position than they might have had the country been solidly behind the government's effort. Luckily, because the democratic system of government was foreign to them, the terrorists misread the internal controversy, and we were able to pressure them into agreeing to evacuate.

As for the media, I do not agree with those who claim that the Israeli press were intentionally involved with aiding or supporting the enemy. I do, however, feel that the press in Israel acted as if it was a neutral force, devoid of any national involvement or responsibility. They did not conduct themselves as a loyal institution of a country at war. I do not think they behaved appropriately and I think there are many lessons to be learned with regard to the method and content of the reporting. During the war the idea of declaring the war area a closed military zone was discussed, but ultimately we rejected the notion, as we felt it was a violation of the concept of a free press. Similarly, the military censor allowed many controversial and negative articles and news reports to pass over his desk, again in an effort to preserve freedom of the press. Yet, in spite of our fairness, we were not accorded the same, and were often the targets of inaccurate and vicious reports. Many of the reports on the war were not guided by the journalists' or editors' sense of national responsibility, but rather by a desire to show the world how free a society we had, and how powerful the press could be. Also, the rush to be the first with a big news story often led to the publication of inaccuracies, which were then picked up by newspapers throughout the world. The gravest example of this was the report that Israel had destroyed 40,000 houses in Lebanon and thus created over 600,000 refugees. Despite the fact that there was no truth behind this report, millions of people around the world were soon reading of this evil deed and believing it was true. The fact that it was first reported by an Israeli newspaper was promoted and offered as proof of the report's validity and truth.

Another great exaggeration occurred when the Israel Air Force engaged in a full day of intensive bombing of terrorist targets in West Beirut. Our policy was to increase the pressure on the terrorists and convince them that they had no option other than to accept our demands to evacuate. The bombing raids that day were indeed intense, but the orders to avoid civilian targets were still in effect. Yet, the Israeli media heaped an incredible barrage of criticism on the government for the action. They described our raids as having caused great damage to schools and hospitals and as having caused thousands of civilian casualties. The American media, and other foreign reporters, picked up the criticism and brought the false reports into the homes of millions of people worldwide.

As a direct result of this negative press, the American government, and other Western governments, began to place a great deal of pressure on the Israeli government. Sensing that Israel's hands were tied, the terrorists began to make counter-demands to our requirement that they evacuate. Had the press not been so critical, and had they been more concerned with the accuracy of their reports instead of whether or not they got the story in before their competitors, the government of Israel might not have been placed under such intense pressure, and the terrorists might not have had the opportunity to extract a price from Israel in exchange for their evacuation.

Our commitment not to harm civilians is aptly illustrated by the fact that, although we had the intelligence data and the opportunity, we did not kill Yasser Arafat. To be sure, Arafat was a definite target, and we would have achieved a great deal if we could have succeeded in neutralizing him, but he understood the restrictions we had imposed on ourselves and situated himself among civilians at all times. Ironically, Arafat understood our commitment not to harm civilians better than many Israelis did.

We also had the opportunity to eliminate Arafat while he was boarding the boat that was evacuating him from Beirut. Although he was clearly within firing distance, and in the scope of our sniper's rifle, I did not order him to fire because we had agreed to allow them to leave safely. I knew that Arafat would not have honored the agreement if the roles were reversed, nor would he have allowed the ships to sail away peacefully instead of sinking them. Still, we kept the agreement, not for him, but for ourselves.

31

War Diary

A war diary is something I have never kept, and I have always been impressed by those who did. I was never able to understand how they managed to find those few moments each night to write down the events of the day. I was always either too busy, or too tired. I always relied on my memory, and for the purpose of this chapter, I will rely on some documents as well. I am not a historian and do not claim to present the facts in a disinterested fashion. I was part of everything I am writing about, and naturally my personal views have contributed to the way I see things.

On Friday, June 4, 1982, two days before the war started, we received authorization from the government to attack eleven separate terrorist targets, two of which were the terrorists' headquarters near Beirut, in retaliation for the attempted assassination of our ambassador to England, Shlomo Argov. Although we did not have the authorization to send ground forces into Lebanon, we had to consider what our reaction would be if the terrorists responded to our raids by attacking our northern villages. It was decided that under those circumstances we would indeed respond with a ground assault. Initially, if it was deemed necessary, the assault was scheduled for Tuesday, and the standing army was assigned the task of stifling the terrorist guns. The reserve units were only to be called in as they were needed. As Chief of Staff I was authorized to order a call up of the reserves, but chose to request the government's authorization for each call up I ordered. It was essential that we conceal the mobilization of our reserves, and I wanted the government to be aware of all the units I was calling up. In addition, I had to consider the possibility that a ground assault on our part would spark a Syrian assault on the Golan Heights. They might view our activity in Lebanon as a sufficient diversion of our attention and resources and attempt to seize the opportunity, or they might choose to attack the Golan as a means of damaging our war effort. In any case, it was my responsibility to ensure the security of the State and I dispatched some additional reserve units to the Golan Heights as well.

Some of the attacks scheduled for Friday were postponed until Saturday due to weather conditions, and that evening the Cabinet met to decide on whether or not additional steps would be taken, and what they would be.

The terrorist response was quite intense. Over the course of less than one day more than 270 Katyusha rockets were fired on our northern towns and villages. Under such an assault, I recommended that the IDF suspend all retaliatory action until after the government decided on a ground assault. I was of the opinion that it was not in our interests to enter into another war of attrition with the terrorists. We had only one means of quieting the terrorist guns, and that was through a ground assault. If the government was not willing to authorize this action then it was pointless to continue with our air raids.

As the terrorists resumed their bombardment on Saturday afternoon, it became evident that the government was strongly considering a ground assault. I was concerned about the possible time frame of the assault, because the American mediator, Philip Habib, was due for a visit in the middle of the next week. From past experience, I knew that there was an excellent possibility that he would try to stop the fighting, and therefore, it was extremely important that we achieve our objectives quickly. In an effort to save time, and in anticipation of governmental authorization, I moved some tanks into the area of Southern Lebanon controlled by Major Haddad and had them camouflaged.

As the artillery barrage on our northern area intensified, I informed the Prime Minister that I had reconsidered my position and requested authorization for renewed air strikes. We resumed our strikes late Saturday afternoon.

In anticipation of governmental authorization, the army prepared to enter Lebanon at twelve noon on Sunday, June 6, 1982. The plan called for our forces to avoid contact with the Syrians in the east, but to reach the Hasbaya-Kawkaba line, which was approximately two and a half miles south of the Syrian's southernmost position. Reaching this area would effectively place our towns of Kiryat Shemona and Metulla out of range of the terrorists' artillery.

Our plan focused on the coastal road, which had a high concentration of terrorist forces. We debated landing forces by sea along the Zaharani and Awali rivers, but I decided to wait and see how far our ground forces got before making a determination. The plan did not speak in terms of kilometers or distances, but included reaching the Beirut-Damascus Highway, linking up with the Christians, closing off Beirut from all areas and destroying the terrorist infrastructure in Southern Lebanon.

In an effort to quell any fears the Syrians might have with regard to our intentions, I instructed the tanks I was sending to the Golan Heights to begin traveling there only after we had entered Lebanon. Furthermore, I advised the Prime Minister to make an announcement upon our entry into Lebanon declaring that we were pursuing the terrorists in Lebanon and did not have any intentions to attack the Syrians.

At the cabinet session that evening we presented the plan and answered all questions. I advised the Cabinet ministers that we could expect the terrorists to resist our ground assault and that most likely they would engage in guerrilla warfare, and hit-and-run assaults. Both, I cautioned, would claim their share of casualties among our men. In response to a question, I estimated that the Syrians would probably make attempts at aerial and artillery intervention during the beginning stages of the war in an effort to fulfill their commitment to their Arab brothers, and would then retreat to a defensive position in the Beka'a Valley and on Mount Lebanon. I did not think the Syrians would court a conflict with us; however, I did expect them to defend their positions in Lebanon. I also advised the cabinet of the possibility that we might, at some point during the conflict, be obligated to destroy the ground-to-air missiles the Syrians had placed in the Beka'a. After hearing our explanations and appraisals, the cabinet authorized our plan and called for us to begin the assault at eleven o'clock in the morning on Sunday, June 6th.

The last Katyusha rocket was fired by the terrorists at 3:40 on Sunday morning. The 180 millimeter cannons the terrorists were using were also of concern to us, because if shot from the Tyre area they had the potential of reaching the Haifa Bay region. We therefore had the destruction of these guns as one of our immediate priorities, to be achieved during the first stages of the war.

On Sunday morning the Minister of Defense joined the command staff and reviewed every minute detail of the operation. I reminded the officers that the authorization for the operation was only up to the Beka'a Awali line and that any further advance would need the government's approval. I reviewed the need for speed and the importance of keeping all roads open for the transportation of men and supplies. Furthermore, it was of the utmost importance that we capture "the iron triangle," the area south of the Litani River where the terrorists had their strongest concentration of force, during the first day of the fighting.

I also told my officers that the UNIFIL forces were to be treated courteously and with respect. They were not the enemies. Furthermore, I instructed them to take special care not to harm civilians or damage their infrastructure. In addition to the humane reasons behind this order, I did not know how long we would be controlling these areas and did not wish to damage an infrastructure we would then be responsible for rebuilding. I also took the opportunity to again remind the officers that the Syrians were not our targets, and that if their intervention required our response, it was best that it happen after we had consolidated our gains against the terrorists.

A half an hour before our troops crossed the border I invited General Callahan, the UNIFIL commander to the headquarters of the Northern Command for a brief meeting. General Callahan came with some of his top commanders and I too had some of my top officers present. I notified the General of our plans and he protested vigorously. I informed him that I did not invite him to our headquarters to receive his blessing, rather I was requesting that he instruct his troops not to confront our forces. Any attempt to clash with Israeli soldiers would be responded to in kind, and that would cause unnecessary bloodshed. We placed a telephone at his disposal and he called his command post and issued the proper orders.

I believe that the original protest expressed by the general was for the benefit of the others present, for after he had called his forces he asked that he and I be left alone for a few moments. Once alone he informed me that his forces would not get in our way and he wished us success in our operation. Unfortunately, as the war progressed, perhaps due to political pressures, Callahan made numerous anti-Israel comments to the press. When he published an open letter to me criticizing the war, I responded by revealing his kind words of support prior to the outbreak of the war.

Once the campaign began I joined the forces in the field, and after a careful examination of our advance, I ordered a night landing at the Alawi River. I wanted to land a large force behind the terrorists so as to isolate and surround them.

Our war effort proceeded according to the plan. On the central axis our forces passed the French and Nigerians attached to UNIFIL and crossed the Litani River over the Aqaya Bridge. On the east and west axes our forces advanced in accordance with the plan and reached the limits of what the government had initially approved. We submitted a proposal to the government to begin deliberations on the next stage of the war, so that we could continue our advance.

The Prime Minister was stationed at the Northern Command headquarters and was updated on the progress of the campaign. He decided to postpone any announcement concerning the war so as not to give the terrorists an idea of our objectives. As early as 1:00 o'clock on Sunday afternoon the American military attaché contacted the foreign relations officer of the General Staff and informed him that the United States was aware of the fact that we were operating on two axes. We informed the attaché that we were acting only against the terrorists and had no intention of initiating hostilities with the Syrians. In fact, according to our government's instructions, we were authorized to attack the Syrians, as they had already fired artillery at our forces.

That evening Sharon returned from a cabinet meeting and informed us that the government had approved the second stage of the campaign and that we were to advance to the Beirut-Damascus highway. Sharon also told us that the Americans were not yet applying any pressure and that Philip Habib would be arriving in Israel to meet with Prime Minister Begin the next day, Monday. We understood that we had very little time before the pressure started to mount and the nations of the world tried to deprive us of our hard fought victory.

32

Racing for the Beirut-Damascus Highway

By midday Monday, the second day of the fighting, we had four primary strategic areas we had not completely captured. Of these, the Tyre axis and the Rashidiyya area were almost totally under control, and the Iron Triangle and Nabatiyya were being advanced upon. A fifth objective, the Beaufort Castle, was an ancient structure situated on a strategic hillside. The terrorists had transformed the building into a fortified complex, and we had attacked it at dawn Monday morning. It was in our hands after a long and courageous battle.

At this stage of the war one of our key objectives was reaching the Beirut-Damascus Highway and linking up with the Christian forces. The plan that had been authorized by the government called for our forces to approach the highway from the Syrian's rear and take over the portion of highway near Dar al-Baydr. On Monday we had a full division advancing along the mountain ridge with the projection that they would reach the highway by Tuesday morning. Our only fear was that the Syrians, who had up until then confined themselves to fulfilling their pan-Arab duty by firing some inconsequential artillery at us, would take some action designed to slow or prevent our advance. Our forces on the mountain ridge were exposed to possible Syrian air strikes, and we considered destroying the Syrian anti-aircraft batteries, so that our planes would be able to respond should the Syrians introduce their air force. In the end, we decided not to act until the Syrians gave a clearer indication of their intentions. We also considered the option of moving our forces and approaching the highway from the west. Again, however, we postponed our decision until we had an idea of what to expect from the Syrians.

On Monday evening, at a meeting between the General Staff and the Minister of Defense, we received information that the Syrians were preparing to intervene on a large scale. We realized that there would be a need for us to divert important forces from their tasks of fighting and destroying the terrorists, so that we could appropriately respond to the Syrian offensive. Moreover, we realized that we had to consolidate our gains, because once we started to rout the Syrians, there would almost certainly be a cease-fire imposed on us.

By seven o'clock Tuesday morning we had information that indicated that the Syrians had moved an armored brigade to the Syrian-Lebanese border in the Jedeydat-Yebus region. Another Syrian brigade was centered in the Lake Kar'oun area. It appeared that the Syrian deployments were defensive in nature, but as a precaution, I continued to delay the advance of our forces on the mountain ridge.

Meanwhile, in an effort to consolidate our gains, the coastal axis, which was firmly under our control, was being mopped up of all terrorist forces that had not fled or been killed or captured. We dropped fliers in Nabatiyya, Sidon and Tyre appealing to the terrorists to surrender and followed with troops sent in to mop up the area. We also strengthened our hold over the Iron Triangle.

I sent a telegram to Bashir Gemayel that included an extremely general description of our troop positions and requested that he consider sending Druze, Christians, or Shiites to the Shouf mountains in the north in order to gather some data as to the status and intentions of the militia there. At the same time, Sharon advised me that a United Nations resolution calling for a cease-fire would be introduced the next day, but he did not feel Israel would be under great political pressure to agree. The American Secretary of State, Alexander Haig, was, according to Sharon, positive with regard to our aims.

Our troops stationed on the mountain ridge advised us that any efforts to advance on their part would most likely result in an encounter with Syrian forces. Their fear was that the Syrians would position their troops along a narrow bridge called Jab'a, and that they would resist any attempt by us to advance beyond that point. Sharon did not agree with this analysis and argued that although the Syrians would have to fight in the Beka'a because the area was vital for them, Jab'a did not have a similar importance. We knew we would have to take Jab'a because it was of strategic importance to our mission. However, the question was whether or not it required a confrontation with the Syrians.

Until our report concerning possible Syrian movement in Jab'a, we had understood the Syrians' behavior as telling us that we were free to confront the terrorists, as long as we maintained our distance from Syrian positions. We understood that Syria's President Assad was under great pressure from the terrorists and other Arab nations to intervene, and we were willing to accept small gestures of pan-Arab unity. As long as the Syrian posture was defensive we would refrain from attacking.

Our primary concern vis-à-vis the Syrians were the anti-aircraft missiles Assad had brought into Lebanon's Beka'a Valley in June 1981. Part of our plan called for removing the terrorist threat from the southern Beka'a and the Syrian missiles posed a great danger to our aircraft and freedom of movement in the area. On the other hand, any attempt on our part to destroy the missiles would almost definitely result in an active Syrian involvement in the war, as they would interpret our strike as a signal that we were challenging Syria's presence in Lebanon.

Our mission, as authorized by the Cabinet and as explained to the United States, United Nations, and other world powers, was strictly to remove the terrorist threat from our northern border. We planned to achieve this by destroying the terrorists and their infrastructure, and pushing their forces away from Israel, beyond the range of their weaponry. We had announced our intentions to avoid a confrontation with Syria. Yet, as the third day of the war progressed, it appeared that the Syrians had decided that they would not tolerate our presence in the southern Beka'a.

In considering how to approach the Syrians, it was felt that a deep flanking movement would be most effective. Sharon had instructed us to prepare to push back any Syrian presence at Jab'a, as was authorized by the Cabinet session the night before.

The war had its lighter moments, such as the time Prime Minister Begin requested that he be taken into Lebanon to review the situation first hand. Both Sharon and I were uncomfortable placing the Prime Minister in danger and attempted to persuade him that this was not a good idea. We expressed our concerns regarding the danger, to which Begin replied "If you're worried about the helicopter, I understand. If you're worried about me, I have two deputies." When I responded that it was best for his deputies to remain in their present posts, the Prime Minister jokingly asked me if I was interfering with the political arena, an act the Chief of Staff should refrain from committing. In the end, Begin settled for a ride to the Beaufort Castle and a detailed description and analysis of the situation, with special attention being given to the prospect of a conflict with Syria. We visited the castle before we knew that we had lost many men in the battle to conquer it, and still the visit was emotionally powerful.

When we returned from the Beaufort Castle we received reports on the progress of our men in the field. We were notified that an exchange of fire had occurred with the Syrians, after the Syrians had fired artillery at our positions in two separate incidents. In the coastal region we had surrounded Nabatiyya and were not encountering great resistance. Many terrorist forces were beginning to surrender in Tyre as well. We had only two major concerns, apart from the Syrians. First, Irish troops attached to the UNIFIL force had blocked the roads leading into the Iron Triangle with stones. Although they did not attempt to prevent our forces from removing the barriers, their action cost us valuable time and was inappropriate. Secondly, the terrorists had informed the Red Cross in Tyre that they had captured an Israeli soldier and were holding him as a prisoner of war. We were not able to identify who this soldier might be.

In an effort to avoid a clash with the Syrians, we had decided to reach the Beirut-Damascus Highway via the coastal road. Such a maneuver would distance our forces from the Syrians and also reduce our need to contend with the Syrian anti-aircraft missiles. Furthermore, we realized that we would be able to control the highway and the entrances to Beirut by capturing the Damur-Khaldeh-Aley axis. The only danger left would be our need to reach Jab'a and the possibility that the Syrians would initiate hostilities.

By Tuesday, June 8th, it became clear that we would have to deal with the Syrian presence in the Beka'a if we were to successfully push all hostile forces twenty-five miles away from our northern border. It was clear to us that the Syrians would not voluntarily retreat, nor would they demand the departure of the thousands of terrorists who had taken refuge in the Syrian-controlled territories. Keeping in mind that confronting the Syrians would require the destruction of their missile sites, and that we did not have government authorization to do that, we designed a plan to advance on the ridge, hoping that the Syrians would pull back to south of Lake Kar'oun to avoid being outflanked.

However, the Syrians chose a more aggressive path. They decided to try to block our route at Jezzine, which would have limited our freedom of movement in the north and west of Lebanon. They accompanied this act with a renewed burst of artillery fire. It became clear that we were going to have to confront the advancing Syrian force. We made our needs and recommendations known to the government and received authorization to attack the Syrians. This authorization did not include permission to destroy the anti-aircraft missile batteries. We were not even given permission to attack the overall Syrian deployment in the Beka'a. We were simply authorized to attack and repel the Syrian force advancing toward Jezzine.

The need to present almost every aspect of the war for cabinet approval was new to the IDF. Never before had the Cabinet sat in what was in effect a war room, authorizing or rejecting various military operations. All of our requests were presented openly and honestly, and we had all of our needs met by the Cabinet. The only concern was that this procedure caused a prolonging of the war, perhaps by several days.

The war with the Syrians was heating up. On Tuesday the commander of the eastern sector, General Yanush Ben-Gal, complained that his forces were under constant Syrian harassment and requested the right to return fire. Sharon granted Yanush the authority to return fire when fired upon, but he was not allowed to advance in the direction of any Syrian position. Later that day the Syrian Air Force tried to attack our forces in Sidon, but were intercepted by our planes and shot down between El-Meri and Marj Ayoun. A few hours later their Air Force was again called to action as they tried to attack some of our fortified structures. Seven of their planes were shot down and we took three MIG-23 pilots captive.

Meanwhile, our Air Force scored accurate hits on the Syrian tank force advancing toward Jezzine. We later positioned a tank force of our own in Jezzine and confronted and destroyed the Syrian force when it arrived.

I requested permission to mobilize additional reserve units and presented Sharon with a plan to attack the Syrian positions in the Beka'a, should the government decide to authorize such a move. The plan called for an advance along a wide front, which would encompass the Arafat Trail in the east and continue up to the border of the western Beka'a.

Sharon was pressuring the army to secure a portion of the Beirut-Damascus Highway before nightfall, but I remarked that I was not sure this would be accomplished. Our major obstacle was still the Syrian anti-aircraft missiles in the Beka'a. These missiles substantially limited the operational ability of our Air Force, which in turn slowed the momentum of our advance. Although the government was reluctant to authorize the Air Force to destroy the missiles, we knew that it would be extremely difficult to achieve our advance within the desired timeframe without destroying them. We even presented Sharon with a plan to destroy the missiles with artillery fire, although this method was less accurate when compared to the Air Force option.

It soon became clear that a great debate had evolved within the government concerning our actions against the Syrians. The Cabinet had decided that the Syrians would be given the opportunity to return to their previous positions in exchange for a commitment that Israeli forces would not attack. Minister of Defense Sharon was very much against the decision, as he felt it lent legitimacy to the Syrian presence in Lebanon. Sharon had remarked to me the day before this decision that Israel's forces would not leave Lebanon unless Syrian forces evacuated as well. Sharon simply felt that the situation presented an opportunity for Israel to rid itself of the menace and threat that Syria had become in Lebanon. This political debate inside the cabinet attached added significance to each move the army made, as some actions were more likely than others to bring about an aggressive Syrian response. However, since we did not know what the Syrian intentions were, it was important that we continue our advance in the Beka'a, so as to be in a flanking position against the Syrians, should an all out war with them erupt.

When the American emissary, Philip Habib, arrived, we understood that his presence would translate into a delay on action against the missile sites. Habib's visit also gave us the first warning signs that Bashir Gemayel was suffering a change of heart with regard to his previously expressed opinions concerning Lebanon's special relationship with Israel. It seemed that he was enjoying playing the role of "leader" of Lebanon and was beginning to see the benefits of remaining a part of the Arab world. Habib's visit also brought the first rumors that the Americans were considering sending troops to help secure a peaceful settlement. Prime Minister Begin supported an active American role, while Minister of Defense Sharon was against the idea.

By Tuesday evening it became clear that the Syrians were positioning forces so as to encourage a confrontation. They were moving their troops directly in front of our forces and were also bringing in additional anti-aircraft batteries. As a result, our forces advancing along the Dar al-Baydr axis met heavy resistance. These new Syrian maneuvers convinced us that the Syrians would not be pushing for an immediate cease-fire, but would wait to see if they would succeed in pushing our forces back. Furthermore, our fears of an imposed cease-fire were eased when Habib met with Begin and Sharon and did not even mention the issue of a cease-fire.

When we discovered that some of the terrorists' leaders were trying to escape to Cyprus by sea I ordered a blockade off the coast of Lebanon. The terrorists could not travel out of the port of Beirut, as it was under Christian control, but were boarding boats slightly to the north. The blockade was a deterrent method, more than an actual instrument to stop the fleeing terrorists, because we did not have the means of identifying the passengers, and not knowing whether women and children were on a specific boat ruled out the option of firing on any boat that tried to run our blockade.

On Tuesday night a plan was developed to destroy the Syrian missile batteries. Our airplanes were to be ready to move at eleven o'clock the following morning, and Sharon would present the plan, and receive Cabinet approval, earlier the same morning, at nine o'clock. I was not personally in favor of the attack, unless we felt that we had no alternative. I believed our forces advancing in the Beka'a would soon be in a position to destroy the batteries with artillery, and I preferred this option. My concerns were the Syrian reaction, and my belief that the assault on the missile batteries would widen the scope of the war. However, I was also convinced that the missiles had to be destroyed, as the Syrians were already expanding their role in the war, and the missiles were limiting our ability to respond properly. The pressure was intensified by our belief that we had to have our forces on the Beirut-Damascus Highway and north of Lake Kar'oun before any cease-fire was called.

Also delaying our progress was the city of Sidon. The main road through the city was lined with houses and our forces were falling victim to snipers hidden in these structures. It was suggested that we destroy the buildings, but I am not in favor of this type of blanket destruction. I simply stated that it would have to take a little longer to mop up the terrorists in the city, and that we would have to make up for the lost time in other sectors.

As the race to the Beirut-Damascus Highway quickened and the war with the Syrians intensified, we awaited the government decision on our plan to destroy the Syrian missiles. We knew we needed some freedom of action, and requested that the government at least authorize us to attack the batteries that were actively directing fire at our planes. In many senses, the course of the war, and the achievement of all we had fought for, rested on this one governmental decision.

33

Destroying the Syrian Missiles

We received permission to attack the missiles on Wednesday, and planned to execute the attack at three o'clock that afternoon. The task that our brave pilots were undertaking was complex and dangerous. No air force in the world had gone against such missile batteries in so direct a manner. We had taken months to discuss, debate, evaluate, analyze, and review the missile sites, the Syrian defense system, and the technology we had developed to counter the heat-seeking system in the missiles. As the attack unfolded, even the pessimists among us, those who did not believe that such a complex plan could be executed, were confident that our pilots would achieve their mission. Their major fear was the cost that the missiles would exact. When the planes returned, even the optimists among us were surprised and elated at the amazing success of the mission. In all, nineteen missile batteries had been destroyed, and not one of our planes was lost. None of the difficulties that had been foreseen materialized, and our pilots performed with incredible skill.

The destruction of the missiles should have resulted in a Syrian transfer of forces to protect the road to Damascus, since they understood that without the missiles we would be able to rule the skies and advance on their positions. When the Syrians responded to the destruction of the missile sites by maintaining their positions in Lebanon, we understood that they had been promised a cease-fire by either the Soviet Union or the Americans.

The Director of our Intelligence Service suggested that the destruction of the missiles presented the Syrians with two options. One possibility was to evacuate their forces from Lebanon due to the lack of a missile and aerial defense system. The other possibility was to increase the number of Syrian forces in Lebanon and attack us to the south. He informed us that the Syrians showed no signs of bringing additional forces into Lebanon, although it did appear that they had been planning to attack us before we destroyed the missiles. The Syrians were also not showing immediate signs of evacuating, but this, we surmised, was due to their expectation of a cease-fire. Had the cease-fire not been imposed, there is every reason to believe that the Syrians would have had little choice but to evacuate their forces from Lebanon.

In an effort to speed up the Syrian decision to remove their forces from Lebanon, I instructed our forces to intensify the pressure they were applying to the Syrian rear flank. Our hope was that such pressure would either convince Damascus to retreat, or cause the local commander to retreat on his own initiative.

A great deal of concern was raised when the Syrian government issued a report that Israeli planes had bombed Damascus. This simply was not so. None of our planes had crossed the Syrian border or penetrated Syrian air space, even when the Syrians were firing at our planes from missile batteries inside Syria. We were not certain why the Syrians had made this announcement, but thought that either they were trying to apply international pressure on our government, or were preparing themselves for a major offensive against us. In the latter case, such an announcement would be seen as a justification for the attack. In the end, the Syrian did not act, and we later found out that the Syrians had thought we bombed Damascus because a Syrian plane that we had shot down over Lebanon had crashed in Damascus while on the way back to its base.

By Wednesday night the effects of the attack on the missiles was being felt. No longer under the protective shield of the missiles, the terrorists' Katyusha and artillery bases in the Syrian occupied area were destroyed by our airplanes. The Syrians had begun a partial retreat and our forces were inflicting heavy damage to their armored corps. We estimated that by late Thursday morning we would have achieved our objective of pushing all terrorist guns far enough back that their guns could no longer reach our border. As we had predicted, the destruction of the missile sites was the turning point of the war.

With the objectives close at hand, Minister of Defense Sharon praised the IDF. He stated that the army's performance, the planning by the General Staff, the control by the Chief of Staff and the Commander of the Northern Command, and the skill and bravery of all the officers and soldiers, from the commanders of divisions and brigades to the junior commanders and enlisted soldiers, all combined to make this campaign one of the most brilliant operations the IDF had ever carried out. It was not that the Israeli Army had not conducted more difficult operations in the past, but the war in Lebanon encountered not only operational difficulties, but also consisted of a series of complex and complicated operations that required a great deal of sophistication and imagination during the planning stages, and during implementation. The coordination of large scale operations between the army, navy and air force also required a great deal of planning and the ability to communicate clearly and precisely. Moreover, Sharon praised the Air Force and remarked that the exemplary control, incredible accuracy, and precise planning displayed by Israel's pilots would be studied in military academies around the world.

As a consequence of the movement of the Syrian armored brigade in the Beka'a, our planes subjected the force to a series of night raids. We were placing a great deal of pressure on the Syrians in the Beka'a by shelling them from our positions on the mountain ridge and from on top of Mount Baruk. Two hours before the cease-fire took effect on Friday, we encountered and destroyed a unit of T-72 tanks.

One of the problems being caused by our routing of the Syrian tanks was that the roadways were becoming congested with abandoned and destroyed tanks. I instructed our Quartermaster Corps to begin removing damaged vehicles and all other equipment found in the areas under our control. I was concerned that the burdened roadways would restrict our ability to move freely, and I recognized that our freedom of movement was in effect dependent on the discipline of our soldiers and our ability to overcome technical mishaps.

On June 10, Minister of Defense Sharon telephoned Prime Minister Begin to inform him that General Yekutiel "Kuti" Adam had been killed during the day's fighting. The jeep he had been traveling in was struck by an anti-tank weapon fired by terrorist forces. The death of Kuti deeply disturbed all of the General Staff, yet his death also served as a reminder that in Israel the Generals do not remain in the safety to be found behind the lines, but rather are actively involved in the war effort. The Israeli slogan, "after me," was still spoken by every officer in the IDF. The senior commanders, including myself, spent most of our time with the troops in the field, as the soldiers were often a great source of pride and encouragement. At times when it was necessary to gather the various commanders together for a planning session or strategic discussion, many senior officers would request a delay in the meeting so that they could see their forces through a particular situation. The IDF is proud that we have a different mode of conduct in this regard than that which is customary in other armies. Our senior officers pride themselves on being involved in the actual fighting, and I, as Chief of Staff, also spent most of my time shuttling from unit to unit, to review the field and listen to the remarks of my soldiers.

The Syrian First Armored Division was quickly losing its ability to fight as a coherent force. Similarly, the Syrian tank units were in disarray and were not functioning in an organized fashion. We were concerned only that the Syrian Third Armored Division was advancing from Syria toward the Syrian-Lebanese border, but we were not sure what its objectives would be. Our concern was intensified because the advance was being conducted under the protection of anti-aircraft missile sites inside Syria. This fact would limit the use of our air force, unless we decided to attack the batteries inside

Syrian territory.

We decided to wait until the force crossed the Lebanese border, at which time we attacked and destroyed over thirty tanks. That same day the Syrians also lost twenty-eight airplanes, as they tried to intercept our aircraft.

It was clear to me that Sharon had a general idea as to when the cease-fire would be imposed on us. He was concerned about our advance and requested an analysis of where our troops would be by Friday at noon. I gave the Minister of Defense an overview based on the present situation and our estimated advance by noon the next day. I informed him that the force in the Beka'a, commanded by Yanush, could control the Beirut-Damascus axis using the unit that was moving below the mountain ridge in the western part of the Beka'a. The Minister inquired whether all sectors had succeeded in pushing enemy fire at least twenty-five miles from our northern border, to which I proudly replied in the affirmative.

I know now that Sharon had been instructed by the Prime Minister to institute a cease-fire at twelve o'clock and that he was unsure whether Begin meant midnight Thursday or noon Friday. After contacting the Prime Minister he informed me that at noon Friday we were to unilaterally declare a cease-fire. From that moment on we were to continue fighting only if the Syrians did not cease hostilities.

With the cease-fire a little more than twelve hours away, we carefully planned our approach to the Syrian Third Armored Division that was advancing its T-72 tanks into the Beka'a from the north. We decided to try to slow their advance through air strikes and artillery, but we also knew that we were in an excellent position to confront the tanks in the Beka'a. We understood that an artillery battle might risk our failing to reach the Beirut-Damascus highway, but it was clear that this battle was more strategically important. If the Syrians moved their tanks into the Beka'a, they would simply become the focus of all our energies. Although we did not know the operational capabilities of the T-72 tank, we knew we had an excellent chance of catching the Third Division in its side, as one of our units was positioned at the foot of the mountain and another was spread across the Beka'a in the shape of the letter "L." Military leaders everywhere dream of having their enemies walk into the center of an "L" position. We knew this would be a classic tank battle, but we were confident that we enjoyed superiority in the air, superior artillery and tanks, better intelligence, a higher quality of soldier, and excellent strategic positioning.

One of the primary reasons Begin decided to unilaterally declare a cease-fire was that the American Secretary of State, Alexander Haig, would be arriving in Israel the following Sunday. The cease-fire would certainly please him. Furthermore, Philip Habib had notified Begin from Damascus that the Syrians, while not willing to expel the terrorists located in the region under their control, were ready to abide by a cease-fire. We were not concerned about the terrorists in the Syrian sector, as we knew we would be expelling them during the upcoming tank battle. The cease-fire also did not concern us, as the government had already decided that we would not allow the Syrians to rebuild their ground-to-air defenses during the lull in the fighting. They simply would not be permitted to install new anti-aircraft missile batteries.

The battle with the Syrian Third Division began at approximately two o'clock Friday morning. Our forward tank unit confronted the spearhead tanks of the Syrian unit, and our air force continued to harass and inflict heavy damage. The Syrian unit that intended to reach the road leading to the Beka'a was totally destroyed by our planes.

The fighting ability of the Syrian brigade in Beirut was crumbling and its commanders had lost control over their units. Still, on Friday morning we were informed that one of our units had strayed from its route, by advancing one intersection more than was planned, and had walked into a Syrian defensive position at Sultan Ya'akub. Although we suffered some losses, the Commander of the Northern Command informed me that the battalion had successfully been rescued from their potentially dangerous situation.

Our planes were being confined by the Syrian missile batteries located along the Syrian-Lebanese border. We had destroyed seven batteries earlier in the war that resulted in a controversy as the Syrians claimed they had been situated in Syrian territory. We argued that they were in fact exactly on the border, and therefore subject to attack. We wanted to refrain from hitting targets in Syria because that would indicate a widening of the theater of war, and we were not interested in providing the Syrians with an excuse to attack Israeli territory. Still, I made the distinction between Syrian territory in general, and Syrian territory that was being used to fire missiles at our planes. I therefore instructed the commander of the air force to continue the attacks on the Syrian Third Division and, if missiles were fired at our planes, to destroy the missile batteries, including those firing at us from within Syrian territory. However, I did not authorize the air force to attack Syrian tanks advancing toward Lebanon from Syrian territory, These tanks could only be attacked once they crossed the Lebanese border.

Early Friday we were also informed by our intelligence service that the terrorists' headquarters in Beirut was still active, although we had bombed the area repeatedly. Convinced that the destruction of their headquarters would strike a great blow at the terrorists' operations, Sharon instructed me to order additional air force strikes against the terrorists.

The Israeli government announced that a cease-fire would be placed into effect on Friday, June 11, at 12 o'clock noon. The government informed the Americans that the cease-fire include all aspects of the hostilities except any Syrian attempt to replace the missile batteries that had been destroyed during the active fighting. The Americans were clearly notified that any such attempt would be considered a violation of the cease-fire agreement and Israel would feel at liberty to once again destroy the missiles. The Americans expressed an interest in separating our forces from the Syrians. As this had been done in previous wars, and always to our disadvantage, we resisted. We explained to the Americans that the Syrians could maintain or violate the cease-fire from any deployment, and that we preferred to hold on to our present positions.

Although this went against their wishes, the Americans understood that Begin and Sharon were firmly set in this position. We simply wanted to guarantee ourselves the benefits our actions during the war would afford us, should the Syrians break the cease-fire.

34

Cease-Fire

At the moment the cease-fire took effect we were in the process of destroying the Syrian T-72 tanks. Our troops were also situated north of Lake Kar'oun, about eight miles away from the Beirut-Damascus highway. In the west, our forces had reached the area around the Beirut airport, in the region of Khaldeh. My estimate was that the cease-fire could last as long as a week, although I expected the Syrians to fire on us daily, risking a collapse of the cease-fire at any time.

The battles with the Syrians were encouraging in that they proved to us that the Merkeva tank, an Israeli produced weapon, was capable of going against, and beating, the Soviet made T-72 tank. With this in mind, we developed a plan to capture a segment of the highway and link up with the Christians, should the cease-fire be broken.

Many of the senior officers in the General Staff believed that our positions at the start of the cease-fire invited the Syrians to engage us in a protracted war of attrition. I believed that the Syrians would maintain the quiet for a short period of time, so as to re-organize their forces in the Beka'a. I did, however, anticipate sniper fire and mining, and suspected that the Syrians would point an accusatory finger at the terrorists still in the area. I informed my officers that we would not tolerate a war of attrition, nor would we allow the Syrians to hide behind the terrorists. Any violation, both big and small, was to be responded to with overwhelming force.

The Syrian forces in the Beka'a were in complete disarray, and as soon as the cease-fire was in effect we received a report that a

Syrian convoy was advancing from Zahleh toward the south. As we
had suspected, the Syrians were planning to use the cease-fire to
improve their standing against us. We understood that they would
do this, and had no plans to intervene, unless they tried to install
new missile batteries.

Throughout Lebanon the terrorists had declared that they
would not recognize or honor the cease-fire agreement. We decided
to take advantage of their foolishness and continue our efforts
against them. In the west we decided to continue our advance until
we reached Aley. In doing so we would have to use infantry, as the
area was wooded and without many wide roads. Our objective was
to push the terrorists into Beirut and then cut the city off. Once
trapped in Beirut, we would bomb the surrounded terrorists from
the air and place tremendous pressure on them until they surrendered. Another option was to hand control of the city over to the
Christians, so that they could weed out the terrorists with the
support of our artillery.

During Friday evening, and into the night, the Syrians violated
the cease-fire by firing on our troops on the mountain ridge. We
believed that the Syrians were firing because they thought our forces
were advancing but this was not so. In any case, we were in an
excellent strategic position to destroy the Syrian forces, and continued to consider various operational plans to achieve this, in the
event the Syrians did not stop firing.

On Saturday, June 12, the Minister of Defense contacted the
Lebanese and informed them that Israel demanded contact with the
Lebanese on the same level as they had with the Syrians. Sharon was
concerned that the Lebanese would press for an Israeli withdrawal,
without demanding the same of the Syrians. This concern remained
and even intensified once Bashir Gemayel was elected President.

Once we had Beirut surrounded and under siege, I suggested to
Sharon that we lift the siege and publicly announce that we were
doing so as a gesture of good will, so that many of the civilians
trapped inside Beirut would be able to flee the city. I understood
that the plan ran a great risk that many of the terrorists and their

leaders would also use the opportunity to flee, but as long as they were fleeing to the north, and not in the direction of the Israeli border, I was not concerned. I also saw our lifting the siege as an opportunity to link up with the Christians, as they controlled the area that many of the fleeing civilians would be passing through. I felt a link with the Christians was important both strategically, but more importantly, symbolically.

During the war we took hundreds of terrorists prisoner. In the beginning, as we had no facilities in which to hold them in Lebanon, we transferred the prisoners to an Israeli prison. I was very much against this policy, as I feared that once a settlement was reached, we could potentially be left with thousands of terrorists inside Israel, with no country agreeing to take them. As a result of my fears we brought the terrorists back into Lebanon and set up a prison facility in the south.

As the cease-fire took effect Sharon detailed for the General Staff what our responses should be in the event of a Syrian violation. We were instructed to use the air force to respond to any artillery firing or mining. Sharon stressed that we were not to get involved in a war of attrition, but rather to respond to each provocation with whatever means were at our disposal. Sharon also informed us that he foresaw a Syrian attempt to slowly advance their forces in the Aley sector, and that were this to happen we were to do all that was necessary to return the Syrian forces to their original positions. In addition, the Minister of Defense outlined for us the approaches the government had determined would guide our policy after the war. Israel would only agree to a withdrawal of forces if all foreign forces evacuated their positions in Lebanon. Furthermore, Israel would not accept a United Nations peacekeeping force, as they were under the control of the Security Council and the influence of the Soviet Union and Arab States. Israel would only agree to a multi-national peacekeeping force.

The terrorists were also pushing for a cease-fire and the Americans were pressuring us to accept a cease-fire beginning Saturday, at nine o'clock in the evening. With a cease-fire on all

fronts, I decided that the standing army would be able to control all
our areas and maintain the level of security without the help of the
reservists. I knew that many businesses and families were suffering
in Israel, as many men had been away for a long time. I issued an
order to release all reserve soldiers.

In a gesture of friendship to the Christians, I ordered my troops
to allow Christians who had fled Jezzine, the Shouf mountains, and
Dir el-Kub during the civil war to return to their homes. I even
offered to arm them, so that they could defend themselves against
terrorist forces and other potential enemies.

By Sunday, June 13, the terrorists had already managed to shatter
the cease-fire that was supposed to have gone into effect the night
before. Prior to nine o'clock the night before, we fought a battle for
the village of Kafr Sil, the last terrorist stronghold before the Beirut
airport. The terrorists used tanks during the battle, but we destroyed
their armor, and proceeded to capture the town. With the cease-fire
broken, our forces continued to advance along the western axis, in
an effort to link up with the Christians.

Once our forces linked up with the Christians outside of East
Beirut we had effective control over the Beirut-Damascus Highway.
We had no intentions of entering East Beirut, and I assumed the
major portion of the war had been completed. I even went so far as
to assign to a senior officer the task of studying the war, isolating
the lessons we should learn, and evaluating the performance of both
our soldiers and our equipment.

After the terrorists had not observed the first attempt at a
cease-fire we suggested another attempt, and set the time for Monday, June 14, at two o'clock in the afternoon. The Americans were
pleased at our suggestion, but had placed a great deal of pressure on
us because the American ambassador in Beirut had reported to
Washington that our forces had captured the presidential palace at
Ba'abda. This report was inaccurate, but the Americans had no way
of verifying it. Unfortunately, this cease-fire was not observed by
the terrorists any more than the previous one had been.

As we captured many of the Palestinian refugee camps we were shocked at the many stories of horror we were told. It was not unusual for the terrorists to punish a father by murdering his child right before his eyes. Any resident that wished to flee or resisted taking up arms against the Israelis was also treated in vicious and violent ways.

During this period the Saudi king, King Khaled, died and all the Arab leaders flew to Saudi Arabia for the funeral. Sensing the opportunity, the Syrian leader used the gathering as an opportunity to chide his Arab brothers for abandoning Syria during its time of war against Israel. The meetings in Saudi Arabia raised our concern, in that we did not rule out the possibility that the Arab states would either form a united front, or pledge their support for a long term war of attrition with Israel. In fact, Assad had voiced his condemnations as a means of countering the Palestinian claims that Syria had abandoned the terrorist forces in Beirut. The PLO was in the world media spotlight and Arafat was using the opportunity to condemn Syria, condemn Israel, and announce that the PLO fighters were heroically withstanding the power of the mighty Israeli army, although we had routed the PLO forces and had surrounded Beirut. The terrorists had proven to be mediocre fighters, primarily because of their lack of organization. Yet, Arafat stood before the world and presented himself as a hero. Sadly, the media centers of the world presented this nonsense to their audiences.

The American approach to the events in Lebanon was twofold, and split between the State Department and the Defense Department. The Defense Department, under Secretary of Defense Caspar Weinberger, wanted to pacify the region. They argued that the Syrians should be allowed to return to the Beirut region, and that the terrorists should be permitted to concentrate and re-organize their forces in Beirut. Israel's security needs were to be met by a twenty-five-mile-deep security zone that would be patrolled by an international force. In Weinberger's view, any attempt to influence events beyond these points would be unnecessary. On the other hand, the State Department, under Secretary of State Alexander Haig, saw an opportunity to have a more far reaching effect on the events about to unfold in Lebanon. However, Haig did not have great confidence in the Christian ability to form a stable government and often questioned how they would enforce their demand that the Syrians withdraw from Lebanese territory. Moreover, Haig was always testing the Soviet Union, and would be greatly influenced by what the Soviets did.

The Soviets were not interested in directly intervening on Syria's behalf in Lebanon. We understood that this position might change should we enter Syria, but were not concerned since we had no plans to do so. The Soviets knew that the present military situation would not allow the Syrians to hold on to their assets in Lebanon, but they chose to try to secure some advantages for the Syrians through the diplomatic process.

The Soviets had an additional problem that was a direct result of the war. Throughout the Third World, the Arab World and the Warsaw Pact, many of the nations that had been supplied with Soviet military hardware were beginning to voice doubts as to the efficiency and quality of the weapon systems. The Israeli forces had routed the Syrians, and in the process had shown the world that the T-72 tank and the Soviet anti-aircraft missiles were inferior and vulnerable to other weapon systems.

Once we had linked up with the Christians, the terrorists once again proposed a cease-fire and we immediately agreed. On this occasion, the third attempt, the cease-fire was maintained and a relative quiet prevailed in the Beirut area. The commander of the Northern Command suggested that we announce to the terrorist and Syrian forces under siege in Beirut that we would guarantee them safe passage out of the city, on condition that they lay down their weapons. I supported the idea, but the Minister of Defense felt that the terrorists were not ready to agree to such an offer.

We chose not to impose any form of military government in Lebanon and operated a civilian system in the areas we had captured. Our task was made easier by Christians who were sent as emissaries from the north. These individuals actually operated the civilian system, while our officers served as an avenue for the appeals of

Lebanese civilians. Many Christian refugees were beginning to return to their original homes and they found their homes and villages had been destroyed by the terrorists. These people bravely began to rebuild their lives and we assisted them in any manner we could. We set up makeshift medical centers with the assistance of the Ministry of Health and the Magan David Adom, Israel's counterpart to the Red Cross. Full scale hospitals were also set up in Tyre and Sidon, where particularly intense fighting had occurred.

We were also actively trying to assist those who had lost their homes due to the fighting. Although the PLO had claimed that over 600,000 people were homeless, the actual numbers were closer to one percent of that ridiculous amount. Still, in the areas under our control we were doing all we could to help people rebuild their homes. Our efforts were again focused on Trye and Sidon, although we also helped in other towns such as Eyn Zahalta, Nabatiyya, and even Damur, which was destroyed by the terrorists before we even entered Lebanon.

During the lull in the fighting I was called before the Knesset Foreign Affairs Committee and was asked to respond to the concerns of the various committee members. We discussed the issue of refugees and I explained that the number of those made homeless by the war was far, far less than was being reported by the press. I informed the committee that we were allowing those who had fled to return to their homes. I also advised the Knesset members that the press reports about the number of civilian casualties were far greater than the actual number of dead and wounded. I reported that our forces had reached the Beirut Airport, but had not bombed the airfield. Any destruction of planes at the airport was the result of artillery being fired by the terrorists. Our activity in Beirut was directed solely at the terrorists and our bombing raids were carefully orchestrated to avoid civilian casualties. In response to other questions, I remarked that the political intentions for Beirut were not known to me, but that the IDF did not have any intentions of entering the city. I concluded my visit with a report on the prisoners we were holding in a prison we had set up near Nabatiyya. We had in our custody terrorists, Syrians, and foreign gunmen, most likely terrorists who were in Lebanon taking courses on the art of murder from the PLO. I also told the committee that we had proposed to the terrorists and the Syrians that they would be permitted to leave Beirut without being harmed if they lay down their weapons. I stressed that every step in this war had been presented to the government before it was executed and that nothing was done without government authorization.

As I was leaving the committee meeting hall, an outspoken critic of mine approached me and demanded that I stop distorting the amount of damage the IDF had done in Sidon and Tyre. He further commented that it was useless for us to try to hide the truth, as the foreign press was able to see all the damage we had done. I responded that just the day before we had taken a group of foreign journalists to Tyre and Sidon so that they would be able to see the towns for themselves. I reminded him that destruction is not easily concealed, and yet the journalists did not see the massive destruction the PLO had told them we had caused. Certainly there was some level of damage — after all the city had been attacked — but the extent of the damage was nowhere near the outrageous lies that were offered to the press. I reminded the Knesset member that it was remarkable that the IDF had taken such care to avoid hitting areas that were not associated with the terrorists, and equally remarkable that we were now in the process of assisting the local Arabs in the immense task of rebuilding their towns. We were supplying materials, equipment, water, food, and medical services. Yet, despite all this, even a member of the Knesset had been drawn into believing the lies and slander of the terrorists' propaganda machine.

Our search of Sidon brought about the discovery of a tremendous amount of weaponry. We found nineteen truckloads of Katyushas, artillery, and guns in just one weapon storage area, located under an apartment building. This storage house was but one of the many we found in Sidon, Tyre, and other areas that had been controlled by the terrorists.

By June 15 we had an estimation that there were twelve to fifteen thousand terrorists in the Beirut area. Although some of their leaders had escaped to Damascus and Kuwait, most of them, including Arafat, were still in Beirut. An additional two or three thousand terrorists were at the Beirut Airport, but we decided not to take the field. We realized we controlled the area by situating ourselves on the surrounding hills, and did not need the airfield for our own purposes. There was also a concentration of terrorists in the Sabra and Shatila refugee camps.

The Syrians in Beirut were also in desperate condition, as only a small remnant of their force was left. One tank brigade had only nine tanks left and their Brigade 42 had suffered a casualty rate of over 35 percent. In addition, their Brigade 72 was severely damaged, and overall they had lost approximately 150 tanks.

The primary advocate for the besieged terrorists was Egypt. At the terrorists' urging, the Egyptians placed a great deal of pressure on the Americans to push Israel to agree to a cease-fire. The Americans were afraid that we would grow tired of waiting for the terrorists to leave and move to capture Beirut. Such a move would be a death blow to the terrorists, but would also have widespread ramifications throughout the Arab world. Yet, there was also a school of thought in the United States that argued that our actions had brought about a unique opportunity to expel all foreign forces from Lebanon and help establish a strong central government. Despite this view, the Americans were pushing us to agree to a separation of forces and the introduction of a UNIFIL type of peacekeeping force.

During the course of the war I constantly emphasized that I did not want my commanders underestimating the strengths of our enemies. I was conscious of the costs that this error extracted from us during the Yom Kippur War. In the end we did underestimate the terrorists, but only because we had no way of knowing the quantities and types of weapons they had. We also did not know how they had organized their forces in the major cities. As soldiers they fought reasonably well and they caused us casualties and damaged some equipment. In many ways they behaved differently from what we had expected. On the other hand, we overestimated the strength of the Syrian forces. Although their soldiers also did not fight poorly, the Syrians were extremely disorganized and the structure of their army simply did not function.

In certain battles we were even able to achieve our objective without losing any men, although we suffered some wounded. There were very few battles in which we suffered a great many casualties. However, the cost of any war is too high when one thinks about the death of a young man, or a reserve soldier with a family. It is the unfortunate cost of securing the future of our nation.

Our intelligence during the war was very good; however it is impossible to expect them to uncover every morsel of information, and it is foolish to plan operations under the assumption that all is known. The system of mobilizing our reserve forces worked properly, as did our system of getting supplies to the front lines. The new equipment we used for the first time proved to be quite effective, and lived up to our greatest expectations. In all areas our armed forces performed well and achieved their objects quickly and unambiguously.

It has been said that the Minister of Defense, and in some scenarios, the Chief of Staff as well, misled the Cabinet and convinced them to approve operations by altering or omitting important details. This accusation is completely false, and a sad commentary on the levels to which some will fall in order to harm Sharon's and my reputations. Our objective, as defined in the governmental authorization, was to push the terrorists and their artillery far enough back so that they would not be able to reach our northern border. The number of miles we would need to force them back was estimated at twenty-five, but at no time was it limited to this number. As we advanced, we discovered new weapons and a structure that required us to continue with our advance. In the end, Sharon was also criticized for not having wanted a UNIFIL force to replace the IDF, but in truth the UNIFIL force had proven ineffective at preventing terrorist attacks on Israel prior to our campaign, and there was very little reason to believe that they would be more effective this time. Sharon wanted a multi-national force similar to that in place in the Sinai. Each nation participating would sign a separate agreement with Israel and would vow to prevent the terrorists from entering the area under their control. Such a force would be in constant communication with Israel, and would be effective in carrying out their mandate.

Yet, the debate on how to assure Israel's security against a terrorist return would have been academic if the siege of Beirut had not been effective. The siege alone was responsible for the evacuation of the terrorists from Lebanon.

35

The Siege of Beirut

It had become clear that the IDF could not withdraw from Lebanon until all other foreign forces, namely the terrorists and the Syrians, removed their forces from Lebanon as well. The government of Israel decided on this policy because it was felt that any arrangement allowing these enemy forces to remain in Lebanon would result to a return to the situation we were faced with prior to our campaign in Lebanon. Without a strong central government the Lebanese could not stop the terrorists from returning to the south and bombarding our northern villages. A central government was impossible as long as the Syrians and terrorists had forces in Lebanon. Furthermore, we intended to hold our positions until we received an acceptable arrangement guaranteeing the safety of our northern border. This being our policy, I began to understand that there was an excellent possibility that our forces would be required to remain in Lebanon for an extended period of time.

While our government was considering the needs of the nation, the army was continuing its siege of West Beirut, where more than six thousand terrorists were trapped in their underground headquarters. We were placing a great deal of pressure on them through our air raids, but we decided that the Lebanese and the Christians, in particular, would be responsible for solving the problem their presence brought.

Yet the Christians preferred not to act. They most likely realized that although we were placing the responsibility on them, the terrorists were our problem as well, and as such, eventually we would stop waiting for the Christians to act and act on our own. When it became clear that the terrorists were stalling and not willing to leave voluntarily, the cabinet began to deliberate on the various options for action.

On June 21 we received a report that a Syrian commando unit was inching its way toward the Aley region, a clear violation of the cease-fire. We realized that the force would probably try to place itself so as to be in an advantageous position should hostilities breakout. Such a force could threaten our positions on the Beirut-Damascus Highway. Thus, we decided to confront the unit and prevent their advance. In the battle, we suffered four wounded, but destroyed four Syrian tanks and successfully stopped the advance.

In an effort to better understand the strategic aspects of our deployment, the Cabinet Ministers visited the Northern Command and received a full briefing. While we were reviewing our positions facing the Syrians, we noticed they were entering "no man's land" and removing their damaged equipment. Under normal circumstances I would have instructed my forces to chase them away with warning shots, but fearing that they might respond and place the ministers in danger, I allowed the Syrians to continue undisturbed.

By June 23 the terrorists still had not agreed to unofficial negotiations through the American mediator, Philip Habib, and so we began to consider tightening our siege of Beirut by utilizing our naval force situated off the Lebanese coast. As the Lebanese began to serve as a channel for communication, we learned that the terrorists were considering various options for their evacuation. Under these circumstances, we understood that the military pressure we were applying was serving to convince the terrorists that we would not allow them to stay in Lebanon, and so we continued to inflict on them heavy losses in personnel and equipment. At this point in the conflict we were focusing our efforts on the Bahamdoun district, where the terrorists had many installations.

In planning our strategy, I had what later became an extremely ironic meeting with a commander of a tank brigade stationed on the outskirts of Beirut. The officer's name was Colonel Eli Geva, and later in the war he would become the first officer in Israeli history ever to refuse orders and to carry out an operation. During this meeting, Geva suggested to me that the IDF could cause the terrorists to flee Beirut by attacking different sectors of the city at different times, and tightening our hold by advancing up to the city limits. Geva suggested that we employ our artillery more liberally, and argued that our effort to spare civilian casualties was causing the IDF to suffer greater losses. Thus, he remarked, we should consider risking greater civilian losses and do all we could to protect our forces. At the time, I thought little of Geva's comments. I did not agree with his view, and knew that the government would not allow us to risk the lives of civilians. Later, when he refused to carry out his orders I understood the absurdity that had taken place.

The one point that Geva made that had some sense to it was the idea that the IDF advance to the city limits and tighten the hold we had on the city. We developed a plan to take the suburb and neighborhood of Burj al Barajneh and Ouzai, and the sector of the airport still controlled by the terrorists. After receiving government authorization, we fired heavy artillery at terrorist installations in the three target areas and advanced our troops. We took the areas with little resistance, and succeeded in pushing the terrorists into West Beirut.

Later that day I met with Bashir Gemayel and he shared with me his assessment that the terrorists and the Syrians would probably not agree to evacuate Beirut. He suggested that Israel stick to its demand that they surrender their weapons before agreeing to any arrangement. I questioned Gemayel about the role his Christian forces were willing to play, but he informed me that he preferred not to play any role. He commented that his forces would have very little actual effect on the course of the fighting, and there was the danger that the fact that they participated would come back to haunt them in the future. I understood his position, and had to admit to myself that it was sensible. During the course of the war the Christians had shown themselves to be wary fighters, and in fact had participated in battles only when their identities as Christian fighters were concealed. In this manner they had disappointed us on numerous occasions, and I reminded Gemayel that we were in Lebanon to fight our war, not theirs, and that we would not engage in any effort that was not directly related to our interests. Bashir understood our position, and recognized it as correct.

Another development influencing Gemayel's behavior was his effort to form a government and his decision to attempt to include the Muslim factions that had been fighting the Christians. Under these circumstances, he was very wary of being perceived as involved in our war effort, and at times acted against our interests to demonstrate his distance from our actions.

After three days of our being fired upon, I ordered our forces in the Beka'a to respond to Syrian provocations after an armored personnel carrier of ours was hit by a Syrian missile. We activated the air force, which inflicted heavy damage on the Syrians, as did our artillery. At the time, Prime Minister Begin was in the United States and he was questioned by the Americans after they received a cry for help from the Syrians. Begin's deputy, Simcha Erlich, contacted me and demanded an explanation. I informed him that we had acted in compliance with the government's authorization and that we would not allow a war of attrition to develop. The Syrians had to learn that, unlike past wars, we were going to respond to their provocations in ways that were most likely to enhance our position. We continued our fire until six o'clock that evening, and also attacked some terrorist targets in Beirut that day.

Meanwhile two additional problems arose that required my attention. I was informed that some of our soldiers had been caught trying to smuggle consumer goods they had looted in Lebanon back into Israel. I was extremely distressed that our soldiers would engage in looting, and instructed that all looters be held in jail until their trial, and voiced my opinion that if found guilty, they should be severely punished. In addition, I ordered a unit of the Military Police to be transferred to East Beirut, so that it could keep an eye on the behavior of our soldiers. Looting is a danger that exists in any war, with any army, but the IDF had extremely high standards of behavior, and I had no intention of tolerating any forms of deviance.

The second problem that was brought to my attention had to do with a unit made up of religious soldiers. This unit had suffered heavy losses at Sultan Ya'akub and the surviving soldiers were having a very difficult time dealing with what had happened. I ordered that those who wished to speak to a professional be given immediate access and also divided the soldiers up and placed them in other units. It was my feeling that this would give them an opportunity to distance themselves from what had happened.

On June 28 we captured another sector of the Beirut-Damascus Highway after the Syrians again violated the cease-fire. The sector was in the Bahamdoun region and was topographically difficult to capture. Although the Syrian resistance was light, it was more difficult to capture than the section we had taken in the Eyn Zahalta - Dar al Baydr area. As always, we did not advance on the area without prior authorization from the government.

Amidst reports that the Syrians were receiving arms from the Soviet Union and Libya, our forces advanced on the Bahamdoun region to the west and the Gamhour region to the east. The Syrians who were in these regions did not attempt to stop us, and many in fact fled before we even arrived.

Meanwhile, the Americans informed us that the PLO was ready to begin negotiating the terms of their evacuation. We decided that the PLO was not in a very good position to make demands upon us, and in an effort to point this out to them we intermittently withheld water and electricity from West Beirut. We also continued to apply tremendous military pressure, which brought Kahaleh and Aley under our control.

The analysis we received from the head of our intelligence service was that the PLO would not agree to leave Beirut. His feeling was that the Palestinian leadership believed that there was too great a political significance attached to the idea of retreat and that such an action would cause grave damage to the "Palestinian struggle." Thus, he concluded that the PLO would not agree to surrender their weapons and leave Lebanon. He felt they would search for an alternative solution that would allow them to leave without it appearing that they were forced out.

In the end the PLO did leave Lebanon, and this was in fact one of the primary accomplishments of the war. As I have said, there is some truth to the argument that the war did not succeed in achieving much of what it had striven for. Yet, with regard to the PLO I believe it is clear that we were extremely successful. The PLO left Lebanon, and with it went its ability to attack our northern towns. In addition, they lost their home base, the land they used to store equipment, train troops, and administer their terrorist activity. They also lost their freedom of action, in that they are now dominated by a variety of Arab States that offered them asylum. In fact, almost all Arab states have at least one faction of the PLO under their control. Thus, it cannot be said that the PLO after our campaign was not significantly weaker than it was prior to the day we entered Lebanon.

The same night that we were told that the PLO was interested in negotiations, Arafat, the Chairman of the PLO, appeared on the British Broadcasting Company's television newscast and claimed that Israel would not intimidate or frighten the PLO. We considered his remarks as proof that the PLO was digging in for a prolonged negotiation process. We knew that Arafat and his close advisors were in favor of an immediate evacuation, under the best conditions they could get, arguing that the battle had been lost and that holding out would only result in more bloodshed. We also knew that within the PLO hierarchy there were also some extremists arguing that the PLO should fight to the very last man. Unfortunately, Arafat's statement on the BBC led us to believe that the extremists were once again in control. The fact that the PLO again broke the cease-fire that evening, re-enforced in our minds their decision to stay and fight. We saw no signs that they were ready to evacuate and surrender their weapons. Rather, they exhausted their efforts on public relations ploys aimed at bringing world pressure on Israel. Their hope was that world opinion would force us to ease up on the pressure we were applying on them, and they would then have time to develop an option other than evacuation.

Yet the Americans knew that we accepted the principle that all foreign forces must leave Lebanon, and that we would be willing, in fact eager, to do so once we saw the Syrians were also withdrawing. It was, later on, the Americans who retreated from this position, as they decided to recognize certain Syrian interests in Lebanon. The Americans withdrew their support for a total Syrian withdrawal and even went so far as to recognize the legitimacy of a Syrian military presence in the Beka'a. The Americans argued that Syria had a legitimate interest in protecting its border, to which Israel responded that we could not accept this argument unless our security needs, with respect to southern Lebanon, were also recognized.

The Americans also were not clear with regard to their policy vis-à-vis the terrorists. Although they voiced support for the idea that the PLO evacuate Beirut, they did not make clear their position on our demand that they surrender their weapons. The Egyptians, who were using the PLO's vulnerability as a means of re-entering the Arab world, pressured the United States to support the idea that they be allowed to take their weapons with them. The Egyptians were interested in preventing the PLO from being too humiliated. The Americans were not unsympathetic to the Egyptian plea, but never officially stated their position. In the end, a compromise was reached allowing the terrorists to take only their personal weapons with them.

While the negotiations over the PLO evacuation were taking place, other negotiations, for the presidency of Lebanon, were also underway. The Syrians were pressuring the Lebanese not to select someone who was unfriendly to Syrian interests. For this reason they were against the candidacy of Bashir Gemayel. Yet, the years of civil war in Lebanon had taken its toll, and the country was completely divided. While the Syrians supported Camille Chamoun, a Christian, the other Christian group, the Phalange, supported Gemayel, their leader. The Druze, however would not even sit at the same table with the Gemayel family, and the Muslims were divided between Shiites and Sunnis. Without presenting an

in-depth history of Lebanon before and after this period, suffice it
to say that to this very day these same forces, and others, are
alternately allies and at war with one another.

Menachem Begin was in the United States during the time that
Philip Habib was most actively involved in the negotiations for the
PLO withdrawal. He informed us that he had been told that an
agreement had been reached, but we did not see any evidence of
that on the ground, as the terrorists continued to fire at our forces.
Also, the terms of the agreement were at this point not yet clear.
Still, in anticipation of a withdrawal, and in an effort to avoid looting
and other more logistical complications, I ordered that as many
forces as possible be withdrawn from the Beirut and Jounieh areas.
I made it clear that we were not to alter our capacity to fight or apply
pressure, but merely to thin out our ranks.

In an effort to ensure that a smaller force would be able to apply
as great an amount of pressure, we planned an assault that would
allow us to capture some of the neighborhoods surrounding the
terrorists' encampment, and also their bases north of Khaldeh. This
action would allow us to control the southern suburbs of the city
and would serve to further box in the terrorist forces. It should be
mentioned that this maneuver was later pointed to by opponents of
the war as proof that we had intended to enter Beirut. This is simply
not so, and those claiming this outrageous lie have no answer when
asked why, if we had intended all along to enter Beirut, did we not
do so before the assassination of Gemayel?

The military pressure we were applying to the terrorists was
designed to force them to understand that they had been militarily
defeated in a war they themselves had instigated, and that they were
not in a position to dictate to us any conditions. The pressure was
manifested through psychological ploys, the movement and advancement of forces, and the use of fire power without advancing our
troops. The Americans understood that our pressure was the only
reason the PLO was considering withdrawal, and recognized that
our continued pressure would only serve to speed up the negotiations process. Unfortunately, the media attached an extremely nega-

tive connotation to what we were doing, and as a result our image around the world was tarnished, and we were exposed to various political pressures.

The Syrian troops in Beirut were also placed under tremendous pressure, as we wanted to secure their withdrawal as well. In the Beka'a the Syrians were rebuilding their forces and had brought in new equipment and forces, and were building ramps for tanks and trenches for troops. Yet, we knew the Syrians were not interested in a war with us. Once we had destroyed their missile batteries, particularly with no losses, they understood that they were not prepared for a war against us. Their losses were listed as 345 tanks, 20 of which were T-72s, 70 Armored Personnel Carriers, 75 pieces of artillery, close to 100 airplanes, and over 400 dead and 1,500 wounded.

Yet, the Syrians were re-enforcing their forces along Mount Lebanon and Mount Sannin in the east. On the Golan Heights the Syrian forces were in a high state of alert, almost to the point of being at war. We realized that the Syrians could not possibly intend to attack, but we took precautionary measures to counter what was clearly a threat. Later we learned that the Syrians had placed their troops on alert in an effort to place pressure on us to ease off their troops in Beirut. Their maneuver did not work, primarily because the threat had very little credibility.

The negotiations for the PLO evacuation were centered on talks between Habib and Gemayel, who at this point was clearly going to be Lebanon's next President. Gemayel demanded that all Palestinian and Syrian forces leave Lebanon, but did not rule out permitting some kind of symbolic Palestinian force to remain as a unit within the Lebanese army. However, he declared himself ready to discuss such issues only after the PLO agreed to the terms of their departure.

Habib, as an American mediator, was supportive of Gemayel's demands. The Americans saw great benefit arising from our actions, as the terrorists and Syrians were weakened, the Soviets were weakened and embarrassed, and Lebanon was on the verge of becoming an independent, free country once again. The public stance of the administration was that it opposed Israel's actions, but being that they were taken, the United States and the free world should take advantage of the new status quo.

At this stage of the conflict we had already suffered 128 dead and 1,578 wounded. These numbers were far greater than I had thought we would lose, but the prolonged nature of the conflict, the terrain, and the modern weaponry had taken their toll.

The amount of weapons the terrorists had accumulated in Lebanon was truly frightening, and served as ample evidence that they were preparing for a large-scale armed confrontation with Israel. By the beginning of July we had already expropriated 1,350 trucks, 36 armored vehicles, 87 tanks, 250 vehicles, 11,000 machine guns, an additional 9,000 Kalashnikov rifles, 1,100 heavy machine guns, 650 anti-tank weapons, 12,000 rockets, 100 rocket launchers, 19 small cannons, 24 130 mm cannons, thousands of pieces of communications and optical equipment, 18,000 82 mm mortar shells, 8,000 120 mm mortar shells, 12,500 rocket-propelled grenades, 6,500,000 rounds of live ammunition, 7,000 mines, and SAM-9 ground-to-air missiles. These quantities of arms had already been found at a time when we had not yet discovered all their weapons depots and were still confiscating between 70-100 truck-loads of arms, weapons systems, armor, and ammunition daily.

The negotiations with the terrorists were quite confusing. Neither the United States nor Israel was willing to engage in direct negotiations with the PLO, and therefore we used Habib as our middleman, and he in turn relayed the messages to the Lebanese Prime Minister, Wazzan. Each party along the way suffered from selective hearing, and unintentionally distorted what the original message had been. Furthermore, although the PLO had in principle agreed to leave Lebanon, there was no Arab country willing to accept them. Egypt, which had at first offered to provide refuge to some, had backed away from its offer. Syria, Libya, and Algeria had not offered their assistance. Saudi Arabia and Jordan had publicly ruled out the possibility that they would accept them. In light of this

problem we began discussing the possibility of allowing the terrorists to transfer to Tripoli, in northern Lebanon. We were against
the idea and believed it would not serve our interests, but we began
to think in terms of a lesser evil. It was argued that transferring them
to Tripoli was preferable to an indefinite siege of Beirut.

In addition to these difficulties, the communal strife that had torn
Lebanon apart during the civil war began to manifest itself in areas
under our control. The Christian community interpreted our control over the area as an opportunity to settle the score they had with
the Druze, who had slaughtered many Christians while allies of the
Syrians and Palestinians. In these communities revenge manifested
itself in only one way, wholesale slaughter. The Druze were now
vulnerable without the Syrians and PLO to protect them. Naturally,
the IDF took upon ourselves the responsibility to spare no effort in
preventing massacres and bloodshed in the areas under our control.

As the negotiations continued, we began to recognize that even
after the terrorists left, our forces would have to remain in Lebanon
for an extended period of time. We began to consider what our needs
would be for the winter. Although it was only July, it was clear that
we would be somewhere in Lebanon when the rains and snow of
December arrived. We had to think in terms of buildings, heating,
clothing, and how to teach our soldiers to deal with the winter
conditions.

We also began to discuss what our possible long-term strategic
positions should be, and how many forces we needed to hold them.
It was clear that we could not keep our reserve soldiers away from
their jobs and families indefinitely and that we had to reconsider
what our needs were. I had already thinned out our forces, and
ordered my officers to release additional reserve soldiers. I told them
that we had to consider the active fighting portion of the war over,
and that we needed only to maintain a force large enough, and
strong enough, to hold our gains. We also had to be sure not to
appear smaller or weaker, so as to not tempt or encourage our
enemies to attack us. We simply had to have enough men and
equipment to defend the areas we were controlling.

I did not believe the Syrians would want to go to war with us when the terrorists left Lebanon. The withdrawal of our forces and theirs would be handled at the political level, and the question was not our military strength, but our political strength in withstanding the pressure being applied by foreign and domestic forces.

By mid-July I had ordered that our Air Force cease performing bombing raids on Beirut. The raids, although extremely effective, were causing an uproar in the international community and the price was too high. We would be able to achieve practically the same results by using artillery. In addition, we had plans to increase the pressure by capturing the area around the racetrack, and the airport at Khaldeh. Both of these actions would bring us to the edge of the terrorists' area, and would certainly serve as a point of pressure. Also, this plan would place the refugee camps of Burj al Barajneh, Sabra, Shatila, and Fakahani behind us, effectively cut off from the terrorist forces.

By the end of July we had concluded that an artillery assault against the Syrian forces in the Beka'a was necessary because of a long series of serious cease-fire violations on their part. It was clear that the Syrians were still interested in forcing a war of attrition on us, as they hoped such a war would wear away our will to remain in Lebanon. A strong response on our part was necessary in order to show them that this assumption was wrong, and also to serve as a deterrent for future violations. There was also an element of retaliation in our intentions. We received governmental approval and proceeded to bombard the Syrians with tank shell fire and air force attacks. We exploited the element of surprise and the Syrians were practically unable to foster a response. We estimated that they suffered twenty dead and dozens wounded and lost 72 tanks, dozens of armored personnel carriers and many vehicles. We also severely damaged the structural foundations of many of their positions.

Our raid had the desired effect, in that the Syrians began to take concrete actions to prevent the terrorists operating in their territory from infiltrating our area and striking at our forces. They also ceased their sniper and artillery fire. Yet, the danger existed that they would encourage and assist the terrorists still situated behind our lines to strike against us. Our fears were heightened when it became apparent that the Syrians had set up some SAM-9 anti-aircraft missile sites near Yatta. These missiles downed one of our Phantom jets, killing one of our pilots. The second pilot was taken captive by the terrorist forces operating in the area. We had previously warned the Syrians not to bring additional anti-aircraft missiles into Lebanon, and we were determined to locate the batteries and destroy them.

36

The Eli Geva Affair

The controversies of the war in Lebanon were most often expressed in the media and the political arena, and opposition to the war was led by groups such as Shalom Achshav (Peace Now) and Yesh Gvul (There Is a Limit). While these organizations often employed misinformation and faulty analysis to condemn the government and army commanders, they also sowed doubts about the wisdom and validity of the war in the minds of many Israelis. Their campaign was felt in the army, as Israel's army is a reservist army and it is very difficult to prevent the influence of events happening in Israel's civilian sector from following the reservist as he assumes the role of soldier. In most instances, the fact that our army is a "people's army" greatly adds to the unity and spirit of the IDF. However, during the Lebanon war, the influence of the public sector was mostly negative. Furthermore, the IDF tradition of encouraging soldiers to speak their minds and allowing for the questioning of orders also had many negative manifestations. Despite the controversies, I can say with satisfaction that there were no violations of discipline and the motivation of our soldiers and officers was not damaged. We had to weather a controversy, but in all there was but one case in which a soldier refused to obey orders.

This lone exception was Colonel Eli Geva, whose case was exploited by the political elements seeking to damage the government and top army officers. What these forces failed to understand was that Geva was not the "hero" they had made of him, and that the implications of his actions were dangerous, not only to the IDF, but to the entire State of Israel.

The first indications that Geva was beginning to waiver in his duty arose a full three weeks prior to the assassination of Gemayel, and at a time when we had no intentions of entering West Beirut. At that time Geva was arguing against any invasion of Beirut, and had said that he would be unable to command his brigade on such a mission, were it to be ordered.

I first heard of Geva's remarks at a meeting of the General Staff and found them serious enough to warrant my personal attention. At this time, we had Beirut under siege and were applying a great deal of pressure. We were not intending to enter Beirut, but as in all situations, we had plans ready should the need arise. In all our plans, Geva's brigade would be called upon to act. Furthermore, I was concerned that a seasoned officer was talking in terms of refusing orders.

In order to take command of what was an uncomfortable situation, I traveled to the outskirts of Beirut and called an officer's meeting. At this meeting Geva, and others, expressed their objections to entering Beirut. I listened carefully, and explained to the officers that at the moment we had no intentions of entering the city, and that all our efforts vis-à-vis Beirut were aimed at pressuring the terrorists and Syrians to evacuate. Furthermore, I reminded them that they, as officers of the IDF, understood the need to have plans already developed for every possible situation. As such, we had developed plans to enter Beirut, but would not be doing so, unless otherwise instructed by the government. After the meeting was over I had my first of three private conversations with Geva, during which I again informed him that we had no plans to enter Beirut. I expressed concern over the statements he had made and left him confident that he would be satisfied, like everyone else, in limiting his actions to comments he was free to make at officers' meetings. I certainly had no idea that he would take the unprecedented and highly controversial step of abandoning his command of his brigade.

The next time I heard from Eli Geva he was requesting to be relieved of his command. He informed me that he would be unable to lead his brigade into West Beirut, should he be ordered to do so.

He claimed the prospect of high casualties among his troops, and the fact that there would also be a large number of civilian casualties, had weighed heavy on his conscience. It was clear to me that Geva was going through a severe emotional crisis, but I sensed that his difficulties went beyond the issue of West Beirut.

Once Geva's request became public his cause was immediately picked up by many forces in Israel against the war. As the matter became more serious I discussed Geva's case with his immediate commanders and found that there were many other reasons that might have possibly been causing Geva to behave as he was. In an effort to better understand his motives, I called Geva to my office and asked him if there were other matters, other events that had happened during the war, that were causing him to make his request. Geva responded by asking me for an example of such a matter.

I informed him that in fact there were three cases that had been called to my attention that had obviously caused him a great amount of sadness. The first concerned a paratrooper battalion that was attached to Geva's brigade. During the first stages of the war this battalion had made an incorrect turn in the area of Tyre and their mistake brought them into the line of fire of a terrorist unit. They suffered many losses, including the battalion commander. After the battle many of the officers criticized the manner in which Geva handled the situation and they complained that he did not do all he could have and should have under the circumstances. I told Geva that I was informed that these opinions, when brought to his attention, deeply saddened him.

The second case involved a Merkava tank from Geva's brigade that was abandoned at the approaches to the Beirut airport. The terrorists had made attempts to bring the tank back to their lines and it was important for us to do all that was necessary to prevent them from succeeding. With no alternative, we dispatched a Golani infantry battalion to attack and rescue the tank. After the incident, reports reached Geva's commanders that he was very upset by the matter and felt responsible for what had happened.

The third matter was very personal and sensitive, yet I felt it was necessary for me to raise it. I reminded Geva that the polarization between the front and home, that is between one's obligations to the pressures of the war versus one's obligations to the pressures of family, was a burden every officer struggled with. I informed him that it had been called to my attention that he was under heavy pressure from his wife.

After listening to the three concerns I had raised, Geva informed me that the paratrooper brigade and the Merkeva tank were not issues for him, but that there was some truth to the story that he was under pressure from home. He made it clear that the crisis at home was centered on his command of the brigade outside of Beirut.

Once Geva admitted this to me I became convinced that his request to leave his command was not because of any possible attack on Beirut. I reminded Geva that he was in command of many soldiers and that these young men had placed their trust in him, a trust that had to be justified. Yet, I was sure that my message was not being received. Geva, it seemed, was using the issue of Beirut to be relieved of his post because he had sensed that the average Israeli would be sympathetic to his cause and that he would be able to avoid any harsh punishment by attracting the support of some within the political arena. His hope was that the public would view him as a man of peace risking his military career, rather than as an officer abandoning his troops in the heat of battle.

During one conversation with Geva he stated that his request was only to be relieved of his command, but that he wished to remain a soldier in his battalion. I told him that this was absurd and asked him how he would be able to act against civilians as a simple soldier, when he was claiming that he was not capable of leading his men into Beirut because of the threat it posed to the civilians. "What would you do," I asked him, "if, we in fact entered West Beirut, and you, as a soldier, were ordered to fire on a building that had both terrorists and civilians inside? How would you deal with your conscience if some of those wounded were civilians?" Geva was unable to answer me and understood that I would not approve this silly request.

Since Geva did not receive any of the requests he made of me, he requested that I arrange a meeting for him with Minister of Defense Sharon, which I did. Sharon was no more sympathetic to Geva's wishes than I was, and Geva asked Sharon to arrange a meeting with Prime Minister Begin. Later, in typical Geva fashion, he claimed to the press that we passed him around from official to official because none of us wanted to take responsibility. Obviously this was not the case, and was an absurd statement from someone turning his back on responsibility. Geva met with a number of officials at his own request and because he was not granted what he wanted from Sharon or myself.

Geva really began to develop a self-image of a national hero. He desperately wanted to be seen as the great humanist who was placing his principles above all else. He actively encouraged the support of the anti-war movement. At one point Geva was so lost in his own fantasy that he proposed to me that I remove him from his post only after giving him a direct order, which he would promptly refuse to obey. He was even willing to be placed in jail. His hope was that under such circumstances he would be perceived as the victim and I would be perceived as the villain. Naturally, I did not comply with this request either.

Geva believed that we would agree to transfer him from his post and appoint him to a different position somewhere else. He thought that the publicity and the circumstances were such that we would be unable to do anything other than accommodate him. Yet, I believed that Geva's actions were extremely dangerous and I decided that I would dismiss him from the army if he did not change his mind after his meeting with the Prime Minister. When he reported to me after meeting with Begin, he informed me that Begin had also denied him his request. I asked him if he was still insisting on leaving his brigade, to which he replied in the affirmative. At that moment, I pulled out a letter of dismissal I had prepared and handed it to him. The letter relieved him of his duties as brigade commander and dismissed him from the IDF. Geva could not hide his emotion; he was absolutely stunned. He was further surprised when I informed him that I would also not be permitting him to officially take leave of his troops, as is the usual custom when a senior officer leaves a unit. I felt the circumstances of his departure were such, and his actions so negative, that his presence would not be healthy or positive for the troops.

I knew that I had made the necessary decision. Geva had made a circus of the IDF and had interjected the political sector and media into the workings of the IDF. He had done much damage in selfish pursuit of his personal needs. Later, I learned that Geva had also stopped showing concern for his troops and had lost their respect. Up until the day of his release from the service, Geva had not bothered to visit even one of the bereaved families of men who had fallen in his brigade. Nor did he visit the wounded in the hospital. These acts of insensitivity, and the errors he had made on the field of battle, aroused in my mind the strong suspicion that Geva had created his whole charade as a means of leaving his post before we removed him. Furthermore, for a man who had expressed reasons of conscience for leaving his units, it was particularly odd that he had not felt the moral obligation to support his troops and their families in their hour of despair and sorrow.

What bothered me the most about Geva was not that he used the issue of Beirut when it meant close to nothing to him. Nor was it that he demanded and received audiences with Sharon and Begin. It was the issue of responsibility. It was the issue every officer must rise to when he is about to send others to fight, and perhaps die. At one of our meetings I asked Geva what right he had to abandon his unit? How could he say to his men, in effect, that he could leave, but that they must stay to fight and die? If we were in fact going to send them into West Beirut, and if in fact the action caused a high casualty count, how could he defend the idea that he would abandon them to do the fighting alone? Clearly, this is not the example an officer should set, particularly in the IDF, where our officers always are on the front lines, literally leading the way.

Geva acted as he did after consulting with many well known and important people in Israel. In addition to the Prime Minister and the Minister of Defense, he spoke with Yitzchak Rabin, who at the time was a member of the opposition in the Knesset. A former Chief of Staff and Prime Minister, Rabin told Geva that an officer in the IDF does not behave as he was behaving. Geva also spoke with General Tal, a reserve general, who simply told him to do as he felt was right. Even his own father, a former general, Yosef Geva, lashed out at his son and told him that his actions were inexcusable. Yet, despite the advice, and despite the consequences, Geva got wrapped up in the folk hero image some people had placed on him, and was either unwilling or unable to reverse his initial decision.

After the Geva episode was resolved, we once again committed all our time and energies to promoting the evacuation of the terrorists and Syrians from West Beirut. Unfortunately, the long period of time that had lapsed since we initially began our siege had served to encourage the PLO to continue to deny our demands, as they became confident that we would not enter the city. They had recovered from the initial shock of our assault, and, although with difficulty, would be able to remain under siege in Beirut for a long time. They began to entertain the notion that the United States was going to recognize them as the official representatives of the Palestinians, and that they would be called upon to set up a Palestinian State. We recognized that they had ceased to consider the option of evacuation, and this was cause for great concern.

We knew that the United States viewed the present situation as an opportunity to advance its own interests vis-à-vis the Soviets , and that as such, they were against any further military clashes. At the moment they were the only mediators, and chances were that a new round of fighting would jeopardize their status. We realized that the Americans' position was in many ways supportive and understanding of our actions and problems, but, we also knew that the United States, from the days of the Rogers Plan in 1967, did not recognize Israel's claims regarding the territories captured in 1967, and even held to the position that East Jerusalem was subject to negotiations.

With the terrorist leaders cornered and on the verge of destruction, it occurred to us that they might attempt to draw the support of the United States by making loose, unbinding statements meeting the U.S.'s long standing conditions that they renounce terrorism and recognize Israel. Were they to do this, the United States would most probably open a dialogue with them, placing us in a very uncomfortable and potentially difficult position. Thus, we began to feel a great deal of pressure to conclude their evacuation from Lebanon

There were other central issues that were under study, such as the effect the damage to the PLO would have on the extremists in Judea and Samaria. We felt that the weakening of the PLO might serve to weaken their allies in the territories, or perhaps serve to moderate them. There were also some who were claiming that the war would lead to an opportunity to lessen the tensions with Syria. The tactical questions being asked included whether it was better to keep the airport at Khaldeh closed and whether we should save the Soviets some embarrassment by issuing a statement that their weapons were not used to their potential during the war.

What was clear was that Israel had many options, and in this sense the advantage was with us, as our adversaries would not be able to guess how we would act and what we would do. At a meeting with the government and General Staff, I argued that time was not pressing and that we were fully in control of the events unfolding in Beirut. Those claiming that the PLO was successfully "waiting us out" were not subscribing to an accurate analysis of the situation on the ground. In truth, the terrorists were under great pressure to leave West Beirut, not only from our artillery, but also from the residents, who had begun to fight against them and block their entry into certain areas of the city. Furthermore, the blows the PLO had suffered were already showing effects in Judea and Samaria, and the Palestinians had taken note of the fact that all the Arab countries had literally abandoned them.

I also argued that the war had brought about unexpected opportunities and that we should try to exploit them For example, although Israel had not entered Lebanon to nullify all Syrian and PLO influence on the presidential elections there, our actions had in fact had this effect. Our continued presence wold serve to guarantee free elections, and would most likely lead to the election of Bashir Gemayel, who would then sign a peace treaty with Israel. I argued that the government should study all the "side benefits" of the war and determine our behavior based on what we stood to gain versus what the potential losses would be. Similarly, the government needed to reflect on the changes in the attitudes and opinions of the Palestinian leadership in Judea and Samaria, and determine whether our actions enhanced the chances to arrive at an agreement for autonomy.

Throughout the war, I was very strict during General Staff and officers' meetings in demanding the absence of political debates. I explained to my commanders that the forum for political debate was the Knesset and that our responsibility was to debate and arrive at the best strategic course of action, so as to fulfill the mandate given us by the government. At the start of the war many members of the political opposition supported the war. As the war progressed, and the political currents against the war grew, many opposition leaders began to speak out against the war, and argued that they had initially supported the war because our forces were scheduled to advance only twenty-five miles. I was able to understand those who argued that we should not have employed the military option to solve the problems we were facing in Lebanon, but I could not understand those who withdrew their support once we passed the twenty-five-mile marker. The truth is that if we had remained only twenty-five miles north of our border, we would have pushed the terrorists beyond their artillery range, but we also would have found ourselves stuck in this deployment and more exposed to terrorist attacks on our troops. Had we not continued, the terrorists simply would have re-organized their forces and structure beyond the point we had pushed them to, and we would have had our forces in Lebanon paying the price of their continued presence in Lebanon. It is my opinion that those who argued against the war because we proceeded beyond the twenty-five-mile marker were either looking for something to convert into a political issue, or simply did not understand the military, and political, risk that would have been assumed if we had stopped.

Those who today express opposition to the war because it lasted far longer than had been anticipated fail to recall that no war has ever ended as planned or when desirable. The Yom Kippur War did not end for seven months, and paradoxically, the Six-Day War, despite its name, lasted for three and one half years, under the name of the War of Attrition. There was no way for anyone to predict the time it would take to secure a PLO evacuation, nor could anyone have known that the IDF would be required to stay in Lebanon for a long period of time following the evacuation.

Similarly, some individuals in Israel voiced criticism of the fact that our forces engaged the Syrians in Lebanon. What these individuals have failed to understand is that Syria, to this day, is officially and actively in a state of war with Israel. They have refused to negotiate with us and have never accepted our existence. Under such circumstances, we are certainly entitled to respond to any and all military provocations emanating from behind Syrian lines. Furthermore, I do not hesitate to say that the Israeli government has an obligation to determine and pursue the national interests of our small, beleaguered country. In doing so they must determine what are the best mechanisms to be used for the attainment of these objectives. Whether political or military, the government is within its mandate to do what it deems necessary to preserve the security of the state. The task of the General Staff is to prepare plans to accomplish the objectives, as expressed by the government.

As far as I was concerned, the siege of Beirut might last a year or more. We were in control and could bomb and pressure the PLO at will. We controlled the water and electricity supply and could block the entry of any supplies we wished to deny the terrorists. I felt no great pressure to bring the siege to a quick resolution. I understood that the world had focused its attention on Beirut, but in my mind it meant that their attention was also off the Palestinians in Judea and Samaria, and pressing Israel to agree to a solution that was not in our interests. I was, like many others, concerned with the casualties a prolonged siege would cause. However, I felt that, although the most difficult aspect of any operation, we had to weigh the costs of casualties into our consideration of all the options. Quite often, when a country fails to act when the opportunity presents itself, it finds itself fighting the war anyway at a later date. Most often when the war is imposed, it is under conditions less favorable, thus resulting in more casualties than would have been suffered if the opportunity had been taken earlier. Therefore in this instance, I felt that Israel need not feel great pressure. The terrorists and not we were under siege. There were no similarities between Beirut and the Suez Canal zone after the Six-Day War. We were in total control. I felt we should exploit this to our benefit and not rush into any agreement that did not totally meet our needs.

Furthermore, I felt that we should take advantage of the weakened PLO and their allies in Judea, Samaria, and Gaza, and strengthen our presence in these areas. The militant Palestinian leadership was no longer able to meet with the PLO and receive instructions. We had the opportunity to cultivate an alternative leadership that would understand our will and need to remain in the area. Although we had tried to cultivate such leaders in the past, they were always silenced by the militants' bullets. Now the militants were weak, and the opportunity stood before us to succeed in this important endeavor.

Although I was sensitive to our need to maintain good relations with the United States, I did not believe it was necessary to submit on all of our ideals and objectives. The Americans were committed to removing the PLO from Lebanon, and we agreed with their objective. Yet, we held the key to their success and at times they tried to pressure us to agree to certain conditions that were not in our interest. We understood that the Americans had effective means of pressuring us, such as economic and military aid, but I felt that we would be better respected and understood if we held firm. Philip Habib was continuing in his efforts and our task was to be as supportive as possible. Yet, there were certain conditions we could not retreat from.

The analysis we received from the head of our intelligence service concluded that Israel had the potential to influence the removal of the PLO from Lebanon, as well as the withdrawal of all foreign forces. However, the report stated that we were not in a position to help secure a stable Lebanese government united around the various factions and militias. The most important objective for us was the removal of the terrorists. Once that was achieved we would begin to consider how to best secure the removal of the Syrians. We understood that Israel's army would not leave Lebanon until the Syrians did, but we also knew that the Syrians would exact a heavy price for their withdrawal.

Even before the PLO evacuated I had my General Staff begin to consider the lessons that were to be learned from the war. Although we had fought well, we all knew that mistakes had been made and concepts had proven to be false. The ability to learn from errors and develop alternative solutions and approaches is extremely important, particularly since we never know how much time will pass before the next war. We had to consider the T-72 tank and try to imagine its full potential. Although we had been quite successful against it, we had to place our success in the context of the war. Our successes came against the Syrians, who were not well organized, and during a war in which we enjoyed complete superiority on the ground and in the skies. We had to try to estimate the damage it could cause, and how we would counter it, should another war erupt. Similarly, we had to assume that the next war would not grant us the luxury of complete control of the skies. We did not use our anti-aircraft missiles, and so we also needed to evaluate how they might have performed.

On July 30, 1982, we were informed that the PLO was prepared to evacuate from Lebanon and would be ready to leave once an international force had taken up positions in Beirut. The terrorists planned to withdraw from the camps and transfer to the Beka'a, where they would stay for two weeks, before moving to other Arab countries. According to their plan, any terrorist forces that did not leave the Beka'a would become part of a Lebanese force, under the command of the Lebanese army.

Naturally, Israel could not agree to such a plan, as it gave no means of guaranteeing that the terrorists would actually leave Lebanon once they moved to the Beka'a. In the Beka'a they would not be under the pressure of our siege, and they could very possibly decide not to evacuate, that is, if they actually had any intentions to. The terrorists also demanded that Israel withdraw its forces from the Beirut-Damascus Highway and five miles away from Beirut before they would evacuate. These conditions were unacceptable to us, as was their evacuation plan. We rejected it and continued to apply pressure by shutting off water and electricity, and selectively employing our Air Force.

Our successful assault on the airport at Khaldeh was instrumental in breaking the morale of many of the terrorist fighters. Although they were prepared for our assault, the manner with which we attacked surprised them, and many fled the battlefield. Their will to resist was further damaged by the Syrians, who were attempting to prevent us from attacking their forces by restricting the terrorists and preventing them from attacking our forces.

The terrorists were also under great pressure from the civilians in West Beirut, as they were recognized as being the source of the hardships. There were many demonstrations against the PLO, and it was clear that, although unorganized, the civilians were capable of damaging the terrorists' efforts to withstand our siege. After considering all these facts, we felt it was only a matter of time before the terrorists agreed to evacuate under terms more suitable to us. All we had to do was maintain the pressure, and wait.

37

The Terrorists Evacuate

After many weeks of intense negotiations the PLO and Syrians finally agreed to evacuate West Beirut during the last week of August. The Syrians left the city looking tired and troubled, and I was surprised to see their brigade commander leaving the city in a new Mercedes Benz. The contrast of him in his shiny new car with his soldiers dirty and defeated walking and riding behind him was extreme, and certainly something that could not happen in the IDF.

We estimated that the terrorists were sending some of their heavy weapons out of Beirut with the Syrians, where it would then be transferred to the forces of Murabitoun, an extremist Moslem organization composed mainly of Lebanese citizens. Among the weapons transferred were recoilless rifles, armored personnel carriers, and mobile Russian vehicles equipped with anti-aircraft guns. We also received intelligence reports that the terrorists with Lebanese papers were being reorganized and would be remaining in West Beirut. Their presence was unacceptable to us, as it was clear that they would seek to re-establish the terrorists' infrastructure in Lebanon. We instructed our intelligence services to set up a network that would allow us to identify and locate all the terrorists that remained in the city after the evacuation was completed. Such information would allow us to arrest these individuals and prevent an underground from developing. In achieving this goal we would naturally work closely with Bashir Gemayel and the Lebanese.

The evacuation was completed on August 31, when Arafat and

his forces left Beirut. (The date was significant for us, as it was forty-three years after the German surrender in World War Two.) Yet, the war, although officially over, still provided many challenges to our forces. An international force, which had been set up to oversee the evacuation, had completed its task and was considering leaving Lebanon. Their absence would create a vacuum that we had to be aware of. Furthermore, the possibility of an underground movement in Beirut was of great concern. We knew that the terrorists had left secret stockpiles of weapons, and we knew that many terrorists had not evacuated the city. The IDF would be called upon by Gemayel to assist in locating these forces, their weapons supplies and their operational facilities. Gemayel did not have the intelligence services necessary to complete this task alone, and recognizing our interests in preventing a resurgence of terrorist activity in Beirut, we agreed to assist in follow-up actions, aimed at locating and neutralizing the remaining terrorist forces in Beirut.

Prior to the evacuation Israel had pledged not to strike the PLO forces as they were leaving Beirut. In exchange for this vow, the terrorists promised not to secretly hide weapons or leave forces in Beirut. Naturally, they disregarded their commitments, but we felt that we could not violate ours. Although we had the opportunity to destroy the terrorists, and more importantly, their leadership, we did not fire on them.

Once the terrorists had left Beirut we held a meeting with Gemayel at the home of an influential senior Lebanese officer. The atmosphere was friendly, and Gemayel, who was at the time President-elect, was confident that the decisions he had made and the plans he had for restoring Lebanon were going to succeed. I sensed a change in the way he viewed Israel, but was not concerned since he expressed an interest in working together to clear Beirut of all the terrorists that had not left.

The plan that Gemayel outlined for us called for a combined force of Phalange and Lebanese army troops to enter Beirut and clear out the terrorists by October 15. Once this was achieved, the barriers between the eastern and western sectors of the city would be torn down, and the city would be reunited. I explained to him that from the Israeli perspective the war was over and that we had achieved our objectives. I understood that his forces would need us to play a supportive role, and we were willing to comply. We were willing to remain in the vicinity of Beirut until the Lebanese had completed their operation, and would offer any intelligence data we uncovered. However, I made it clear that Israeli forces would not be entering Beirut.

As the meeting concluded we once again touched on Israeli-Lebanese relations and Gemayel repeated his feelings that Lebanon had been abandoned and isolated from the Arab world and that Israel was its natural ally in the region. I believed that Gemayel was sincere, although many doubted that he would succeed in his ambitious plans. Three days later Bashir Gemayel was assassinated. In addition to the loss of a potential friend and ally, we had to consider the consequences of the vacuum created and the opportunity this presented to the thousands of terrorists that had remained in West Beirut.

38

The Murder of Gemayel and the Taking of Beirut

During the few days between our final meeting with Gemayel and his assassination we had begun releasing reserve forces and sending many regular units back to training. It was clear to us that the war was over, and the quiet that prevailed reinforced our conclusion. We had no reason to believe that we would be forced to dust off our contingency plans for entering Beirut.

On Tuesday, September 14, at two o'clock in the afternoon, a gigantic explosion shook the Phalange headquarters building in Beirut. At first there was a tremendous amount of confusion, and we received reports that, although there were many people killed and wounded in the explosion, Bashir Gemayel had escaped unharmed. By eight o'clock that evening I was informed by the Minister of Defense that our initial information was mistaken, and the Gemayel had been killed in the explosion. Sharon and I discussed the implications of his death and decided to assist the Lebanese by sending rescue equipment and medical teams to the bomb site.

Our attention was focused on the military implications of the attack. We did not know who was behind it or what they hoped Gemayel's death would bring them. We feared that the Syrians and the terrorists had orchestrated the attack so as to create chaos and provide the terrorists with an opportunity to return to Beirut.

The Minister of Defense and I agreed that the situation required us to place the IDF on alert. We also instructed our intelligence forces to follow all developments and provide us with regular updates. In discussing the options before us, Sharon expressed his opinion that, if we were required to enter West Beirut, we should not allow the Phalange to avoid playing a central role. The IDF should not suffer casualties and do the work of the Christians. During the war we had often asked the Christians to participate in various battles, or initiate an assault on their own, and we had usually received evasive responses. We had no intentions of entering Beirut by ourselves. We would demand that the Phalange play an active role.

At midnight Sharon called me at home and informed me that Gemayel's death had been confirmed and that the IDF would be entering Beirut. He requested that the operation be initiated as quickly as possible, and we decided our troops would move at dawn. I immediately ordered a helicopter and flew to the Northern Command, where preparations were already underway. I informed my commanders that I did not want heavy cannons or the Air Force to be employed, so as to minimize the risk of civilian casualties. I ordered the Air Force to place planes in the air beginning at dawn, so as to be ready for every possibility.

After authorization of our plan, I traveled to the Phalange headquarters in Karantina. It was two o'clock in the morning. The military commanders at the headquarters were confused and stunned by the death of their leader. I explained to them that Bashir's murder had the potential of sparking a new round of violence, and that it also could be the first act in an attempt by the Syrians and terrorists to return to Beirut. For these reasons the IDF had decided to place its forces inside the city. I asked them if their forces would be prepared to assist us, and to my surprise received an immediate affirmative answer. I asked them to place a curfew on all the areas under their control, as we were doing, and asked that they prepare to capture the Palestinian camps Sabra, Shatila, and Fakahani. I was told they would be ready to capture the camps the following evening.

The plan to gain control of West Beirut began exactly at dawn on Wednesday, September 15. As planned, our ground forces already in Lebanon entered first while we called up reserves to help man the subsequent stages of the operation. The operation was large and logistically complex. Soldiers and equipment were flown in on planes and helicopters, as well as by boat. We did not meet a great deal of resistance and lost eight soldiers during the entire operation.

By Thursday morning West Beirut was already under our control. I left the city at seven o'clock in the morning and on my way out of the city I observed the Phalange troops preparing to enter Sabra and Shatila. I did not speak with any of their commanders, but was impressed by the manner with which they were approaching their task. They appeared to be highly motivated and well organized. As I left their position I saw no evidence to indicate that these forces would engage in the kind of brutal rampage that they conducted in the camps. I had no reason to expect such behavior from them, as they had conducted themselves according to the accepted rules of war in all the other battles they had fought. I did not imagine they would behave differently this time.

Late that afternoon I flew to Jerusalem to report to the Cabinet. I informed the ministers that the Phalange, in cooperation with the Northern Command, would be entering the Palestinian camps at eight o'clock that evening. None of the Cabinet ministers objected to the plan. I responded to the one inquiry about the possibility that the Phalange would seek revenge by stating that they appeared to be motivated to fulfill the objective of their mission, and that they had never displayed a tendency toward misconduct. I informed the Cabinet that the high level of motivation was most likely a result of the assassination of their leader. I also mentioned that I was able to see "the long knives and the eagerness for vengeance in their eyes," a comment that was misunderstood after the slaughter that took place in the camps was discovered. I merely meant that the Phalange forces were clearly anxious to participate in the war effort. I had no idea, nor did I even consider it a possibility, that they would massacre innocent people.

I explained to the Cabinet that one of the reasons we had decided to enter Beirut was to prevent the outbreak of bloodshed. Lebanon was still a very divided country and we feared each militia would seek to exploit the lack of a visible authority in Beirut to avenge the acts of their enemies. This remark was also interpreted after the events at Sabra and Shatila as having been an indication of the possibility of a massacre. In fact, however, I was referring to forces with no association with us. I was not referring to the Phalange forces entering Sabra and Shatila. I viewed that mission as an organized military body going into an area with a specific mission, and under the command of its officers. My statement referred to the other militias that had less direction and were not tightly structured.

The Phalange mission in Sabra and Shatila was performed in coordination with our Northern Command, in that we had a liaison officer with one of their officers stationed at their headquarters. This officer was to receive updates from the Phalange forces on the ground. None of our soldiers were accompanying the Phalange, nor, as some reported, did our forces guard the exits of the camps while the massacre was taking place. We had no information that the massacre was happening while it was in progress. The only assistance we provided was illuminating shells, so as to provide light during the night operation. Furthermore, we informed the Phalange that we had not used artillery or the Air Force while taking West Beirut so as to avoid civilian casualties. We made it clear to them that we would hold them to the same high level of conduct.

39

Sabra and Shatila

By Friday, the first evening of Rosh Hashanah, the Jewish New Year, the entire city was under our control and the fighting was coming to a halt. At around noon I received a telephone call from the Commander of the Northern Command informing me that he was putting a stop to the Phalange operation in Sabra and Shatila. He told me "it seems that the Phalange are going too far." As I pressed for a better understanding of what was happening, he informed me that they were "mopping up houses without removing the civilians and were shooting at people randomly." The Phalange had entered the camps the night before, and we had an officer at their headquarters who was supposed to be receiving updates from the Phalange forces on the ground. They were distorting the information they were sending, as they knew that we would never allow them to embark on such a brutal and barbaric rampage.

I immediately notified the Minister of Defense and left my home for the Northern Command post. I was extremely upset by the report I had received. As I arrived in Beirut I met with General Amir who was not able to provide any additional information. I reached the Phalange headquarters at 3:30 and was met by the Phalange headquarters staff. When I asked for an update on their progress in the camps I was told that all was well and that they had completed the capture of Sabra and Shatila. They told me they had suffered several wounded and killed and requested that we provide them with tractors, so they would be able to destroy the tunnels and trenches they had discovered. I continued to inquire about the course of the battles and was not given any indication that the headquarters staff knew what had actually taken place in the camps.

At first I was inclined to provide the Phalange with some tractors, but then reconsidered in light of all that had happened. In the end I gave them one tractor, which sat unused, as they had no one capable of operating it. As I returned to Israel later that night I still did not have a clear picture of what the Phalange forces had done in the camps. I only knew that we had stopped the operation because the Commander of the Northern Command received reports of civilian casualties and random shootings.

The following morning, Saturday, I was awakened by the Prime Minister who asked me to check into an American complaint that the Phalange had broken into Gaza Hospital in West Beirut. I contacted my officers in the area and was informed that the American report was inaccurate. I relayed this information to Begin. Meanwhile, information regarding the massacre at Sabra and Shatila was beginning to surface. Naturally, many of the forces that are inherently against us began to report that our forces were present while the massacre was taking place. Some reports even went so far as to claim that our forces participated. Many reports suggested that we were responsible. The Prime Minister and Sharon decided that I should be the one to go before the press the following morning to refute the charges and clarify what had happened. It was important that we stop the spread of damaging rumors and false reports as quickly and clearly as possible.

When I went before the press in Beirut on Sunday morning, I was clearly at a disadvantage. Many of the journalists had already visited the camps and had seen what had happened. I had not been there and was still unaware of the extent of the slaughter. I did however know for certain that none of our troops had been involved and that we had taken quick and decisive steps to restrict the Phalange troops once we became aware of the fact that they were deviating from the plan. My goal at the press conference was to explain the operation, as it should have been carried out, and remove all questions of guilt from the IDF.

The reporters asked technical questions that they thought would implicate the IDF, at least as a passive observer. They wanted to know from which direction the Phalange entered the camps, to which I replied that they entered from the east and the south, and that our forces could not have seen them from either direction. I was asked whether we knew the Phalange was entering the camp, to which I replied that we did, but that we had received certain guarantees that they would behave according to the proper rules of warfare. As they began to ask questions about the details of the massacres my credibility was greatly damaged. I found myself answering "I do not know" to many of the questions, to which one of the reporters wondered aloud how it was that the Chief of Staff did not have an in-depth understanding of what had happened. In truth, I should have had more information, but obviously the Phalange were not sharing with us the details of what they had done, and I was not allowing our troops to enter the camps to investigate for fear that their presence would give rise to accusations against us.

After I left the press conference I went immediately to the Phalange headquarters, and in a strict tone scolded them for what had happened and demanded that they issue a statement accepting responsibility for their actions and clarifying the fact that Israel and the IDF were in no way associated with what they had done. Although I received a promise from their political officer, no statement was ever made. Either they lacked the political courage or they were comfortable with letting Israel take the blame. It was clear to me that they did not feel anything particularly barbaric had taken place, as in their minds Christians slaughtering Moslems and Moslems slaughtering Christians was simply a part of life in Lebanon. They saw no reason for an investigation, and certainly were not considering punishing those responsible.

The domestic political scene in Israel became inflamed after the massacres. Many Israelis were accusing the IDF of complicity. The most radical accused us of participating, and others of not acting to prevent the bloodshed. The uproar in Israel fed the foreign press, which in turn created an international uproar. Before long, the IDF and Israel's top political leaders were on trial for acts that we had

had absolutely nothing to do with. The damage that this caused the nation was far greater than any political gain those who orchestrated the opposition could have possibly achieved. The shame was that they either didn't consider this important fact, or sadder, they did not care.

Immediately after the massacres I assigned a Colonel to investigate the events surrounding the massacre. His chief conclusion was that there had been a need to take into account the possibility of a massacre before the Phalanges were allowed to enter the Sabra and Shatila camps. Furthermore, he concluded that an officer in the Beirut sector had been slow in reporting the Phalange activities, as was an IDF unit that failed to immediately report what they believed was happening. As the Colonel was completing his report the government decided to initiate its own investigation, to be called the Kahan Commission. Once this commission was established I saw no reason to publicize the results of the IDF investigation, although I did make the report available to the commission.

The Prime Minister set up the commission after he was placed under great pressure from both domestic and international forces. In Israel a mass demonstration was held in Tel Aviv demanding an investigation. Many Cabinet members, specifically Minister of Education Zvulen Hammer, were also in favor of an investigation. I responded to Begin's inquiry about my own feelings by informing him that the IDF had nothing to hide and would support whatever he felt was best for the nation.

The evening before Begin announced the formation of the commission he called me to his home in Jerusalem. Again he asked my personal opinion, and again I expressed support for whatever decision he arrived at. He concluded that he would conduct the investigation because there was "no way out."

I was not concerned about the possibility of being damaged by the commission's investigation. I knew that the Phalange had acted on their own and that the IDF, and I as the Chief of Staff, were in no way connected with the massacre. I was so confident that I did not see any need to prepare for my testimony before the commis-

sion. I believed that I would enter and simply tell the truth. I
certainly saw no reason for legal counsel. The Chief Military
Prosecutor informed me that my approach was naive and that my
lack of preparedness could lead to complications. He suggested that
he provide a staff to gather important materials and prepare me for
my testimony. I unenthusiastically agreed and he assigned a
Lieutenant Colonel and a small staff to assist me.

The testimony I presented to the commission members was
based partly on my memory and partly on the documents I had in
my possession. I had issued instructions to all echelons of the IDF
to fully cooperate, without exception, with the investigation, and to
place all documents requested at the disposal of the commission. My
order remained even after the commission, in compliance with the
law, published a listing of individuals who could be damaged by its
findings. Although my name was on this list, I remained unconcerned. I was confident of my innocence and believed that the
commission could conclude nothing other than that I was totally
innocent.

On the other hand, Minister of Defense Sharon was quite
concerned. He requested of me that I recall exactly what I had told
him on that Friday night when I called to tell him that the Phalange
had exceeded the scope of their mission. He asked me to go before
the commission and explain to them that I had reported to him that
"a lot of people are getting killed in the camps, a massacre is going
on." I was not able to report this to the commission, as my recollec-
tion of our conversation was only that I had repeated what the
Commander of the Northern Command had told me, that the
Phalange "were going too far."

My testimony before the commission was rather unemotional as
I stated the facts. Once the conclusions were published I remained
calm. Despite the fact that the commission concluded that I was
among those who should have foreseen the possibility of a massacre, I knew that the situation before the war did not lend to such
suspicions. It is always easy to look back and say "you should
have," but there were good reasons why we didn't. The Phalange

gave us no reason to fear their actions, and we had taken the precaution of warning them to behave in a proper fashion many times. Furthermore, we had every reason to conclude that they would conduct themselves properly because they were going to be fighting in close proximity to our forces. We had allowed the Phalange to enter the camps because it was in our interests. We did not want our forces to have to fight there. My conscience was at peace, and I knew that I had acted in a professional and moral manner.

There were also some other conclusions in the commission's report that concerned others that I found to be unfair. The commission did not draw the proper conclusions with regard to the lack of intelligence data that might have allowed us to better predict the possibility of a massacre. The commission focused the blame on the Commander of Military Intelligence, General Yehoshua Saguy. Yet, the responsibility for the day to day contact with the Phalange was that of the Mossad, the civilian intelligence agency. The head of the Mossad had assumed office only a few days prior to the massacres, and so the commission did not focus on what his role could have been. However, the outgoing head of the Mossad was also not considered. Instead, they concluded that Saguy had somehow failed to meet his obligations, when if fact he was not responsible at all.

I cannot comment as to whether the commission treated Minister of Defense Sharon with undo severity in recommending his resignation. I do, however, believe that the commission's conclusions concerning Sharon should have been seen as a statement about the entire Cabinet because not one action during the war was taken without the express consent of the entire Cabinet. Sharon was merely the contact person between the government and the army. He decided nothing alone, including whether the Phalange should be allowed to enter the camps. Indeed, during the briefing I gave prior to their entry, Deputy Prime Minister David Levy questioned me with regard to the possibility that the Phalange would seek revenge. The Cabinet heard my response and did not raise further objections. David Levy did not insist that we postpone the mission until we could better assess the Phalange's intentions. Nor did any other Minister. In my mind, this implicates them to the same extent that the commission implicated Sharon. Furthermore, during the massacre the Minister of Communications was informed by a journalist of what was taking place. He informed the Foreign Minister who did not believe the report. Was not the Foreign Minister obligated to pursue the information? Shouldn't the Minister of Communications have contacted the Prime Minister and the Chief of Staff? Sharon was not alone among the Cabinet ministers, he was but one, and yet the commission singled him out as being solely responsible.

I do not know what influences the commission's report had on the IDF, but I am sure that its effect was not helpful. Clearly the public censure and punishment of top officers serves as a deterrent to future deviations. However, since it is relatively clear in my mind that the commission showed itself to be unfair, I believe that it will serve to curb legitimate, and more importantly, necessary action. It would not be unreasonable for an officer to hesitate before ordering his forces to conduct a legitimate action for fear that he will be called before a commission. Furthermore, the commission's conclusions and the punishments handed down also served to confuse many officers with regard to what kinds of actions were permitted and what kinds were not. Clearly our forces had not participated in the massacres. Yet, we conducted an inquiry, and even found some of our leaders at fault. How could men lead when such an absurdity was possible? In addition to stifling the creativity and leadership of our officers, the commission's report also made many soldiers feel as if they had been placed on trial for events that they had nothing to do with. The effect this had on the morale of our troops was very damaging and could harm the fighting ability of our men.

Yet the Kahan Commission was not the first time that the political echelon had tried to avoid taking responsibility for their actions by placing the blame on the IDF. After the Yom Kippur War, the Agranot Commission found our Chief of Staff David "Dado" Elazar guilty of acts of omission and commission, even when the evidence clearly pointed to Moshe Dayan, the Minister of Defense. Both the Agranat and the Kahan Commissions are part of a dangerous trend. As a democratic nation, Israel must place authority and responsibility in the hands of the same individuals. Any attempt to place the authority in the hands of the government and the responsibility in the hands of the army could lead to great frustration within the ranks of the IDF. Under such conditions, it would not be inconceivable that the army officers, upon whom the responsibility is being placed, would try to secure for themselves the authority as well. Even if such an unfortunate event does not take place, it is clear that the contradiction evident in Israeli life is dangerous and undermines our democratic institutions.

To his credit, Prime Minister Begin had no inclination to place the blame on the IDF. He told me from the beginning that he viewed the whole government and the General Staff as equal partners. He was not interested in passing on any allegations of guilt and was ready to stand behind his decisions.

The cabinet meeting held after the commission issued its report was very tense and emotional. I attended this meeting accompanied by the three officers implicated in the report; the Commander of the Northern Command, the Chief of Military Intelligence and the Division Commander of the division that was stationed on the outskirts of the camps. Each man spoke in turn and repeated what they had told the commission, that they were in no way responsible for the actions of the Phalange. Minister of Defense Sharon also spoke quite passionately, as he was literally fighting for his political life. The commission report had recommended that Sharon be relieved of his post, a conclusion Sharon felt was absurd. He argued that the Jews should not be punishing themselves because Christians killed Moslems. He pointed out the irony of our actions, while the actual perpetrators of the massacre were not being punished at all. He also warned his fellow Cabinet members that their acceptance of the commission's finding would be paramount to admitting responsibility, and that Israel and the IDF would be placed under an international cloud of guilt.

When we had completed our remarks I informed the Cabinet that we were not demanding that they act in any particular manner, and that we would accept whatever decision they arrived at. After deliberation it became clear that the Cabinet was willing to spare the careers of the IDF officers on condition that Sharon resign and accept responsibility. Obviously these were conditions that Sharon could not agree to, and the Cabinet concluded that they would accept the findings of the commission in its entirety. This, of course, meant that Sharon would be relieved of his post without accepting the blame, and the officers would be removed from their positions as well.

What I found most distressing about the commission was the pride so many Israelis took in the fact that it was set up, and conducted in such an independent manner. Although I agree that this was an indication of the strength of our democratic system, I saw it as yet another manifestation of the concept that Israel must behave in a manner that is more moral than the other nations of the world. We must do so, the concept dictates, no matter how unfair it is to certain individuals, or how dangerous it is to our national security.

Although many Israelis were proud of the commission, there was also a strong expression of anger from those who felt that the commission had been unfair. These individuals argued that the commission had tainted Israel and the IDF by implying guilt where none existed. They mocked those who were proud of it by reminding them that for every person in the world who was impressed by Israel's working democracy, there were at least ten others who were rejoicing at the damage the commission had caused.

My personal feelings were that the commission did nothing to enhance Israel or the IDF. It did not cleanse us of the guilty or rid us of the unworthy. It failed to do this simply because there were no guilty and unworthy individuals among us. We had done nothing to warrant the commission, and had certainly not been guilty of the acts of commission and omission as described in the report. We had absolutely nothing to do with the massacres at Sabra and Shatila.

The IDF applied the findings of the commission and I removed the officers from their posts. I did allow General Saguy to remain Chief of Intelligence for a short while before he assumed a different post. The government also acted in accordance with the commission's recommendations and Sharon resigned his position. He was replaced by Professor Moshe Arens, who at the time was serving as Israel's Ambassador to the United States. As my date of retirement from the IDF was approaching, Arens and I did not discuss military policy at any great length. We did however spend a great deal of time discussing who would be replacing me. I believed in the military leadership of General Avigdor "Yanush" Ben-Gal and strongly recommended his appointment. Defense Minister Arens however chose to overlook my recommendation and proposed to the cabinet the appointment of General Moshe Levy. The cabinet approved Levy's nomination.

40

Concern for Israel's Fighting Men

During my tenure as Chief of Staff, and particularly during the war, I often sought to remind my officers of the supreme importance the IDF placed on removing the wounded from the field and retrieving the bodies of our soldiers killed in action. I believed that in addition to being the proper policy, our dedication was awarded by higher morale among our troops. Our men knew that if they were wounded in action they would receive care on the spot and be taken to a hospital as soon as possible. Similarly, they knew that if they were to fall in action they would receive a proper burial and their bodies would not be left on the battlefield. Indeed, during the war we launch a number of raids so as to retrieve the bodies of our dear fallen soldiers.

I ordered my officers to provide the Medical Corps and the Military Rabbinate with the necessary means to carry out this important mandate. I was even willing to transfer troops from combat formations so as to guarantee a sufficient number of forces. Furthermore, I instructed the commanders of these units to develop plans to deal with each situation, both in wars that we initiate, and in wars that are forced upon us. My aim was to enable these units to function under extreme pressure with speed and maximum effectiveness.

In order to achieve this crucial mission the unit needed to understand better the conditions under which our troops have been wounded. They needed to determine the casualty rates we suffered during daytime fighting, and similarly, our casualty rates during night fighting. Other questions, such as the types of wounds and the enemy weaponry most likely to cause injury, were also fully researched. By the time the Lebanon War began, our Medical Corps troops were prepared to help our wounded based on the lessons we had learned from the Yom Kippur War and the War of Attrition. These wars had taught us to be wary of the damages caused by the Arabs' artillery. The war in Lebanon found us suffering many losses due to the short-range anti-tank weapons carried by the terrorists. The Medical Corps proved to be skilled and brave and saved the lives of many men wounded in the field.

In addition to the physical damage that war so often causes young soldiers, there are many times that the experiences of war and the horrors one often sees cause emotional and mental damage as well. I saw these injuries as being no less severe and no less deserving of our attention. Our approach was initially to train our officers in the tactics to be used to help ease a soldier through a difficult moment. We believed that immediate care would help prevent the problem from developing into a more serious disorder. Our training was born out of the lessons we had learned during our many wars. We studied the emotional problems that had arisen from these wars, and with the assistance of researchers and other medical and psychological professionals, developed a program designed to sensitize our officers to the problem and educate them on methods of dealing with these stressful situations. We also emphasized the need for each officer to establish and maintain a personal relationship with his men. Although modern technology has provided means for an officer to relay orders over advanced communications systems, we recognize that only direct orders, given "face to face" allow soldiers to feel connected and an integral part of the operation at hand. We demand of our officers that they take upon themselves the responsibility for the young men whose lives are literally in their hands. I believe every officer in the IDF, from the Chief of Staff to the newest lieutenant, has an obligation to recognize that his troops are dependent on him in combat situations and that this places upon him the responsibility to be conscious of their needs and feelings.

The war in Lebanon gave rise to much discussion over the problem of combat fatigue. In my experience as a career soldier and veteran of numerous wars, I have learned that combat fatigue is inevitable among some soldiers. Even during the War of Independence we suffered many cases of this paralyzing condition. The fourth battalion of the Palmach, stationed in Jerusalem, had a whole company that suffered from battle shock. Some soldiers are more sensitive than others, and some soldiers see horrifying sights that others do not see. Some men suffer as a result of the loss of a good friend who died before them, others feel great pressure due to the damage they have caused. There are literally hundreds of legitimate reasons why a strong man could break down during a war. Our task was to train them to withstand the pressures, and help them to the best of our ability if in fact they cracked.

Before a soldier's first battle, he is a man of great courage. It always takes courage to proceed into a situation you understand you must fear, without fully understanding why. After a soldier's first battle he is usually less of a hero, however he is no less brave. Often a soldier is transformed during a battle from an easy-spirited individual to a solemn, sober young man. He is forever to be affected by the filth, the blood, and the destruction he witnessed. It is at these moments that the commander must do all he can to speak to his forces and allow them the opportunity to express their feelings. The officer must assist them in understanding what they have just experienced and what changes their experiences will have on them. The information the officers provide can have a profound effect, as many soldiers learn not to internalize their feelings and also learn that what they are feeling is natural and normal.

The relationship between our soldiers and officers is unique unto the IDF. Most other modern armies do not encourage such open relationships, nor do they place their officers on the frontlines. Our history has many examples of officers who heroically led their men into battle at great personal risk and were killed. In the War of Independence the commander of the raid on Nebi Yoshua, Dudu

Cherkassy, was killed. In the Six-Day War and Yom Kippur Wars we lost many officers. During the Lebanese War a full forty percent of our casualties were officers. This number is even higher when one considers that only three percent of the overall American casualty count were officers during the United States' involvement in Vietnam. We believe that this difference provides us with an advantage and allows us to expect, and receive, more from our soldiers. Our officers ask nothing of them that they are unprepared to do themselves. Our soldiers and officers are partners, and they fight together for a common purpose. For this reason we invite our soldiers to question their officers and make suggestions. We want every fighting man to feel that he has a personal role to play, and our experience has shown us that this encourages them to play their role with greater dedication.

We also developed training sessions that were designed to simulate a true battle experience as accurately as possible. Our goal was to bridge the gap between what our soldiers thought a war would be like, and an actual combat situation. By closing the gap between expectation and reality we felt we could reduce the number of soldiers who became overwhelmed and emotionally disturbed during an actual war. We also had seminars on the danger of being captured and taken captive as a prisoner of war. Although we tried to set rules of behavior, we understood that once in captivity many of the rules would be broken. Yet, we could not expect our men to return to the days of the War of Independence when we understood that death was preferable to captivity. Many men committed suicide rather than be taken prisoner, as did my friend Zerubabel Horovitz, who blew himself up together with his armored car in Nebi Daniel so that he would not fall into captivity.

As an officer in the IDF, and then as Chief of Staff, I was very conscious of the fact that my role was to lead. I believed my soldiers would judge me on three different levels, and I strove to be the best I could on all three. The first level was my professionalism. I needed to know every weapons system, how they were to be used, how to deploy my forces, and what orders to issue at what times. I needed to be able to lead under pressure and maintain my self-control. Secondly, I would be judged on my courage. I had to lead my men into battle and remain by their side throughout. I could not shy away from danger or expect my men to assume more risk than I personally assumed. Finally, I would be judged by the example I set. I would not eat until all my men had eaten. I had to recognize that I was their leader based on trust and confidence and had to do all I could to preserve the respect and faith of my men. I had to play the role of educator and motivator, yet I had to be willing to learn and eager to act as well.

The Lebanon War produced a great deal of criticism. Although I am in favor of vibrant democracy and agree that discussion is a healthy development in any society, I must confess to a lack of understanding with regard to the level and basis of the criticism generated by the war. We were at first criticized for not sufficiently preparing the public for the war, that is, that we did not explain the reasons for the war in clear enough terms. Perhaps this is so, but we had no way of knowing that some segments of the public did not realize that we had the need and right to rid ourselves of a terrorist force that had concentrated on our border and was engaging in rocket attacks and ground assaults against our civilian population. We believed that the public would understand that, just as we had launched the Litani Operation after the terrorists killed over thirty civilians on a coastal bus route, we were initiating this assault in an effort to destroy the terrorists. Can anyone actually expect us to wait for the next attack before we acted, or did we not have the right to act first, thus preventing the deaths of additional civilians? The opposition to the war made no sense, in that after a terrorist attack there were cries for revenge and demands that the government do all that was necessary to prevent further attacks. Yet, when we launch a war designed to achieve exactly those objectives, we are criticized and condemned.

My confusion is increased by those who argue that Israel must come to a consensus on defense and the borders of the Land of Israel. Yet, they also emphasize the value of debate. Furthermore these individuals would demand that Israel not take the initiative and refrain from aggressively pursuing its security needs. However, these are the same forces that joined the cry of outrage after the Yom Kippur War when the government was asked why Israel did not strike first.

In truth there can be no strict guidelines determining when and where Israel can exercise its military option. Certainly the Arab states, who are still in an official state of war with us, would take advantage of any system that was designed to regulate, and in effect, stifle, Israel's use of force. We have an obligation to our citizens, and to history, to defend our state. I personally can not think of even one military exercise that Israel engaged in when we were not justified in using force. We are always fighting for our survival, whether we are blowing up a nuclear reactor in Baghdad that was going to produce atom bombs to be used against us, or freeing innocent civilians from the hands of terrorists in Entebbe, or destroying the dangerous terrorist infrastructure in Lebanon.

The educational system in Israel has to bear much of the responsibility for this great opposition, as does the press, and the politicians who are putting their own interests before those of the state. Our young are not being taught the essentials of Zionism and their education no longer focuses on the land. Instead our young are at times questioning the rights of the state, and are often supportive of compromises that would lead to war and present a grave threat to our very existence.

The educational system must teach our children to love the land. They must learn to know the land by walking it, enjoying the views, and smelling the flowers. We must teach our young that the land is to be appreciated and respected, and that this nation is their home. We must teach our young the essence of Zionism and implant in them a national pride. We must focus on the flag and the symbols of the state and teach the children the value of community.

Our young are the inheritors of our efforts, yet they must also bear the burden of our errors. They must fight wars as we fought and they must sacrifice as we did. Our young people must be motivated for these tasks and must approach them with the willingness to do what must be done. They too are responsible to the generations that will follow. They must not grow weary of the struggle and must continue to be ready for war, even as they search and long for peace.

This sizeable challenge will call for leadership. Our politicians must rediscover their connection to the people. Our leaders must set personal examples of financial responsibility and respect for others. Only through leadership and personal example will we be able to overcome the difficulties we face today, and thus offer our children and grandchildren the opportunity for a better life.

41

People

Throughout the thirty-seven years of my military service I have met many magnificent people. Although I cannot mention them all, and hope that those I do not mention will forgive me, I would like to note those individuals, aside from my family, who have had a special influence on my life.

The first man of great esteem, and the man whose place is at the top of those I have admired, is Chaim "Poza" Poznansky, the commander of the platoon I was assigned to in the Palmach. Poza was killed in the War of Independence at Nebi Samuili only two weeks after his brother had died at Beit Keshet. He was the first living example I had seen of the perfect qualities of leadership. He was a brave man of great skill who made a special effort to set a personal example. He took great interest in the well-being of his men and often shared with us his seemingly limitless knowledge of the Land of Israel. Poza made it clear to us all that he would not request of us any action he was not prepared to do himself, and he fought beside us at all times.

Although I have a great respect for and admire Ariel Sharon, I did not have the stability in my relationship with Sharon, as I did with Poza. Sharon, however, was a magnificent military leader, and as commander of the paratrooper battalion was the motivational force for many necessary operations. He was a man of great dedication and had a vitality that never tired. Furthermore, Sharon had a special talent to analyze and plan military operations. He has had an influence on the tactical thinking of many IDF officers, and greatly influenced the way I approached a military situation. My only hesitation with Arik was that he was an "operator," a man in pursuit of more, whether it be status, position, or authority.

My company commander during the War of Independence was Uri Banner, who later adopted the Hebrew last name Ben-Ari. Uri was the classic commander of what later became the IDF tradition of officers in the lead. He wore a big Australian hat and was always in the front, leading us into action. His bravery has served as an inspiration.

Two men who have in many ways become legendary soldiers in Israel are Meir Har-Tzion and Obed Lajinsky. Har-Tzion was an officer in the famous Unit 101 and was responsible for the execution of the anti-terrorist and retaliatory raids performed by this legendary unit. He was a man of amazing bravery who possessed an uncanny mind for tactical understanding. He was a quiet man who performed all functions during combat. Conversely, Lajinsky was an impatient, restless man whose major task was leading his men. He was not as versatile as Har-Tzion, but he too was a man of extraordinary bravery and skill.

There were also two men who made a special impression on me while I was their commanding officer. The first was Gad Manella, whom I met when he was a corporal and I was a brigade commander. Gad was a quiet, shy man who spent a great deal of his time alone. He had a difficult time adjusting to the discipline and structure of the army, yet as an officer demanded great discipline from his soldiers. He was an extremely brave man and a great leader. Similarly, Arik Regev was a man of great intelligence who was able to foresee certain events by following actions to their logic consequence. Regev greatly contributed to my ability to serve as an effective officer. Both of these men are no longer alive, and yet their contributions continue to make their mark.

During the Yom Kippur War I was given the opportunity to serve beside many men of tremendous stature. Any combat situation serves as a test of courage and self-sacrifice. Yet, the Yom Kippur War was an even greater test due to the extremely difficult circumstances. One great soldier to shine during this war was Avigdor

"Yanush" Ben-Gal. Yanush was a commander of genuine heroic proportions. During the war his unit withstood the enemy advance in a desperate and amazing battle of survival. After fighting literally until the last ounce of strength, Yanush was able to regroup his unit and continue fighting after only twenty four hours. Ben-Gal's skill as a leader and his professionalism as a soldier were such that he was one of the few men who stood out at a time when so many were heroes. He was truly one of the great men of the war.

Similarly, Uri Orr was another man who displayed incredible courage. Whereas Yanush distinguished himself by commanding a unit that fought brilliantly, Uri was the commander of a loosely organized, incoherent unit of reservists. In an effort to mobilize and motivate his men, Orr personally led his men into difficult and dangerous battles. Bravery of this magnitude is simply beyond the ability of description. Suffice it to say that Uri Orr risked his life on many, many occasions in his valiant defense of Israel.

After the war I recommended to the Chief of Staff that both Yanush and Uri Orr be awarded merit citations for the brilliant manner with which they withstood the challenges. Unfortunately merit citations are not awarded to soldiers with the rank of colonel or above. Were it not for this regulation, however, both men would have been officially commended for their valor and fearlessness.

One man who did receive a citation of merit was Avigdor Kahalani, another man who displayed incredible levels of personal bravery. Kahalani was serving as a battalion commander and demonstrated a stubborn ability to withstand the severest tests of war. Kahalani's devotion, capabilities, and self-sacrifice were so impressive that his performance has come to serve as an example for Israeli youth today. He was an excellent commander and fighter, so much so that he was awarded a citation of merit in both the Six-Day War and the Yom Kippur War.

Another soldier whose performance was acknowledged through a citation of merit and who has since become part of the IDF folklore is Meir "Tiger" Zamir. As a company commander with only nine tanks, Zamir's unit engaged an entire Syrian brigade in an intense nighttime battle. Under Zamir's command the company destroyed many Syrian tanks without suffering any losses, and effectively stemmed a Syrian advance that would have altered the course of the war had it succeeded in breaking through. Zamir was a leader of impressive qualities and enjoyed the support and respect of his troops.

One Israeli military and political leader who greatly influenced me was Yigal Allon. When I first joined the Palmach it was initially for one year. As the War of Independence neared, I wanted to extend my service. My problem was that my father needed my assistance on the farm. It was Allon who convinced my father that I should continue my service.

Yigal was a great leader. He was at separate times during his years of service a great military commander and a keen, intelligent politician. Yet, he was a simple man, a man of the soil, who was modest and careful with his authority. I always enjoyed learning from him, and continued to discuss issues with him casually, even as I advanced to the position of Chief of Staff. We had become great friends and I used to bring him to the front and solicit his advice on many occasions. He first suffered a heart attack in my office when I was head of the General Staff Branch. I was very sad when he passed away, as he was a man I admired and loved. He was an unusual combination of leader and simple man.

An unlikely figure to have served as an influence in my life is George Berling, a Christian from Canada who was a hero during the Second World War. His heroics as a young pilot in the British Air Force were immortalized in his book "Spitfire Over Malta." He was a man of intense bravery, who volunteered to serve because he felt an obligation to fight against evil. After the war, although he had no prior connection with Jews or Israel, George volunteered for the Haganah and began to fly Norseman aircraft to Israel. On one particular flight he crashed near Rome and was killed. His tale of sacrifice and his sense of justice have always served as an inspiration to me.

The wars and conflicts with the Arabs have brought a great deal of death to Israel. I remember as a child feeling the pain when the husband of one of my teachers was killed as he rode his bicycle to Afula. Although no clear answers were available, it appeared that the Arab driver who struck him had done so intentionally. Our need to learn to defend ourselves also took the life of a close family friend, Yitzchak Leopold, who was killed in a training accident.

My first encounter with the death that comes in war was during the War of Independence when a convoy I was part of was making its way past what is today Moshav Shahar. Our convoy was ambushed and four of the men I had trained were killed. In addition, I went with a few other men to scout out a position, and on the way we discovered the mutilated bodies of some of our men who had been taken prisoner. This sight, still fresh and haunting in my mind, truly introduced me to the brutality of war. Also for the first time, I understood the concept of purity of arms and the need to restrain the impulse for revenge. Only in this way would we be able to preserve our humanity.

It was during these years that I learned that I had to accept things I could not change. There was little to be gained from losing one's temper, and often it harmed one's ability to think rationally. Conversely, I also learned to fight until the end for the things I could change. Yet, death was not one of those things. I learned to mourn alone, privately. I never felt it was an emotion to be displayed to all. Only happiness should be shared.

The two hardest tests of this personal policy were when my son and my nephew died. I was notified that my nephew had died on the first day of the Six-Day War. The son of my brother Shmuel, Giora and I were very close. Ironically, earlier that same day he had brought me a bottle of whiskey, and left me to fight the war. Although I was deeply hurt by his death, I knew I had a war ahead and men dependent on my leadership. I had little choice but to put his death behind me. My obligation was to those still alive. Yet, his bottle of whiskey was in my half-track and each morning I took a small sip, remembering Giora.

My son Yoram died when I was Chief of Staff. I was involved in

discussions with the Prime Minister when I was notified that his
plane had gone down and he was not seen parachuting to safety. I
immediately notified my wife not to come to Tel Aviv as we had
planned, and went home to her. When I arrived she did not ask why
I had come, although I suspect she understood. When I told her,
she reacted as I did. There was little we could do to bring our beloved
son back. All that was left was to silently mourn. Still, to this day,
on the anniversary of his death, we go to his grave in Tel Adashim
and care for the trees and pull the weeds.

The accident occurred during the time when we were planning
the raid on the Iraqi nuclear reactor. I could not allow his death to
postpone this important mission, nor could I ask that others proceed
without me. I had little choice but to return to my duties.

Yoram's death was due to the failure of the hydraulic system in
the Kfir jet he was piloting. He lost a great deal of altitude and bailed
out too low; his parachute never had the time to open. I was at his
base when the planes leaving for the Iraqi reactor took off and I
visited his room, requesting a few moments to be by myself. Oddly,
Yoram had survived two other crashes, one in a Fouga and the other
in a Skyhawk. The accident with the Skyhawk had caused him a
great deal of stress because he had tried to save the expensive
airplane, but could not. Ironically, it was his attempt to save the Kfir
that took his life, as he would have survived if he had bailed out as
little as five seconds earlier.

42

On to the Knesset

My last day of active service in the Israel Defense Forces was April 19, 1983, five years and three days after assuming the position of Chief of Staff. I took leave of my duties at an official ceremony at the Prime Minister's office and took leave of the soldiers at a parade and ceremony at the IDF headquarters. Although it was a milestone in my life, it was not, as it is for some, a sad occasion. I had devoted over thirty-five years to the defense of my country because I had felt a sense of mission. However, unlike many senior officers who retire from the army without an alternative career, I was looking forward to returning to the farm and my carpentry shop.

Although I was entitled to remain in the army for an additional year, that is, to receive a full salary and keep my vehicle, I felt it was not the correct thing to do. Thus, ten days after leaving my post as Chief of Staff, I officially retired from the IDF. By the end of April I was a civilian. I was even assigned a task in the reserve forces, where I was to be a pilot.

A short time after I retired I began receiving many invitations to lecture at schools and community centers. In the beginning it was difficult to respond to all the mail and arrive at all my destinations, as I was without a secretary or a driver. Still, I worked hard and answered every letter I received and spoke at literally hundreds of sites throughout the country. I did not demand a fee for my services and only accepted reimbursement for my expenses. Many times I would ask the organization to donate money to my favorite charity, LIBI, instead of paying me a fee.

As I traveled around the country, I soon found myself in the lead and at the center of a new movement that was developing. At first we thought of trying to revive an old non-political Zionist organization called "Ein Vered Circle." We later decided to establish a non-political organization dedicated to a Zionist revival. Our organization was to be based on five key principles: settlement, education, aliyah (immigration), work as a value, and unconditional support for the Land of Israel. In an effort to implement our program we established four major objectives: we were to support the security of the State of Israel and oppose any move that would place the nation in danger; promote economic development so as to reduce our dependency; educate our society so as to be more attractive to new immigrants; and campaign for international recognition of Israel's right to maintain control over all of the Land of Israel. To our delight after a short period of time we began to attract support as more than five thousand people signed up.

Initially our movement, called Tzomet, or Crossroads, was to be non-political, in that it would not offer any of its leaders for public office. However, once the Tenth Knesset was dissolved before its term expired, we decided to join forces with the already established political party Techiya, which had secured a number of Knesset mandates in previous elections. After negotiating with the Techiya party leaders, it was decided that one individual from our movement would be placed on a "safe" spot on the Techiya-Tzomet Knesset list. In Israel Knesset elections are presented to the voter by way of party lists. The whole nation serves as one constituency and each voter votes for the party of his or her choice. Once the votes are counted, each party that received over one percent of the overall vote is awarded a Knesset seat in direct proportion to the percentage of the overall vote they received. The members of each respective party become members of the Knesset only if their party receives the number of mandates that correspond or exceed his or her position on the party election list. Thus, a "safe" spot on a party list is a place high enough on the list to guarantee election. I was chosen to represent Tzomet and began my "political career" in the Eleventh Knesset.

Initially, I did not become an active participant in Knesset debates. I did not shout out my view out of turn and preferred to observe and learn. I had some experience with the Knesset, as I had addressed many committees when I was Chief of Staff, but I felt that I would be more effective after learning exactly how the system functioned. I was surprised to find that the Knesset was actually quite organized, as I, like many Israelis, had the perception that the Knesset did not function properly.

My major dispute with many members of the Knesset centered on the level of compensation we received. Although our salaries were not excessive, there were many benefits that I saw as unnecessary, and perhaps even unfair. I felt that the Knesset had an obligation to make certain sacrifices, mainly because the state of the economy required it, but also as an example to the people, who were being called upon to make sacrifices. At a time when the economy was suffering I thought the Knesset members should set the national tone by reducing their salaries and benefits. Only by personal example would we be in a position to ask others to voluntarily accept a reduction in their standard of living. I decided to personally lead the way and donated fifty percent of my monthly salary to LIBI.

There were other issues in the Knesset that were of importance to me, and required that I take a personal stand. I was extremely distressed to learn that the Israeli flag does not fly in the Knesset. Though not an issue of strategic national importance, I believed it was symptomatic of the lack of Zionist enthusiasm in Israel. Thus, I began to build a stand for the flag in my carpentry shop. Soon the Knesset secretary informed me that they would not be able to use my stand, but that architects would be designing a flag stand. This procedure frustrated me because it was costly and I reacted by donating 100,000 shekels to the Knesset secretariat to be used specifically for the flag stand. My action influenced other Knesset members and soon Nahman Raz and others also donated money for the stand. Although the Speaker of the Knesset objected to our actions and argued that we were not paupers, we insisted that the government recognize the severity of our economic situation. Unfortunately, to this day my check, and the others, remain in the drawers of the secretariat.

During my first term in the Knesset the internal debate on the merits and wisdom of the Peace for Galilee War in Lebanon continued to rage. Many commentators, journalists, and politicians argued that the war did not achieve its objectives. This simply is not the case, and it angered me to see so many people use the war as a political tool. The war in Lebanon succeeded in destroying the terrorist infrastructure in Lebanon and removed the vast majority of terrorist forces from Lebanese soil. In addition, the war greatly damaged Syria's influence in Lebanon. Also, an agreement between the governments of Lebanon and Israel was signed calling for peaceful relations, and a multi-national force was established in Lebanon. Finally, and most importantly, our northern villages were able to return to a normal way of life as the terrorists were no longer able to fire their rockets randomly at our civilians.

When people criticize the war today they do so because none of the advantages gained through the war lasted very long. This is not the fault of the leaders who orchestrated the war, but rather of those who followed. It was they who allowed the advantages to slip away as we retreated from the Shouf mountains and evacuated the Beirut-Damascus Highway. We acted without proper foresight and in response to internal pressures. We allowed the Syrians access into Lebanon and then watched as they effectively undid much of what we had accomplished. They succeeded in pressuring Amin Gemayel, Lebanon's President, to annul the agreement he had signed with us. They chased the multi-national force out of Lebanon by using terrorism. They employed terrorism against our forces, which also had the effect of pushing us out. All of these actions were made possible by our lack of staying power and our eagerness to withdraw. Had we stayed, the situation in Lebanon would be much different. But, these are not actions directly related to the war; these are actions taken after the war. The war itself was a success and achieved much, if not all, of what it had strived to attain.

Furthermore, our lack of resolve, and willingness to allow the

Syrian-sponsored Shiite terrorists to dictate our actions was an absolute disgrace. In addition to being weak and without precedent, it presented a grave threat to all of Israel. We had shown the Arabs that they could defeat us through the use of terrorism. Such a message could lead to an increase in terrorism, and certainly an increase in terrorist demands. It is not for no reason that the terrorists were able to demand, and obtain, the release of over one thousand terrorists in our jails in exchange for the release of six of our soldiers. We had shown them that we will respond to their demands and we had given them confidence. It was a very dark hour in Israel's history.

The army's weakness made it hard for me to believe that the senior officers had been trained and nurtured in the IDF. Their actions were so contrary to every approach we have ever taken when confronted by a threat. Yet, they were influenced by the internal debate and lost sight of their mandate. The army's inability to cope properly with the challenges of Lebanon in turn influenced the government, and ultimately led to our premature evacuation. Many of the initial benefits gained by the IDF could have been preserved had we kept control over the entire length of the Litani River. Although this should have been clear to the top military leaders, we did not maintain control of the region, and opened the way for the terrorists to re-establish bases in Southern Lebanon.

Many of those who were against the war argued that the IDF had been used to advance political objectives. What these individuals fail to understand is that every army is created to serve as a policy tool of the government, and every war is fought for some political objectives. The only difference between the war in Lebanon and our other wars was that this war was initiated by a Likud government. The left wing of the Israeli political spectrum are supporters of, or at least allies with, the Labor party, and they objected to the war solely on political grounds. It was they who were using the IDF as a political tool, using the memory of our dead and the suffering of our wounded. The real tragedy is that their manipulation of those who fought and sacrificed led the government to act in a manner which was not in the best interests of the country.

Another issue that I was involved in as a Member of the Knesset was the increasingly dangerous threat against our survival. As the Arab states continue in their quest for nuclear and chemical weapons, we must do all we can to prevent their successful acquisition, and short of that, develop weapons that will neutralize the dangers. I am convinced that the Arabs would not hesitate to use these weapons against us, as they have already used them against other Arabs in Yemen, other Moslems in Iran, and the Kurdish people in Iraq. It was for this reason that we destroyed the Iraqi nuclear reactor, and we must continue to take the initiative and do what is necessary to insure the safety of our people.

As I serve in the Knesset I am guided by the words of the Hashomer HaTzair movement of 1937. During those trying times the movement's newspaper wrote: "We cannot abandon one single inch of the soil of the Land of Israel. The needs of the Jewish people throughout the world, and the Jewish community in the Land of Israel, require not reduction of the area of the Zionist state, but its expansion. Not partition of the country, but its expansion and the development of all its territory." Sadly, those who now claim to be the inheritors of the rich traditions of Hashomer HaTzair no longer embrace these sentiments, but rather struggle against the government and advocate capitulation to the Arabs and a return to the 1967 borders. Somewhere over the years of intense struggle they lost the will to fight, even though the need has not lessened. My hope is that they will return to their roots and once again join in the valiant struggle to rebuild the Jewish homeland.

43

The Intifada

The Arabs have never accepted the fact that Israel exists as an independent, sovereign state in the Middle East. Since we declared our independence in May, 1948, the Arab states and the Palestinians have tried many different strategies in their effort to eradicate our small Jewish country. At times they have tried to destroy us through war, and at times they have taken the path of insincere gestures of moderation. Presently, they have taken to stones and Molotov cocktails.

During the years 1936-1939, before the creation of Israel, while the British were still in control of the area, the Arabs embarked on what they called "The Great Arab Revolt." Although the leaders of this rebellion made statements against the British rulers, most of the violence and angry rhetoric was directed toward the Jews. It was clear then, as it is now, that the Arabs were against any Jewish presence in the region.

The Arab war against the Jews began in the late nineteenth century, when the first Zionist pioneers moved to Palestine. The Arabs realized that the Jews intended to remain permanently, and perceived this as a conquest of their land. In some ways they were not mistaken, as Zionism viewed the land as belonging to the Jews and sought to reclaim it and rebuild the Jewish state. Zionism was a movement that sought to conquer not only the land, but the soil, to emphasize labor, and provide the Jew with the opportunity to shed the traumas of centuries of persecution. The Zionist slogan, "To build and to be built," signified the yearning to build a nation and to be transformed while doing so.

In the beginning the Zionist leaders believed the Arabs would welcome the Jews. They hoped the Arabs would see the benefits of a Jewish presence, as they brought with them technology, agricultural innovations, new medical knowledge, and methods of enhancing industry. The Jew would raise the Arab's standard of living and improve the lot of the average Arab worker. As history has shown, the Arabs, unconcerned about issues such as standard of living, chose to reject the promise of progress the Jews brought with them.

After close to fifty years of conflict with the Arabs, and thirty years of struggle against the British, the State of Israel was born. The economic and social infrastructure and system of government set up by the Jews in Palestine helped convince a guilt-ridden world of the need for a Jewish state once the horrors of the Holocaust were revealed. Had the Zionists not established settlements, health-care institutions, semi-official agencies, and cultural establishments, it is unlikely that Israel would have been proclaimed. Similarly, it is unclear as to whether the State would have been formed as early as 1948 had the Holocaust not occurred. In addition to these important elements, the lack of organization and structure in the Arab community, where they had no educational system or health-care system, or any foundation on which to build a state, also contributed to the founding of Israel. The Arabs had not focused their energies on building a structure similar to ours, but rather directed their attention to destroying what we were building. To this day, this has been the Arab approach to our conflict. And to this day, no Arab state has given up the ultimate objective of destroying Israel.

The Arab states do not want, nor do they need, peace with Israel. The Arabs do not subscribe to the Western logic that values peace as an end unto itself. Nor do they see peace as a means of progress. They do not care if peace would allow them to stop purchasing weapons and allow them to direct those resources to health, education, and economic enhancement. They are involved in a holy struggle and will not cease until the alien Zionist entity is removed from the midst of the Arab Moslem region.

Furthermore, peace is not pursued by the Arab states because it would lead to the demise of their present governments. Today, every Arab state is ruled by a dictator, in control of and supported by the armed forces. These leaders explain the poor economy and lack of technology on their dedication to the armed struggle against Israel. They explain to their people that certain fundamentals are lacking, but that all must suffer as part of the holy war. If peace were to come tomorrow, the peoples of these lands would legitimately ask for the economic benefits of peace. Yet the leader would need to maintain his strong army for domestic reasons, and would not be able to provide the people with their due. This would naturally lead to a de-stabilization. Thus, most Arab leaders do not seek peace.

Furthermore, many Arab leaders are quite brutal to their own people, but deflect attention away from their own atrocities by manipulating the blind hatred their people feel toward Israel. If there were peace between these nations and Israel, the people would begin to examine the brutality of their leaders more closely. Obviously, the leaders are not anxious for this to occur, and thus are not anxious to achieve peace.

The lack of peace does not necessarily mean that an active war is inevitable, just as a peace treaty does not always serve as a barrier to war. What determines whether Israel and the Arabs have a war is Israel's deterrent capability and the international environment. As long as Israel has the military strength to convincingly defeat the Arabs they will refrain from attacking us. Similarly, when the international community is supportive of Israel then the Arabs are less likely to initiate a war, as they know that the world would prevent them from enjoying the fruits of their labor, should they be victorious.

Still, the lack of a viable war option has never prevented the Arabs from perpetrating acts of violence against Jews. During the 1920s, the Arabs used to engage in pogrom-like assaults on Jewish villages. In the 1930s, the Arabs embarked on their "Great Arab Revolt." In the 1950s and early 1960s, the "fedayin" used to cross into Israel and murder civilians. In the late 1960s and throughout the 1970s, the PLO terrorist campaign was waged without any considerations given to the concept of innocence. In the 1980s, the Arabs initiated the "Intifada" — a violent uprising directed toward all Jews, civilian and soldier.

Each of these violent manifestations occurred at times when the Arabs felt they did not have a viable war option against Israel and had the same goal of harassing and weakening Israel. The Arabs sought to weaken our resolve, burden our economy, and endanger the lives of our civilians. The Intifada of today is yet another episode in this long, bitter struggle. Although the image is that of a Palestinian with a stone against an armed Israeli soldier, in truth the Palestinians are backed by the economic and political support of every Arab government. The Palestinians hope that the chaos they bring to the territories, together with the political prestige bestowed upon their leader, Yasir Arafat, in many of the world's capitals, will bring pressure upon Israel.

The terrorists' war has not been particularly successful when one considers the frequency of terror attempts. A great majority of the infiltration attempts were intercepted by our forces before the terrorists succeeded in crossing our borders. Similarly, many other terrorist squads were captured or killed inside Israeli territory before they reached their civilian target. It is the nature of terrorism, however, to specifically strike against the innocent, the young, and the vulnerable. Under such circumstances even one successful attack has an enormous impact on Israel. We are a people particularly sensitive to the slaughter of our innocents.

Our strategy against the terrorists had two major components. We enhanced our efforts aimed at interception by increasing the number of patrols, setting up early warning stations, and fortifying our borders. In addition, we stepped up our offensive campaign against the terrorists' bases and command posts. Our objective was to damage them operationally, exact a price for their actions, and knock them off balance. Both of these strategies led to a sharp decline in the operational level of the terrorists, which in turn created a great deal of frustration within their ranks.

In part, their failure to successfully infiltrate Israel led to their decision to begin striking at our northern border with artillery. The artillery assaults afforded them the option of striking at us without placing their troops in danger. Furthermore, it allowed them to claim successes and boost the morale of their men. It was these rocket attacks that made our campaign in Lebanon necessary.

Despite all the criticism, the war had the potential to provide Israel with peace and quiet, not only on the northern border, but in Judea, Samaria, and Gaza as well. Had the government authorized the Israel Defense Forces to complete its campaign against the Syrians, the Syrian army would not have been in a position to promote Syrian policy in Lebanon. The weakening of the Syrians, combined with the destruction of the PLO, would have led the residents of the territories to conclude that their interests lay in reaching an agreement with Israel. However, as it was, we did not destroy the Syrians or the PLO, and as a result both are active in promoting the disturbances and riots presently referred to as the Intifada.

Yet, the erroneous decisions that led to the disintegration of all we had gained in Lebanon were not the first governmental mistakes that brought us to the Intifada. When the IDF liberated Judea, Samaria, and Gaza from the Jordanians and Egyptians in 1967, the government believed that the Arab residents would recognize the benefits of living under Israeli rule. They argued that the Arabs would realize that Israel, as a democracy, would provide them with greater freedoms, better living conditions, higher standards of education, and greater health facilities than they had been receiving under Arab rule.

Thus, under these assumptions, the government failed to extend Israeli law to these areas, hesitated in the founding of Jewish settlements, and formulated no policy aimed at encouraging Arab emigration. This approach left Judea, Samaria, and Gaza undefined and with a large Arab population. This, in turn, stirred Arab hopes for control over the land, which in turn led to frustration when they began to understand that this would not be possible. The riots we are fighting today are the consequences of these frustrations, born out of poor governmental decisions.

In fact, the government of Prime Minister Levi Eshkol did not wait more than two weeks after the Six Day War to announce to the world that the territories captured would be returned to the Arabs in exchange for peace. This statement, rather than encouraging the Arabs to make peace, was perceived as a sign of weakness and only served to strengthen the Arabs' resolve to destroy us. As it was, no Arab state came forward; in fact, Egypt responded by initiating the War of Attrition along the banks of the Suez Canal. Six years later, the Arabs tried to destroy us once again with their infamous Yom Kippur assault.

Rather than pledge to return the territories, Eshkol should have announced to the world that Judea, Samaria, and Gaza are parts of the Land of Israel and that on the basis of history and our rights as the victor in a war imposed upon us, we intend to maintain control over these areas indefinitely. Such a statement would have won the respect of the Arabs and given them a clear indication that Israel is strong and will not be intimidated. For only through strength and confidence will we be able to convince the Arabs to accept our existence. By displaying weakness and insecurities we only tempt the Arab and encourage his dreams of destroying us.

The large Arab population in the areas is also a direct result of government folly. After the 1967 War the Israeli government did not encourage the residents to join their families in Jordan and Saudi Arabia. Rather, in an effort to show how gentle Israeli rule would be, the government allowed 100,000 Arabs to enter Judea, Samaria, and Gaza. In addition, whereas the Turks and the British had failed to prevent the Jews from settling in these areas, ironically, the Jewish government succeeded. By preventing Jews from moving into the area, and allowing Arabs to enter, we created our own demographic problem and contributed to the environment that made the Intifada possible.

By never officially claiming that the land was ours, and by hindering Jewish settlement, we never showed the Arabs that we view the land as ours; we never established a claim. Thus they have concluded that the land is theirs, and have chosen to use violence as a means of obtaining it.

The government of Israel contributed to the Intifada. In 1984 the first National Unity Government was formed when the Labor and Likud parties joined together to form a government. This government of contradictions projected confusion and weakness, as both parties simultaneously sat together in government and worked against one another. The second National Unity Government of 1988 strengthened the Arabs perceptions that we were a divided nation, torn by controversy and internal debate. The balance of power dictates that the weaker the government, the more powerful the Palestinian Arabs are. The riots that began in December 1987 were not the first riots in Gaza. However, the inability of the government to develop an immediate concrete approach to the threat posed by the violence gave the riots the time to spread to Judea and Samaria, and develop into a coordinated uprising.

In truth, we must recognize that Israel has never had a well defined policy toward Judea, Samaria, and Gaza. Since 1967, we have had seven Ministers of Defense, and each minister has approached the territories differently. This lack of long-term policy planning is also a contributing factor to the causes of the Intifada. Furthermore, they are a clear indication that the policies pursued in the past have failed.

It must be recognized that our uncertainty vis-à-vis Judea, Samaria, and Gaza led to confusion and an inability to function properly. The Intifada began after a traffic accident in Gaza, during which a Jewish truck driver struck a car, killing the Arab passengers inside. It was a car accident not unlike other car accidents. However, shortly after the accident a rumor spread throughout the Gaza Strip that the Jewish truck driver had intentionally crashed his vehicle into the Arab's car. The falsehood of this rumor notwithstanding, riots broke out across the Gaza Strip. Yet, these riots were not unlike other riots that had taken place in the Gaza Strip.

The only difference was our response. The Minister of Defense, Yitzchak Rabin, was in the United States and failed to rush home to direct policy. This vacuum, and the lack of a defined policy, led the IDF to hesitate before acting to quell the riots. The Arabs were surprised and encouraged by the lack of a stern Israeli response and continued to riot, ultimately putting their efforts into an organized structure. However, it must be clearly stated that in the initial stages of the Intifada the Arabs had no planned course of action. They simply responded to the actions — and lack of actions — on our part. The result has not only been the casualties we have suffered, but also great damage to our international standing, both diplomatically and in terms of popular support. Also, the Intifada once again placed the Palestinians, and their claims to Judea, Samaria, and Gaza, on the international agenda. As a result the United States even opened a dialogue with the PLO. Literally, our indecisiveness and inability to act from a position of strength, helped transform a simple traffic accident into a mass, popular uprising for Palestinian independence.

The Palestinian leadership tells the Western nations that they only seek to establish their own state in the areas Israel gained control of in 1967. Naturally, suspicion arises when one considers the fact that they did not attempt to create their own state while that land was under Arab control. Furthermore, their claim is even more curious when one recalls that the Arab States went to war against Israel three times before we controlled these areas. If all they want is Judea, Samaria, and Gaza, what did they want before we had Judea, Samaria, and Gaza?

In truth, the Arabs wish to destroy Israel. They have concluded that, at the moment, they are unable to do so through a full-scale war, and thus have decided to attempt to gain some land from us through insincere diplomacy. Their plan is to gain control over parts of our land, thus making us vulnerable. Once we are reduced in size, and less defensible, they will attack us in an effort to totally conquer us. This policy of conquering us through stages is dependent on our willingness to withdraw from Judea, Samaria, and Gaza in exchange for peace. This concept of land for peace was actually introduced to the world by Adolf Hitler who promised the French and British that he would not bring war to Europe if they granted him control over the Sudetenland in Czechoslovakia. The result of this act of weakness will bear a heavy mark on history forevermore. Israel cannot afford to make a similar error of judgment.

What the Palestinians fail to understand is that our refusal to grant them control over these areas stems from our assessment that the territories are vital to our security needs. Even if one wishes to ignore the historical connection of the Jewish people to these areas, or that we obtained control in a defensive war initiated against us by countries still at war with us, there is no way to overcome the fact that these areas dominate the entire State of Israel. The mountainous region from Jenin to Arad, and the Jordan Valley to the coastal inlands consist of 2,500 square miles that control all of Israel's transportation arteries, airports, power stations, governmental centers, communications centers, and major industrial areas. In addition, a full 80% of our population would be placed within the range of enemy fire were we to return to the borders of pre-1967.

In the event of a combined eastern assault by Jordan, Syria, Iraq, and Saudi Arabia, Israeli control of this mountainous region would be crucial. There are only four major roads or transport arteries that travel from east to west. As long as we control the high points above these roads, the threat of an attack from the east can be neutralized. The narrow roads would allow us to slow down an enemy attack with a relatively small force, which would in turn give us the time we would need to mobilize our reserve forces.

It is our control of Judea and Samaria that provides us with these defensive advantages. The Arabs are aware of this, and are attempting to secure our withdrawal from the area so as to make us more vulnerable.

In fact had Israel not launched a preemptive strike in 1967, it is doubtful that the Jewish State would even exist today. Many supporters of the land-for-peace option argue that Israel was able to survive the war of 1967 despite the fact that Judea and Samaria were in Arab hands. This argument fails to consider our preemptive action, the advances of military technology since 1967, and the dangers of a surprise attack. Simply stated, the Israel Defense Forces would not be able to guarantee the security and survival of the State of Israel if the borders of the state were to return to the pre-1967 demarcations.

In addition to security considerations, we must also weigh the consequences to our water supply. Over 60% of the water supply for the area of pre-1967 Israel has its sources in Judea and Samaria. If the Arabs were to control the highlands they would be able to control our water supply, a power that should not be underestimated. The Arabs would be free to pollute or poison our water, or they could simply stop its flow. Israel, like every other nation, would not be able to survive without water. Any action by the Arabs to prevent or pollute our water supply would lead to great tensions, and possibly war. We have not seen any gestures of good will from the Arabs in the forty-two years we have existed as a State. I see no reason to believe that we could trust them with our water supply.

The only solution is for us to remain strong and determined. We cannot show signs of weakness, as this only encourages the Arabs and increases their violence. We cannot have the Chief of Staff of the IDF making statements, as he recently did, that there is no military solution to Palestinian violence. This statement marked the first time in Israel's history that a military leader announced that we could not resolve the problems presented by Arab violence. The message this foolish statement sent to the Palestinians was that the mighty IDF, with its excellent soldiers and modern equipment, lacks the ability and will to suppress their violence. They are the victors and we the defeated. They therefore conclude that they are close to the realization of their goals, and thus continue and increase their violent efforts. If we have publicly announced that we have no solution to their violence, then clearly they will continue until we capitulate, and grant them their wish, a Palestinian State in Judea, Samaria, and Gaza. Furthermore, such statements of weakness lead others interested in the peace process, such as the Americans and Western Europeans, to conclude that the only solution is a territory-for-peace compromise.

The territory-for-peace solution is a falsehood. The Arab leaders have openly stated that they view the "return" of Judea, Samaria, and Gaza as the first step in the "complete liberation of Palestine." Yet, by mishandling the Intifada, and voicing statements of frustration and weakness, Israel has done more than the Arabs to promote this concept throughout the world.

The Intifada has also brought out the Palestinian loyalties of Israel's Arabs. We are now witnessing riots in Nazareth and Jaffa, in Haifa, and throughout the Galilee. These Arabs, although they have been born and raised in Israel, are also dedicated to the destruction of the Jewish State. The Arab-Israeli wars have caused the division of the Palestinians into four geographic groups: the Israeli Arabs, the permanent residents of Judea and Samaria, the permanent residents of the Gaza Strip, and the refugees living in Judea, Samaria, and Gaza. Each of these groups is equally dedicated to the destruction of the State of Israel. Although our leaders often like to comment that Israel's Arabs are loyal citizens of Israel, it is clear from their actions that this is not so. They too lie in wait for the Jews to show signs of weakness, for the Jews to be vulnerable. The struggle is over the Land of Israel, and the Arabs have not changed their approach for the last seventy years. Even before the formation of the Jewish State the Arabs were rioting against the very presence of Jews. The riots of 1926, and the Great Arab Riots of 1936-1939 were examples of their hatred. They are not willing to resign themselves to the fact that the Jews have established a permanent presence in the Middle East.

Yet, we can stop the Arab violence today, as we did fifty years ago by proving to the Arabs that we are strong and committed and determined to stay. We must immediately renew our settlement activity in Judea, Samaria, and Gaza and increase the number of Jews in the region. This will send a strong message to the Arabs that we view the land as ours and will continue to build on it, farm on it, and raise our children on it.

We must also deploy sophisticated anti-violence methods against the Arabs. The use of military force will not be effective, as it cannot

be used to its maximal potential against the forces of violence in
Judea, Samaria, and Gaza. The IDF should have used military force
in the beginning stages of the Intifada, but since we failed to do so
then, I do not believe it would be effective now.

The first weapon we should employ is the deportation of the
uprising's leadership, including the commanders, ideologues, PLO
journalists, and all others promoting and encouraging violence. The
deportations should be systematic. When a deported person's role
has been filled by another individual, this person should be deported
also. Many people argue that deportations violate the Fourth
Geneva Convention, but it has been ruled in many courts of law that
the Geneva Convention did not intend to provide a blanket prohibi-
tion against deportations. The Geneva Convention sought to
prevent the mass deportations of civilian populations so as to protect
them from slave labor and mass murder. The Convention recog-
nizes the rights of the "Occupying Force" to deport any and all
natives engaged in the promotion of disobedience and violent
resistance to the occupation. Israel has a legal duty to maintain law
and order in Judea, Samaria, and Gaza and we are within our rights
to deport any and all individuals who hinder our pursuit of law and
order.

In addition to deportations, I would employ collective punishment. Again, although many see this as an immoral weapon, I believe
it is a preferred alternative to the use of live ammunition. Collective
punishment disrupts the lives of all and would serve to place pressure
on the troublemakers. Thus, if riots occur in an Arab village, the
whole village should be punished collectively. In the times of the
British, the village Muktar was held personally responsible for all
disorders. It was the Muktar who was fined, jailed, deported, and
even hanged, for the actions of those in his village. We must take
similar steps, in making the young Arabs realize that their whole
village will suffer the consequences of their actions.

Furthermore, we should make the villagers understand that we
hold the economic health of the village in our hands and we will not
hesitate to employ economic pressures. If a town engages in violent

protest, we should inform the village leaders that a fine of fifty thousand shekels has been placed on the village. If this fine is not paid by eight o'clock that evening it will increase to 100,000 shekels. If the fine is not paid by midnight, the two largest houses in the village will be destroyed. If by morning the fine has still not been paid, then we will destroy the next two largest homes. The next day of violent actions in the town will result in an initial fine of 1,000,000 shekels. Failure to pay will result in a cut off of all electricity and telephone services. We will prohibit the village residents from working in Israel, and will not allow the village produce to be exported to Jordan. I would agree with anyone who would suggest that these measures are severe. But, is there anyone who would not agree with me that the alternative, the shooting of Palestinians, is worse?

We do not permit ourselves to behave like the Egyptians at Rafiah, or the Syrians at Hama. We are not like the Jordanians or the Chinese. We do not crush riots with maximum force. Yet, we also cannot expect our army to behave like a civil defense unit. Armies are trained to employ force. Thus, we must develop non-lethal, but dramatically effective means of controlling and putting an end to the Intifada. Still, we cannot lose sight of the fact that the battle we are fighting now, called the Intifada, is but another battle in the war the Arabs have been waging against our very existence since the creation of Israel in 1948. Just as we were justified in destroying the Iraqi nuclear reactor, and just as we were justified in bombing the PLO headquarters in Tunis, so too are we justified in doing all that is necessary to defeat the forces of violence that fuel the Intifada and seek our destruction.

I am not to be counted among those that argue that negotiations with the Palestinians cannot begin until the Intifada has ended. I do not believe the Palestinians will ever end their Intifada, and am confident that any movement toward negotiations will only lead to an increase in violence. Israel must negotiate with the Arab states, not with the Palestinians. We have proven with Egypt that we are ready to talk peace with any Arab nation that wishes to end its conflict with us. This holds true for Jordan, Iraq, Saudi Arabia, Lebanon, Syria, Libya, and the other Arab States that participate in the Arab world's war against us. We have very little to negotiate with the Palestinians. The land is ours. We will not consider any "land-for-peace" formulas.

The residents of the territories are going to have to negotiate some kind of living agreement with us that will regulate their presence. I am not in favor of the radical solution of transfer of the Arab populations. I believe this is promoted by those seeking an easy answer to a complex problem and I think transfer would damage Israel's political-security needs. A transfer of populations can only be performed upon complete agreement by all sides. It is not possible to execute a forced transfer. Anyone believing that the Arabs will agree to transfer is operating under an illusion. A Jewish majority in the Land of Israel has to be ensured through the promotion of settlement and immigration.

Since the Palestinians from Judea, Samaria, and Gaza cannot be removed and since Israel cannot afford to partition the land, we must develop a new approach to all the Arabs under our control. The Arabs living in the pre-1967 borders of Israel must be made to serve some kind of national service. These Arabs remained in Israel in 1948 and have since enjoyed all the benefits of citizenship, without having to serve the country. Although they are not permitted to serve in the IDF, as they are an "enemy identified minority" and their service might lead to conflicts of interest, we must find alternative ways for them to serve the nation. The Israeli Arabs must be obligated to perform concrete acts of loyalty and contribute to society. Any Israeli Arab who breaks the law for nationalist reasons should be stripped of his or her Israeli citizenship and deported. Furthermore, the government must clamp down on illegal Arab buildings on state-owned lands.

The Arabs of Judea and Samaria cannot be offered citizenship. Under international law they are residents of these areas and citizens of Jordan. The fact that Jordan withdrew their citizenship in July 1988 is none of our affair. They cannot and will not ever be citizens of Israel. We must provide these individuals with the right to live peacefully. They can work in Israel and benefit from our health and educational systems. If they seek political rights that Israel cannot grant them, then they are free to emigrate to the country of their choice. Any actions, violent or otherwise, that are designed to promote the overthrow of Israel's control will result in immediate deportation.

The Arabs of Gaza are in a similar situation, except that they do not have Egyptian citizenship and only about 80,000 have Jordanian citizenship. Yet, Israel does not have a solution for their political ambitions. We must act in accordance with our security needs, and they must pay the consequences of voluntarily becoming our enemy. It was they who created our security dilemma. It is their burden to carry.

The Palestinian refugees are the pretext for the Arab war against Israel. It is for them that the Arabs seek to restore the "stolen soil" and demand the "right of return." These unfortunate people are refugees because of a war that their leaders forced on us. Furthermore, they have stayed refugees over the last forty-two years so that they could be used as a political pawn by the Arab states. In the late 1940s and early 1950s an identical number of Jews were expelled from the Arab states as there were Arab refugees from Palestine, Arabs who, for the most part, voluntarily left. The Israelis absorbed the Jews while the Arabs chose to allow their brethren to waste away in appalling conditions. We are not responsible for their plight or their conditions. They have allowed themselves to be exploited for political purposes, because they support the objective of their exploitation — the destruction of Israel. Israel is not obligated to find a solution to their problems. The Arab States and the refugees themselves have this responsibility.

The demographic problem Israel faces can be overcome by allowing those Israeli Arabs who fulfill their obligation to the State to vote, while permitting the Arabs of Judea, Samaria, and Gaza to live as peaceful residents. Their political rights can be expressed locally, but not nationally. At the same time, we must promote settlement and immigration. We must encourage large Jewish families by ensuring good living conditions. We must make ourselves attractive to Jews throughout the world, particularly in the Western world, where Jews do not suffer from persecution.

Most importantly, in our struggle for survival we must not grow impatient. We must remain strong and steadfast. We must wait until the winds of change that are sweeping through eastern Europe bring similar changes to our region. We must wait until our Arab neighbors see the advantages of peace and give up their campaign to destroy us. Only through strength can peace be achieved.